Lecture Notes in Computer Science

Lecture Notes in Artificial Intelligence 16348

Founding Editor

Jörg Siekmann

The series Lecture Notes in Artificial Intelligence (LNAI) was established in 1988 as a topical subseries of LNCS devoted to artificial intelligence.

The series publishes state-of-the-art research results at a high level. As with the LNCS mother series, the mission of the series is to serve the international R & D community by providing an invaluable service, mainly focused on the publication of conference and workshop proceedings and postproceedings.

Angela Lombardi · Elvira Brattico ·
Shuqiang Wang · Hongzhi Kuai
Editors

Brain Informatics

18th International Conference, BI 2025
Bari, Italy, November 11–13, 2025
Proceedings, Part II

Editors
Angela Lombardi
Polytechnic University of Bari
Bari, Italy

Elvira Brattico
University of Bari
Bari, Italy

Shuqiang Wang
Shenzhen Institute of Advanced Technology
Shenzhen, China

Hongzhi Kuai
Chongqing University of Posts
and Telecommunications
Chongqing, China

ISSN 0302-9743 ISSN 1611-3349 (electronic)
Lecture Notes in Artificial Intelligence
ISBN 978-981-95-9577-8 ISBN 978-981-95-9578-5 (eBook)
https://doi.org/10.1007/978-981-95-9578-5

LNCS Sublibrary: SL7 – Artificial Intelligence

This Springer imprint is published by the registered company Springer Nature Singapore Pte Ltd.
The registered company address is: 152 Beach Road, #21-01/04 Gateway East, Singapore 189721, Singapore

Preface

The International Conference on Brain Informatics (BI) series has established itself as the world's leading research conference in the field of brain informatics—an emerging interdisciplinary and multidisciplinary domain that synergizes cognitive science, neuroscience, medical science, data science, machine learning, artificial intelligence (AI), and information and communication technology (ICT) to address the interplay between human brain studies and informatics research. The 18th International Conference on Brain Informatics (BI 2025) continued this tradition, providing an international platform for researchers and practitioners from diverse fields to showcase original research findings, exchange innovative ideas, and disseminate practical development experiences in brain informatics. The primary theme of BI 2025, "Human-Centric AI in Brain Research", encompassed the following tracks: Cognitive and Computational Foundations of Brain Science; Human Information Processing Systems; Brain Big Data Analytics, Curation, and Management; Informatics Paradigms for Brain and Mental Health Research; and Brain-Machine Intelligence and Brain-Inspired Computing.

The inception of the Brain Informatics conference series can be traced back to the WICI International Workshop on "Web Intelligence Meets Brain Informatics," held in Beijing, China, in 2006. As one of the pioneering conferences to explore the application of informatics in brain sciences, it laid the groundwork for subsequent BI conferences. The 2nd, 3rd, 4th, and 5th BI conferences were held in Beijing (China, 2009), Toronto (Canada, 2010), Lanzhou (China, 2011), and Macau (China, 2012), respectively. In 2013, the conference title evolved to Brain Informatics and Health (BIH), highlighting real-world applications of brain research in human health and well-being. BIH 2013, BIH 2014, BIH 2015, and BIH 2016 took place in Maebashi (Japan), Warsaw (Poland), London (UK), and Omaha (USA). In 2017, the conference returned to its original vision, centered on investigating the brain from an informatics perspective and fostering a brain-inspired information technology revolution, returning to the original BI title. The subsequent BI conferences were held in Beijing (China, 2017), Arlington, Texas (USA, 2018), and Haikou (China, 2019).

The COVID-19 pandemic significantly affected BI 2020, originally planned in Padua, Italy, which was reorganized into a one-day virtual event. BI 2021 remained online. In order to broaden participation, the conference resumed a full three-day program including workshops, keynote talks, and technical sessions. Based on the experience gained from offline and online editions, BI 2022 successfully experimented with a hybrid format co-hosted in Padua, Italy (in person), and Queensland, Australia (online), and was part of the celebrations for the 800th anniversary of the University of Padua. BI 2023, held in Hoboken, New Jersey, USA, marked the first fully in-person edition after the pandemic. BI 2024, held in Bangkok, Thailand, continued this momentum with a high-quality hybrid program featuring world-class keynote speeches, workshops, special sessions, and technical presentations from researchers representing nearly 30 countries/regions across Europe, Africa, Asia, Australia, and North and South America.

The BI 2025 conference, held in Bari, Italy, from November 11 to 13, 2025, offered a rich program that combined in-person and online participation. The conference featured high-quality papers, world-renowned keynote speakers, workshops, and special sessions, attracting leading experts in brain sciences and informatics technologies from across the globe. Through a rigorous single-blind peer review process in which submissions received two reviews each on average, 44 high-quality papers were selected for inclusion in the BI 2025 proceedings from a total of 129 submissions, including 31 regular papers and 13 workshop papers. Together, these contributions offer comprehensive insights into brain informatics, spanning multiple scales from neural circuits to cognition and behavior. They reflect the state of the art in methodologies, theoretical frameworks, enabling technologies, and real-world applications, showcasing the rapid advancement and growing impact of this interdisciplinary field.

Distinguished keynote speakers of BI 2025 included:

- Islem Rekik
  Brain And SIgnal Research and Analysis (BASIRA) Laboratory, Imperial College London (UK)
  TITLE: Brains and AI: A Two-Way Journey
- Giorgio A. Ascoli
  George Mason University, USA
  TITLE: From Neuron Classification to Spiking Neural Network Simulations: A Neuroinformatics Approach to Data-Driven Computational Models
- Giulio Pergola
  University of Bari Aldo Moro, Italy
  TITLE: The Human Brain Wasn't Built in a Day: The Building Blocks of Psychiatric Risk Trajectories
- Morten L. Kringelbach
  University of Oxford, UK and Aarhus University, Denmark
  TITLE: Whole-brain Modelling: Cartography of Eudaimonia and Flourishing in the Human Brain
- Luca Longo
  University College Cork, Ireland
  TITLE: Explainable Artificial Intelligence for EEG Research and Scientific Discovery

We extend our heartfelt gratitude to all BI 2025 committee members for their indispensable support. The success of BI 2025 was largely due to the dedication of the Program Committee, which diligently reviewed the submissions and ensured the scientific excellence of the conference. We also express our profound appreciation to the institutions and sponsors who supported the organization of BI 2025, including Polytechnic University of Bari, IEEE, the Web Intelligence Consortium (WIC), the International Neural Network Society, IEEE Computational Intelligence Society (CIS) Brain Informatics Task Force, Asia-Pacific Neural Network Society (APNNS), the Chinese Association for Artificial Intelligence, the Chinese Society for Cognitive Science, PsyTech, Myservice, and Brain Products Italia SRL. We also gratefully acknowledge that the BI 2025 conference received partial support from the DEMETRA project, "Development of an ensemble learning-based, multidimensional sensory impairment score to predict cognitive impairment in an elderly cohort of Southern Italy" (CUP D99J22001970006), funded under Mission 6, Component 2, Investment 2.1 "Strengthening and enhancing biomedical research of the Italian National Health Service", European Commission—NextGenerationEU. Our sincere thanks go to the local organizing team from the Polytechnic University of Bari and the University of Bari Aldo Moro for their invaluable efforts in delivering a successful event. We are grateful to Springer's LNCS/LNAI team for their professional support in coordinating and publishing this special volume. Our heartfelt thanks go to Ning Zhong, Chair of the Steering Committee and Advisory Board, whose outstanding commitment and contributions were instrumental in the organization and promotion of BI 2025. Finally, we would like to express our deep appreciation to all authors, participants, and volunteers whose contributions ensured the success of BI 2025.

November 2025

Angela Lombardi
Elvira Brattico
Shuqiang Wang
Hongzhi Kuai

Organization

General Chairs

Angela Lombardi	Polytechnic University of Bari, Italy
Elvira Brattico	University of Bari, Italy & Aarhus University, Denmark

Program Committee Chairs

Carmelo Ardito	Polytechnic University of Bari, Italy
Hasan Ayaz	Drexel University, USA
Sirawaj Itthipuripat	King Mongkut's University of Technology Thonburi, Thailand
Shuqiang Wang	Shenzhen Institute of Advanced Technology, CAS, China

Local Organization Chairs

Tommaso Colafiglio	Polytechnic University of Bari, Italy
Maria Luigia Natalia De Bonis	Polytechnic University of Bari, Italy
Giulio Carraturo	University of Bari, Italy
Danilo Danese	Polytechnic University of Bari, Italy
Marianna Delussi	University of Bari, Italy
Giuseppe Fasano	Polytechnic University of Bari, Italy
Mariangela Lippolis	University of Bari, Italy
Benedetta Mattarelli	University of Bari, Italy
Paolo Sorino	Polytechnic University of Bari, Italy

Workshop/Special Session Chairs

Vito Walter Anelli	Polytechnic University of Bari, Italy
Xiaofu He	Columbia University, USA
Xinwei Li	Chongqing University of Posts and Telecommunications, China
Paolo Taurisano	University of Bari, Italy

Publicity Chairs

Antonio Ferrara	Polytechnic University of Bari, Italy
Hongzhi Kuai	Chongqing University of Posts and Telecommunications, China
Jing Meng	Chongqing Normal University, China

Tutorial Chairs

Sebastiano Stramaglia	University of Bari, Italy
Paola Galdi	University of Edinburgh, UK

Poster Session Chairs

Domenico Lofù	Polytechnic University of Bari, Italy
Tiziana Lanciano	University of Bari, Italy

Publication Chair

Hongzhi Kuai	Chongqing University of Posts and Telecommunications, China

Advisory Board

Ning Zhong (Chair)	Maebashi Institute of Technology, Japan
Guoming Luan	Sanbo Brain Hospital, China
Mufti Mahmud	Nottingham Trent University, UK
Nikola Kasabov	Auckland University of Technology, New Zealand
Hanchuan Peng	SEU-Allen Institute for Brain & Intelligence, China
Hesheng Liu	Massachusetts General Hospital, Harvard Medical School, USA
Shinsuke Shimojo	California Institute of Technology, USA
Stefano Panzeri	University Medical Center Hamburg-Eppendorf, Germany
Tianzi Jiang	Institute of Automation, CAS, China
Tommaso Di Noia	Polytechnic University of Bari, Italy

Contents

The International Workshop on Neural Data Analysis for Brain-Computer Interfaces and Brain Disorders

The Special Session on Spatio-Temporal Brain Data Modelling: New Approaches to Understanding Brain Dynamics

Brain Informatics 2025 Workshop on Web Intelligence Meets Brain Informatics

A Graph-Aware Transformer Model for Event Extraction in Hotline Texts

Zining Luo[1], Zhiyi Tang[2,3,4], and Jianhui Chen[2,3,4](✉)

[1] Beijing-Dublin International College, Beijing University of Technology, Beijing, China

[2] The School of Information Science and Technology, Beijing University of Technology, No. 100, Pingleyuan, Chaoyang District, Beijing 100020, China
chenjianhui@bjut.edu.cn

[3] Engineering Research Center of Intelligent Perception and Autonomous Control, Ministry of Education, Beijing 100124, China

[4] Engineering Research Center of Digital Community, Ministry of Education, Beijing 100124, China

Abstract. Hotline text data, characterized by their colloquial, fragmented, and noisy nature, present significant challenges for traditional event extraction methods based on formal written text. To address these challenges, this study proposes EENE, a Graph-Aware Transformer model that reformulates multi-stage hotline event extraction as a graph-structured decoding task centered on trigger words to achieve efficient event extraction from fragmented and noisy hotline texts. By integrating BERT-based semantic encoding with Transformer-based dependency modeling, EENE effectively captures long-range contextual dependencies and fine-grained semantic associations for accurately extracting token-token association from fragmented and noisy texts. Furthermore, these connections are utilized to construct a tokentoken association matrix in which triggers serve as central nodes and arguments as edge nodes, thereby enabling event extraction by structured graph reasoning. Multi-stage event extraction is thus transformed into a single-step association extraction task, effectively avoiding cascading errors and improving the accuracy of event extraction. Experimental results on two self-built Chinese hotline datasets covering urban flooding, public complaints, and help requests demonstrate that EENE achieves state-of-the-art performance, surpassing representative baselines such as EDEE and CASEE by 5.15% and 15.44% in average F1-score, respectively. These findings confirm that graph-structured event modeling can robustly extract complete event information from noisy, colloquial hotline text, supporting applications in urban governance, emergency response, and public service monitoring.

Keywords: Event Extraction · Graph-Structured Transformer · Hotline Text Mining · Information Extraction · Urban Governance

A. Lombardi et al. (Eds.): BI 2025, LNAI 16348, pp. 3–14, 2026.
https://doi.org/10.1007/978-981-95-9578-5_1

1 Introduction

Government hotline records typically consist of concise and semi-structured entries that are curated by trained professionals following institutional classification protocols [21]. However, the semi-structured format and high information density of such records pose considerable challenges for manual inspection, thereby necessitating the adoption of automated text processing techniques [1,21]. Hotline text mining can be defined as the process of automatically analyzing and extracting structured information from public service hotline records, call center logs, or transcribed speech data, within the broader domain of applied natural language processing. This process involves not only analyzing surface-level linguistic structures but also uncovering latent semantic relationships and contextual dependencies that reflect citizens' real-world concerns. The ultimate objective is to extract actionable knowledge, such as topics, entities, associations, and events, from noisy and fragmented oral transcriptions. Such extraction provides crucial support for data-driven urban governance, emergency management, and public service monitoring [1]. This is a technically challenging task due to disfluency, ambiguity, and domain variability [1].

To achieve the aforementioned objective of extracting actionable knowledge, hotline text mining typically comprises a set of interrelated subtasks designed to capture information across multiple linguistic and semantic layers. From a broader natural language processing perspective, the major subtasks of text mining include text classification [11], topic modeling [2], sentiment analysis [14], named entity recognition [13], association extraction [20], and event extraction [16]. Recent advances have further integrated these subtasks through pre-trained language models and multi-task learning models [3,7]. Among these subtasks, information extraction, including topic modeling, named entity recognition, association extraction, event extraction, etc., plays a central role, as it forms the foundation for deriving structured knowledge from unstructured or semi-structured textual data [4]. It functions as a bridge between low-level linguistic analysis and higher-level applications such as event understanding, knowledge-graph construction, and data-driven decision support.

Early computational approaches for information extraction from hotline texts primarily employedtopic modeling techniquesto uncover the thematic structures within call transcripts [2]. These methods facilitated downstream applications such aspublic opinion monitoringandservice categorization. While effective in providing ahigh-level thematic overview, topic modeling is inherently limited in capturingfine-grained semantic elementsandinter-entity associations, thereby hindering a deeper understanding of theevent-level structuresembedded in the text. In recent years, research has increasingly shifted towardevent-centric information extraction, focusing on identifying entities and their associations, and has demonstrated strong practical applicability in real-world settings [8]. However, hotline texts are typicallytranscriptions of spoken interactions, which are oftenhighly colloquial, fragmented, andsusceptible to transcription errors or automatic speech recognition (ASR) noise[22]. These characteristicsexacerbate the limitationsof traditional information extraction models, which are mainly designed forwritten, formal, and syntactically well-structured text. Consequently, they tend to producefragmented or incomplete event representations, underscoring the need forrobust and adaptive methodscapable of handlingnoisy, conversational, and less-structured data.

Event extraction constructs structured event representations through a multi-stage task that includes the identification of triggers, arguments, and the semantic roles between them [5,23]. It provides a powerful approach for understanding complex interactive associations in text. Recent studies have explored various approaches to enhance the robustness of event extraction in noisy or informal textual environments. For instance, Wu et al. [18] proposed a pipeline-based event extraction model in the biomedical domain by integrating trigger identification, argument role recognition, and final event construction in a sequential manner. Meanwhile, Peng et al. [10] emphasized that many event extraction systems are formalized as a two-stage pipeline (event detection then argument extraction), and highlight the pitfalls inherent in such architectures. Collectively, these studies illustrate that many existing methods still rely on rigid pipeline structures, which can lead to cascading errors when one stage fails. In particular, when processing hotline data—which are noisy, fragmented and colloquial due to ASR errors and spoken-language disfluencies [22]—the error in one stage can propagate to subsequent stages, undermining overall performance.

To address the challenges of extracting complete events from noisy, colloquial hotline texts, this study proposes EENE, aGraph-Aware Transformer modelthat reformulates multi-stage hotline event extraction as a graph-structured decoding task to achieve efficient event extraction from fragmented and noisy hotline texts.

To sum up, the main contributions of this work are twofold.

This study proposes a Graph-Aware Transformer model EENE forjoint event element extractionin hotline texts, designed to automatically identify critical information in public opinion texts related to rainstorm and flood events. This method first encodes contextual and semantic dependencies between triggers and potential arguments through a multi-layer transformer encoder, enabling association extraction between event elements at the token and sentence levels. Based on these extracted associations, a triggerargument association sub-graph is constructed and an event decoding mechanism is further designed to perform graph reasoning, enabling the joint extraction of triggers, arguments, and their semantic roles. By such a "graph construction - graph reasoning" process, this study transforms the traditional four-stage pipeline event extraction process of trigger word recognition - event type classification - argument recognition - argument role classification into a single- stage association extraction, thereby effectively avoiding the cascading errors problem caused by stage dependence in the pipeline method and significantly enhancing the event extraction capability on fragmented and noisy hotline texts.

The experimental evaluation conducted on the self-built public opinion event dataset (covering typical scenarios such as flooding, water disasters, complaints and requests for help) shows that the model proposed in this study has achieved significant advantages in the task of jointly extracting event trigger words and arguments. Compared with the two representative contrast models EDEE and CASEE, this model has increased the average F1 value by 5.15% points and 15.44% points respectively, and has achieved an accuracy rate, recall rate and F1 score of nearly 90% in single-event scenarios such as "Waterlogging". The results verify the stability, robustness and practical application value of this method in event extraction tasks. Compared with complex Transformers or specialized structures for overlapping events, the model proposed in this study demonstrates better generalization ability and lower error propagation risk in real contexts.

2 Methodology

This study redefines document-level event extraction as a graph-structured decoding task centered on event triggers, employing a two-stage model of graph construction and graph inference. By transforming the traditional multi-stage event extraction pipeline into a single-stage trigger-centered graph decoding process, the proposed method effectively reduces error propagation and enhances robustness for complex events in noisy hotline texts. The overall architecture is shown in Fig. 1.

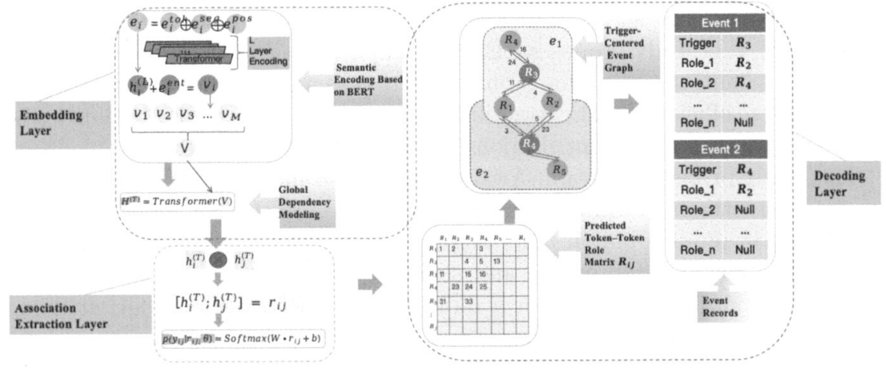

Fig. 1. The overall architecture.

2.1 Embedding Layer

The embedding layer employs the contextualized embedding mechanism of BERT to transform textual tokens into dense vector representations that integrate semantic, positional, and sentence-level contextual information.

Leveraging the global self-attention modeling capability of the Transformer encoder [15] on which BERT is built, this architecture effectively captures long-range semantic dependencies and fine-grained semantic associations within the text. Consequently, it provides token-level feature representations enriched with pre-trained linguistic knowledge, laying a solid foundation for subsequent event trigger identification and argument-role association modeling. Its design consists of the following two parts:

Semantic Encoding Based on BERT. Using the pre-trained Chinese BERT model, this study models the contextual semantics of hotline text by generating dynamic, context-dependent vector representations for each token. Consistent with prior findings that leverage BERT for document-level event extraction [19]. During preprocessing, input sequences are normalized to a fixed length M, with shorter sequences padded and longer ones truncated, forming an $N \times M$ input matrix, where N denotes the number of sentences.

Let the initial embedding of the i-th token be denoted as $e_i \in R^d$.

Each embedding e_i is computed as the sum of three sub-embeddings:

$$e_i = e_i^{tok} + e_i^{seg} + e_i^{pos} \tag{1}$$

where e_i^{tok} represents the token embedding capturing lexical semantics, e_i^{seg} is the segment embedding distinguishing different sentence segments within hotline records, and e_i^{pos} is the positional embedding encoding the token's order within the sentence.

This combination allows the model to capture not only lexical meaning but also cross-sentence and sequential dependencies frequently present in hotline event descriptions (e.g., "heavy rain → flooding → urban flooding"). The input tokens are fed into BERT to obtain contextualized token embeddings that capture semantic, positional, and sentence-level information, represented as e_i^{tok}. The segment identifiers are fed into BERT to obtain segment embeddings that distinguish different sentence segments within hotline records, represented as e_i^{seg}. The positional indices are fed into BERT to obtain positional embeddings that encode the absolute order of tokens within each sentence, represented as e_i^{pos}.

To enhance event recognition, entity-type information is incorporated into each token representation. Specifically, each contextual token vector e_i is fused with its corresponding entity-type embedding e_i^{ent} as follows:

$$v_i = \mathbf{e}_i + \mathbf{e}_i^{ent} \tag{2}$$

where v_i denotes the fused representation of the i-th token, integrating contextual semantics and entity-type features. The sequence of fused vectors is expressed as:

$$\mathbf{V} = [\mathbf{v}_1, \mathbf{v}_2, \ldots, \mathbf{v}_M] \tag{3}$$

To further construct a unifiedsentence-level representation, all token embeddings are concatenated and pooled into a sentence vector:

$$V_s = f\left([h_1^{(L)}; h_2^{(L)}; \ldots; h_M^{(L)}]\right) \tag{4}$$

where $f\left([h_1^{(L)}; h_2^{(L)}; \ldots; h_M^{(L)}]\right)$ denotes a pooling or concatenation operation that aggregates token-level features into a sentence-level contextual vector. All sentence-level contextual vectors are subsequently used as input to the Transformer based global dependency modeling layer.

Global Dependency Modeling Based on Transformer. Based on the fused token sequence $\mathbf{V} = [\mathbf{v}_1, \mathbf{v}_2, \ldots, \mathbf{v}_M]$ obtained from the previous encoding stage, the Transformer encoder [15] is employed to capture long-range semantic dependencies across sentences.

By leveraging multi-head self-attention and position-wise feed-forward layers, the encoder refines contextual interactions among tokens and generates enhanced hidden representations. The process is formulated as:

$$H^{(T)} = \text{Transformer}(V) \tag{5}$$

where $H^{(T)} = [h_1^{(T)}, h_2^{(T)}, \ldots, h_M^{(T)}]$, and $h_i^{(T)} \in \mathbb{R}^d$, and denotes the hidden representation of the i-th token after multi-head self-attention encoding.

To strengthen the modeling of contextual correlations between token pairs, the embeddings of any token pair (i, j) are concatenated to form a joint representation:

$$r_{i,j} = [h_i^{(T)}; h_j^{(T)}],\ r_{i,j} \in \mathbb{R}^{2d} \tag{6}$$

where d is the dimension of the Transformer hidden state and $[h_i^{(T)}; h_j^{(T)}]$ denotes vector concatenation. This operation enables the model to explicitly represent pairwise semantic associations, facilitating the subsequent triggerargument association extraction and event-role identification tasks.

2.2 Association Extraction Layer

Based on the sequence representations $\{h_i\}_{i=1}^{M}$ produced by the Transformer encoder in the global dependency modeling module, amax-pooling operationis applied to extract the most salient features related toevent arguments and trigger words, resulting in a pooled vector H. This operation effectively filters decisive semantic information for event extraction.

The pooled vector H is subsequently mapped into theevent argument label spacethrough alinear transformation with weight matrix W and bias vector b, followed by aSoftmax classifierto compute the probability distribution over argument roles:

$$p(y_{i,j}|r_{i,j};\theta) = \text{Softmax}(Wr_{i,j} + b) \tag{7}$$

where $y_{i,j}$ denotes the label of the token pair (i, j) under model parameters θ; $r_{i,j} = [h_i^{(T)}; h_j^{(T)}]$ is the concatenated embedding of the token pair; $\mathrm{W} \in \mathbb{R}^{|C| \times 2d}$ is the weight matrix mapping from feature space to label space C; $b \in \mathbb{R}^{|C|}$ is the bias vector. The label with the highest probability is selected as the final trigger word - argument association labels.

Considering the class imbalance problem—where the number of "O" (non-argument) labels greatly exceeds that of valid association labels the classification layer adopts a weighted cross-entropy objective [17] to emphasize minority association classes and reduce bias toward non-association pairs. The detailed formulation of the loss function is presented in Sect. 4 (Model Training).

By integrating Transformer-based contextual representations with label rebalancing, this classification layer effectively captures both local and global semantic dependencies while mitigating the adverse effects of class imbalance [9].

2.3 Decoding Layer

Building upon the association extraction outputs, the model first constructs a tokentoken adjacency matrix TT_p, where each entry encodes the learned association strength between token pairs. The matrix is then decoded into a token-level event graph: token pairs with non-zero association scores are linked as edges, forming subgraphs in which trigger tokens serve as central nodes and their corresponding arguments act as connected nodes. Each subgraph represents a distinct event instance that can be further decoded into structured event representations.

For each event type, the corresponding triggers and argument roles are recovered through an edge-type mapping function $f_{\text{map}}(E_{i,j})$, which converts the predicted edge-type identifiers in each subgraph into explicit semantic triplets:

$$f_{\text{map}}(E_{i,j}) = (\text{trigger}_i, \text{role}_{i,j}, \text{event\_type}) \tag{8}$$

where $E_{i,j}$ denotes the association type predicted for the token pair (i, j).

This mapping process reconstructs the event schema by translating edge labels in the event graph into roleassociation structures, thereby yielding a structured list of event instances.

Subsequently, the decoding mechanism performs iterative traversal and reasoning over the constructed event graph. Figure 2 illustrates the key graph reasoning step. By traversing the adjacency matrix TT_p and applying the mapping function $f_{\text{map}}(E_{i,j})$, potential triggerargument associations are identified and reconstructed into event subgraphs. This procedure ensures accurate event parsing from learned token associations and produces structured outputs.

Algorithm: Graph-Based Event Decoding via Token-Token Association Matrix

Input: Learned token-token adjacency matrix TT_P

Output: Structured list of events E

1.Initialize an empty event list E=[ ].

2.Construct an event graph $G = (V, E_g)$, where vertices V correspond to tokens and edges E_g are derived from non-zero entries in TT_P.

3.For each token pair (i, j) in TT_P :

3.1 If $TT_p[i][j] \neq 0$, a potential semantic relation exists.

3.2 Use $f_{map}(TT_p[i][j])$ to obtain the edge-type label (event_type, role).

3.3 If no event of this type exists in **E**, create a new event node.

3.4 If the role=trigger, assign token **i** as the event trigger.

3.5 If the role =argument, append token **j** to the argument list of the corresponding event.

4.Apply graph reasoning over each event subgraph G_k using attention-based message passing to propagate contextual information among connected nodes.

5.Aggregate node representations to form complete event instances.

6.Return the final structured event list E, where each record includes the event type, trigger, and its associated argument roles.

Fig. 2. Pseudocode for the graph reasoning in event decoding.

2.4 Model Training

The model is trained using aweighted cross-entropy loss function, which effectively enhances the learning of minority association classes and alleviates the bias caused by the dominance of "*O*" (non-association) labels. The loss function is defined as:

$$\mathcal{L}(\theta) = -\frac{1}{N} \sum_{(i,j)} w_{y_{i,j}} \log P(y_{i,j} \mid r_{i,j}; \theta) \tag{9}$$

where N denotes the total number of token pairs in the document, $w_{y_{i,j}}$ is the weight assigned to the label $y_{i,j}$, $P(y_{i,j} \mid r_{i,j}; \theta)$ is the predicted probability of assigning label $y_{i,j}$ to token pair (i, j) under parameters θ.

3 Experiments and Results

3.1 Dataset and Evaluation Metrics

Two self-constructed Chinese event extraction datasets were employed, covering three representative event types: urban flooding, public complaints, and requests for assistance, comprising a total of 32,040 documents. The datasets were partitioned into training, development, and test sets with a ratio of 8:1:1, following common practice in event extraction research (Fig. 3). Model performance was evaluated using standard metrics in the field—Precision (P), Recall (R), and F1-score (F1). Following Wan et al.'s study [17], the "*O*" (non-event) label was excluded from evaluation due to the significant imbalance between non-event tokens and valid event tokens. This setting yields an unbiased evaluation of event trigger and argument identification performance.

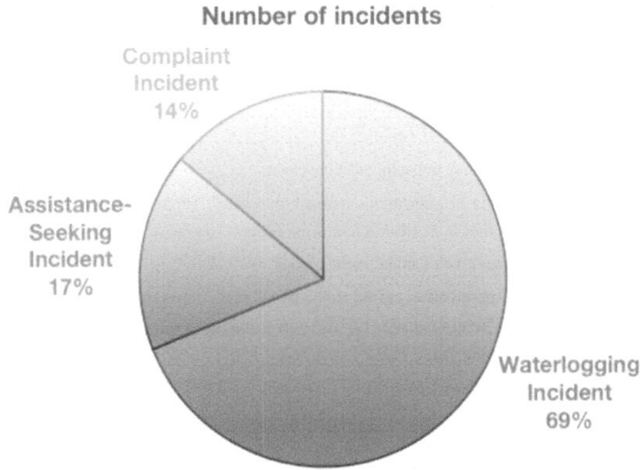

Fig. 3. Proportion distribution of different incident types in the self-constructed Chinese event datasets.

3.2 Hyperparameter Settings and Baselines

All models were optimized using the Adam optimizer [6]with a learning rate of $1e^{-3}$, batch size of 32, dropout rate of 0.2, and a maximum of 15 training epochs. The embedding dimension was set to 768, consistent with the BERT-base encoder [3]. The Transformer encoder comprised six layers and eight attention heads per layer. All experiments were implemented in Python 3.7 using PyTorch 1.12.0 and executed on an NVIDIA RTX 3090 (24 GB) GPU.

To assess model effectiveness, comparisons were made with two competitive baselines, including EDEE [17] and CasEE [12]. EDEE integrates multi-level contextual information by combining tokentoken global dependencies, sequential dependencies, and entity type features. CasEE adopts a cascaded conditional sequence-labeling model that performs argument recognition under trigger and type constraints.

Table 1. Results of comparative experiments

Incident Type	EENE			EDEE			CasEE		
	P	R	F1	P	R	F1	P	R	F1
Waterlogging Incident	92.39%	92.39%	92.39%	88.72%	88.72%	88.72%	79.25%	68.35%	71.02%
Complaint Incident	82.29%	82.29%	82.29%	74.31%	74.31%	74.31%	70.38%	60.18%	65.08%
Assistance-Seeking Incident	81.36%	81.36%	81.36%	77.56%	77.56%	77.56%	76.42%	67.07%	73.63%
Average	85.35%	85.35%	85.35%	80.20%	80.20%	80.20%	75.35%	65.20%	69.91%

3.3 Experimental Results and Analysis

Table 1 presents the comparative results of the proposedEENEmodel against EDEE [17] and CasEE [12] across all event types under the metrics ofPrecision (P),Recall (R), andF1-score (F1). TheEENEmodel achieves the best overall performance, with an average F1-score of85.35%, outperforming EDEE (80.20%) and CasEE (69.91%) by5.15and15.44% points, respectively. CasEE originally reports an F1-score of approximately71.4%on the financial-domain datasetFewFC[12]; thus, the lower score observed in this study is likely attributed to domain discrepancy between financial and urban event corpora. Insingle-event scenarios(e.g.,urban floodingandpublic complaints), EENE attains a Precision close to90%, indicating its strong capability to capture semantic dependencies between triggers and arguments.

3.4 Model Performance Analysis

The superior performance of EENE primarily stems from its graph-structured single-stage decoding model, which reformulates traditional multi-stage event extraction into a unified association extraction task. By replacing the conventional pipeline of trigger recognition → event type classification → argument recognition → role classification with a single-step graph decoding process, EENE effectively mitigates cascading errors caused by stage dependencies and improves overall extraction consistency across complex hotline texts.

In addition, its Transformer-based semantic encoder [15] serves as a secondary advantage by capturing long-range contextual dependencies through self-attention while maintaining a compact and computationally efficient structure. This encoder provides high-quality semantic representations that strengthen the model's capability to identify and associate event elements. Compared with multi-stage architectures such as EDEE (Bi-LSTM + graph convolution) and CasEE (cascaded sequence labeling + conditional logic network), EENE demonstrates enhanced stability, robustness, and interpretability during both training and inference.

The lightweight Transformer encoder facilitates faster convergence and improved generalization under noisy or irregular linguistic inputs, such as transcription errors and colloquial speech patterns. In addition, EENE demonstrates strong robustness across event types with significantly imbalanced sample sizes—for example, the model maintains stable precision and recall even when rare event categories (e.g., emergency assistance) contain far fewer samples than frequent ones (e.g., urban flooding). This stability indicates that the model effectively captures generalized semantic patterns rather than overfitting to dominant event types. Moreover, the tokentoken association structures learned during training provide transparent intermediate representations that can be intuitively aligned with event logic, thereby enhancing the interpretability of the extraction process and supporting downstream applications such as event reasoning and knowledge-graph construction.

Overall Performance. Across diverse event types and linguistic conditions, EENE consistently surpasses EDEE and CasEE in Precision, Recall, and F1-score. The average F1 improvement of approximately5%and15%, respectively, demonstrates itseffectiveness, stability, and domain adaptabilityin complex Chinese urban event extraction scenarios.

4 Conclusions

The work introduces aGraph-Aware Transformer model EENEfor event extraction, which formulates the task as atrigger-centered graph decoding process. Through the construction of atokentoken association matrix and the integration ofTransformer-based contextual representations, the method effectively captures the semantic dependencies between triggers and arguments. Event element recognition and role classification are unified within a single probabilistic structure, reducing the error accumulation common in multi-stage pipelines. Experimental evaluation on twoChinese hotline datasets, encompassingurban flooding, complaint, and assistance request, shows that the model achieves consistent improvements over representative baselines such asEDEEandCasEE. The average F1-score increases by5.15%and15.44%compared with these baselines, and single-event accuracy approaches90%in waterlogging scenarios. The results demonstrate that the propose EENE can enhance accuracy and robustness of event extraction inmulti-event and noisy text environments, providing a reliable foundation for downstream applications includingevent reasoning,public information analysis, andknowledge graph construction.

5 Limitations and Future Work

Several aspects of the proposed model require further refinement. Firstly, as the datasets are in Chinese, dependency onword segmentationintroduces potential tokenization errors, which may affect subsequent association modeling. Secondly, the construction ofpairwise token association matricesleads toquadratic computational complexity, limiting efficiency on long documents or large corpora. Thirdly, although the method performs well on multiple events, it may stillconfuse argument rolesinnested or causally linked events, for example, when a primary flooding incident leads to secondary disasters.

Future research may focus ongraph pruning and association-aware attention mechanismsto improve computational efficiency, and on expanding the approach tomultilingual and cross-domain applications, such as cross-domain term extraction for painting creation assisted by large language models. The incorporation ofcausal reasoningandhierarchical event schema learningis also expected to strengthen interpretability and generalization in complex real-world event extraction tasks.

Acknowledgments. The work is supported by 2025 Educational and Teaching Research Project of Beijing University of Technology (Project No. ER2025ZXA013) and Beijing Natural Science Foundation (No. 4222022)

References

1. Allam, Z., Dhunny, Z.A.: On big data, artificial intelligence and smart cities. Cities **89**, 80–91 (2019). https://doi.org/10.1016/j.cities.2019.01.032
2. Blei, D.M., Ng, A.Y., Jordan, M.I.: Latent Dirichlet allocation. J. Mach. Learn. Res. **3**(4–5), 993–1022 (2003). https://doi.org/10.5555/944919.944937
3. Devlin, J., Chang, M.-W., Lee, K., Toutanova, K.: BERT: pre-training of deep bidirectional transformers for language understanding. In: Proceedings of NAACL-HLT (2018). https://doi.org/10.18653/v1/N19-1423
4. Grishman, R.: Information extraction: techniques and challenges. In: Pazienza, M.T. (ed.) Information Extraction: A Multidisciplinary Approach to an Emerging Information Technology, pp. 10–27. Springer, Heidelberg (2005; 1997). https://doi.org/10.1007/3-540-63438-X_2
5. Ji, H., Grishman, R.: Refining event extraction through cross-document inference. In: Proceedings of ACL-08: HLT, pp. 254–262. Association for Computational Linguistics, Columbus (2008). https://doi.org/10.18653/v1/P08-1030

6. Kingma, D.P., Ba, J.: Adam: a method for stochastic optimization. arXiv preprint (2014). https://doi.org/10.48550/arXiv.1412.6980
7. Liu, Y., et al.: RoBERTa: a robustly optimized BERT pretraining approach. Inf. Syst. Res. (2019). https://doi.org/10.48550/arXiv.1907.11692
8. Mohapatra, P., Dasgupta, G.: A framework for mining speech-to-text transcripts of the customer for automated problem remediation. In: Proceedings of AAAI Conference on Artificial Intelligence (2024). https://doi.org/10.1609/aaai.v38i21.30333
9. Nguyen, T., Grishman, R.: Graph convolutional networks with argument-aware pooling for event detection. In: Proceedings of AAAI Conference on Artificial Intelligence, vol. 32, no. 1 (2018). https://doi.org/10.1609/aaai.v32i1.12039
10. Peng, H., et al.: The devil is in the details: on the pitfalls of event extraction evaluation (2023). https://doi.org/10.18653/v1/2023.findings-acl.586
11. Sebastiani, F.: Machine learning in automated text categorization. ACM Comput. Surv. **34**(1), 1–47 (2002). https://doi.org/10.48550/arXiv.cs/0110053
12. Sheng, J., et al.: CasEE: a joint learning framework with cascade decoding for overlapping event extraction (2021). https://doi.org/10.18653/v1/2021.findings-acl.14
13. Tjong Kim Sang, E.F., De Meulder, F.: Introduction to the CoNLL-2003 shared task: language-independent named entity recognition. In: Proceedings of CoNLL-2003 (2003). https://doi.org/10.18653/v1/W03-0419
14. Turney, P.D., Littman, M.L.: Unsupervised learning of semantic orientation from a hundred-billion-word corpus (2002). https://doi.org/10.48550/arXiv.cs/0212012
15. Vaswani, A., et al.: Attention is all you need. arXiv preprint. Cornell University Library, Ithaca (2023). https://doi.org/10.48550/arXiv.1706.03762
16. Wadden, D., Wennberg, U., Luan, Y., Hajishirzi, H.: Entity, relation, and event extraction with contextualized span representations (2019). https://doi.org/10.18653/v1/D19-1585
17. Wan, Q., Wan, C., Xiao, K., Hu, R., Liu, D., Liu, X.: CFERE: multi-type Chinese financial event relation extraction. Inf. Sci. **630**, 119–134 (2023). https://doi.org/10.1016/j.ins.2023.01.143
18. Wu, P., Li, X., Gu, J., Qian, L., Zhou, G.: Pipelined biomedical event extraction rivaling joint learning. Methods **226**, 9–18 (2024). https://doi.org/10.48550/arXiv.2403.12386
19. Xu, R., Liu, T., Li, L., Chang, B.B.: Document-level event extraction via heterogeneous graph-based interaction model with a tracker (2021). https://doi.org/10.18653/v1/2021.acl-long.274
20. Zelenko, D., Aone, C., Richardella, A.: Kernel methods for relation extraction. Mach. Learn. (2003). https://doi.org/10.3115/1118693.1118703
21. Zhang, Z., Lin, X., Shan, S.: Big data-assisted urban governance: an intelligent real-time monitoring and early warning system for public opinion in government hotline. Future Gener. Comput. Syst. **144**, 90–104 (2023). https://doi.org/10.1016/j.future.2023.03.004
22. Zhuang, X., et al.: Towards ASR robust spoken language understanding through in-context learning with word confusion networks. In: Proceedings of IEEE International Conference on Acoustics, Speech and Signal Processing (ICASSP) (2024). https://doi.org/10.18653/v1/2024.acl-long.286
23. Liu, J., Chen, Y., Liu, K., Bi, W., Liu, X.: Event extraction as machine reading comprehension. In: Proceedings of 2020 Conference on Empirical Methods in Natural Language Processing (EMNLP), pp. 1641–1651 (2020). https://doi.org/10.18653/v1/2020.emnlp-main.128

LFT-Transformer: FT-Transformer with Linear Dimensionality Reduction for Renal Cell Carcinoma Prediction

Jiatong Fan[1], Zitong Zhang[2], and Jianhui Chen[2,3,4,5](✉)

[1] Beijing-DubLin International College, Beijing University of Technology, Beijing 100124, China

[2] College of Information Science and Technology, Beijing University of Technology, Beijing 100124, China
chenjianhui@bjut.edu.cn

[3] Engineering Research Center of Intelligent Perception and Autonomous Control, Beijing 100124, China

[4] Beijing International Collaboration Base On Brain Informatics and Wisdom Services, Beijing 100124, China

[5] Ministry of Education, and Engineering Research Center of Digital Community, Ministry of Education, Beijing 100124, China

Abstract. Early detection of renal cell carcinoma (RCC) is crucial for improving patient survival and reducing mortality. As models based on deep learning have been proven to improve the remarkable performance of disease risk prediction, yet they are mainly applied to imaging data rather than tabular data, which are frequently applied in real-world clinical practice. This study proposes a deep learning model based on the Transformer called LFT-Transformer for early RCC predictions. Aiming at a total of 2940 high-dimensional clinical and radiological features, this study uses feature embedding to convert heterogeneous features into learnable Token embeddings for effectively processing both numerical and categorical features. Furthermore, this study modifies the self-attention mechanism to compute the contextual mapping in linear time complexity, which can improve the ability to process high-dimensional structured data, making it particularly well-suited for multimodal structured inputs in this study. Experiments were conducted on a real-world medical dataset. Results highlight the model's superiority over current state-of -the-art machine learning methods in RCC risk predictions, with significant potential to enhance RCC screening and early diagnosis.

Keywords: Transformer · Tabular clinical data · Projection matrix · Renal cell carcinoma prediction

1 Introduction

Renal cell carcinoma is a common genitourinary system tumor, which affects human health and life, accounting for about 4.2% of all malignant tumors [1]. It accounts for 90% of renal carcinoma, which represents the primary type of kidney cancer, responsible

A. Lombardi et al. (Eds.): BI 2025, LNAI 16348, pp. 15–25, 2026.
https://doi.org/10.1007/978-981-95-9578-5_2

for approximately 85% of kidney cancer-related fatalities [2]. Detecting RCC early significantly improves survival rates, so accurately detecting renal cell carcinoma (RCC) is important in establishing the most suitable treatment strategy for patients. Currently, the primary method for initial screening is through imaging techniques, such as CT, MRI, and ultrasound [3, 4]. Although these methods have a high accuracy rate, they have certain limitations, such as expensive equipment, reliance on manual experience, complex operation, and low efficiency.

Traditional shallow machine learning (ML) methods have been widely applied in the prediction of kidney cancer due to their relatively low modeling costs. SVM, random forest, and decision trees are vital in improving the disease prediction accuracy, particularly in cancer prognosis using structured tabular data [5]. Ayad et al. utilized RFE-SVM and XGBoost in tabular clinical datasets to achieve effective feature selection and classification for accurate lung cancer prediction [6]. Similarly, Agarwal et al. demonstrated the performance of various ML models in lung cancer prediction [7]. The research pointed out that leveraging the tabular radiological feature, shallow ML models can automatically uncover the underlying patterns in data, thereby achieving satisfactory prediction outcomes [8].

In recent years, an increasing number of studies have focused on integrating clinical data with medical imaging to achieve precise cancer prediction. Moreover, with the aim of enhancing interpretability and controllability, these studies still frequently rely on tabular clinical data and radiological features extracted from medical imaging data using specialized tools. Wang et al. employed a classification tree model and multivariate regression to integrate multi-dimensional information from imaging, clinical and follow-up features for risk stratification of malignancy [9]. Aronow et al. conducted a study on glioma subtype classification using histopathology images and clinical data, where they implemented shallow ML models, such as SVM and RF, for the classification task [10]. These studies demonstrated the feasibility of shallow ML models in disease prediction based on tubular data. However, shallow ML models have limited modeling capabilities for high-dimensional data [11]. When confronted with a vast array of clinical and radiological features, most studies typically employed the Mann-Whitney U test or Spearman's rank correlation analysis for feature selection and screening, which often leads to issues such as statistical rigidity and dimensionality fragility.

Many state-of-the-art disease prediction methods focus on designing deep learning models for nonlinear fitting ability and feature extraction ability. Chen et al. proposed a system, RPMSNet, which leveraged stochastic configuration networks to predict radiopathomics mesothelin based on CT images [12]. The experiments demonstrated that the system achieved 73.67% accuracy. Maqsood et al. proposed the Efficient Enhanced Feature Framework (EFF-Net) for RCC grading based on histopathological image [2]. However, the mainstream deep learning models, including CNN and RNN are mainly applied to imaging data rather than tabular data [13–15]. These deep learning models are not capable of handling structured tabular data, many tabular datasets are relatively small, which leads to overfitting in complex deep learning models. In addition, the data in the table usually contains numerous features, so the interactions between features are non-local and complex. Although these proposed models are specifically designed for multimodal data, they still employ machine learning models during the prediction and classification stages. The FT-Transformer was proposed to process tabular data and effectively capture complex associations between fields, but its computational speed significantly declines when handling massive tabular datasets [16]. To address the aforementioned challenges, this study aims to develop a deep learning model called LFT-Transformer for RCC prediction based on structured tabular clinical data and radiological features. On the Transformer architecture, feature tokenization is adopted to rich tabular features for uncovering complex associations between features. A linear dimensionality reduction method is introduced to transform the contextual mapping via projection matrices. This approach effectively addresses the issue of an exponential surge in computational complexity, which arises from the excessive number of feature dimensions in the conventional FT-Transformer architecture.

2 Materials and Method

2.1 Data Description

Data were reviewed from patients diagnosed with pRCC at the Hospital between January 2010 and December 2023. The inclusion criteria were: (1) Postoperative pathology diagnosed with pRCC; (2) Complete preoperative plain and enhanced magnetic resonance images of the kidneys; (3) The patient underwent surgical treatment within one month after the MRI scan; (4) Not receiving preoperative neoadjuvant therapy or radiotherapy. The exclusion criteria were: (1) Poor image quality or significant image artifacts exist; (2) Incomplete clinical data; (3) The pathology is of another type of renal cell carcinoma. Ultimately, the dataset consists of 153 samples and 2,907 features. Among these features, there are both clinical and pathological characteristics, as well as radiological features obtained from MRI.

2.2 Data Collection

Clinical Data Collection. Clinical data included age, BMI, gender, height, weight, history of hypertension, history of diabetes, tumor location, pathological results, imaging reports, surgical methods, and clinical test indicators etc. This study also included several systemic inflammatory indicators: the systemic immune inflammation index (SII), the neutrophil to lymphocyte ratio (NLR), the platelet to lymphocyte ratio (PLR), and the systemic inflammation response index (SIRI). The calculation formula for each system's inflammatory indicators: SII = Platelet count × Neutrophil count/Lymphocyte count; NLR = Neutrophil count/Lymphocyte count; PLR = Platelet count/Lymphocyte count; SIRI = Neutrophil count × Monocyte count/Lymphocyte count. According to the fifth edition of the WHO/ISUP classification criteria, the nuclear grades of each pRCC sample were re-evaluated. Disagreements in the reported results were resolved through joint discussion by two histopathologists.

Radiological Features Collection. All the radiological features were derived from MRI images. The renal MRI scanning protocol included coronal and axial fat-suppressed T2-weighted imaging (T2WI), diffusion-weighted imaging (DWI), axial T1-weighted imaging, and contrast-enhanced T1-weighted imaging (CE-T1WI).

The obtained 4 MRI sequence images: T2WI (T2), Corticomedullary Phase (CMP), Parenchymal Phase (NP), and DWI were imported into the 3D Slicer software (ver-sion 5.6.1) for manual delineation and feature extraction of the region of interest (ROI). A radiologist with 7 years of experience in abdominal imaging carefully and manually delineated the ROI layer by layer without knowing the pathological results. Another radiologist with 10 years of experience then verified the ROI. One month later, 30 patients were randomly selected from the study population. The images were re-sketched, and the intraclass correlation coefficient (ICC) value within the observers was calculated to evaluate the consistency and reproducibility of feature extraction. Features with an ICC value greater than 0.90 were included in the subsequent analysis.

Using the 3D slicer software, features were extracted from the ROIs of four sequences. The features include seven categories: first-order statistics, shape, gray level co-occurrence matrix (GLCM), gray level run length matrix (GLRLM), gray level size zone matrix (GLSZM), gray level dependence matrix (GLDM), and neighboring gray tone difference matrix (NGTDM).

2.3 Data Processing

Handling of Missing Values in Clinical. During the data preprocessing phase, this study systematically addressed null values in the dataset. To minimize sample attrition and model bias arising from missing data, we implemented distinct imputation strategies for numerical and categorical features:

Numerical Features (e.g., BMI, Albumin, LDH, SII). They underwent mean imputation, where missing values were replaced by the column-wise mean (rounded to one decimal place). This method ensured that the data remained representative of the data's central tendency and effectively reduced the interference with the overall distribution.

Categorical Features (e.g., Hypertension Status, Smoking History, Alcohol Consumption). They were encoded numerically, with missing entries assigned a default value of 1.0. This approach allowed us to maintain a consistent format across the dataset, facilitating the model's correct learning of category features, and also avoiding abnormal model training caused by the absence of encoding.

Data Normalization. In this study, StandardScaler is used to convert raw data into a more suitable format for DL algorithms. This method enhances data quality by addressing redundancy, outlciers, noise, and inconsistencies that may arise when integrating data from diverse sources [17]. For each feature, calculate the mean and scale it to a standard deviation of 1. Once the mean and standard deviation are computed, the StandardScaler transforms each feature x into a standardized value X_{scaled} using the equation:

$$X_{scaled} = \frac{x - \mu}{\sigma} \tag{1}$$

where X_{scaled} is the standardized value of the feature X, X is the original value of the feature, μ is the mean of the feature, and σ is the standard deviation of the feature.

2.4 LFT-Transformer

This study proposes an early prediction model for RCC that integrates the FT-Transformer with linear dimensionality reduction. This Transformer model improves the linear self-attention mechanism by adding two linear projection matrices when computing key and value. By leveraging the attention mechanism, hybrid architecture, and transformer-based methods, it presents a novel approach to address the inherent challenges of high-dimensional tabular data. As shown in Fig. 1, the model structure mainly consists of the feature embedding (Feature Tokenizer) and the Transformer encoder layer.

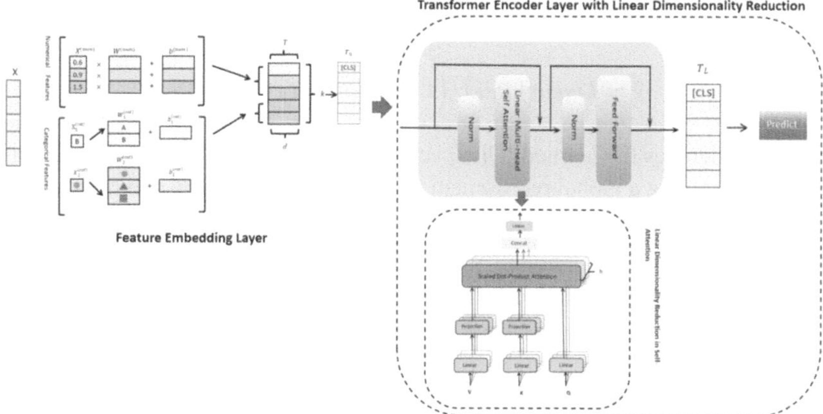

Fig. 1. The architecture of LFT-Transformer

Feature Embedding Layer. The feature embedding layer transforms the input features x to embeddings $T \in \mathbb{R}^{k \times d}$, where k is the number of features and d is the embedding dimension. The embedding for a given feature x_j is computed as follows:

$$T_j = b_j + f_j(x_j) \in \mathbb{R}^d \; fj : xj \in \mathbb{R}d \tag{2}$$

where $b_j^{(num)} \in R^d$ is the j-th feature bias, $f_j^{(num)}$ is implemented as the element-wise multiplication with the vector $W_j^{(num)} \in R^d$. $f_j^{(cat)}$ is implemented as the lookup table $W_j^{(cat)} \in R^{S_j \times d}$ or categorical features,, where S_j represents the number of categories for feature j. And e_j^T is a one-hot vector for the corresponding categorical feature. Next, the embeddings for all numerical and categorical features are stacked to form the final embedding matrix $T = stack\left[T_1^{(num)}, ..., T_{k^{(num)}}^{(num)}, T_1^{(cat)}, ..., T_{k^{(cat)}}^{(cat)}\right] \in \mathbb{R}^{k \times d}$.

Overall:

$$T_j^{(num)} = b_j^{(num)} + x_j^{(num)} \cdot W_j^{(num)} \in \mathbb{R}^d \tag{3}$$

$$T_j^{(cat)} = b_j^{(cat)} + e_j^T W_j^{(cat)} \in \mathbb{R}^d \tag{4}$$

$$T = stack\left[T_1^{(num)}, \ldots, T_{k^{(num)}}^{(num)}, T_1^{(cat)}, \ldots, T_{k^{(cat)}}^{(cat)}\right] \in \mathbb{R}^{k \times d} \tag{5}$$

Transformer Encoder Layer with Linear Dimensionality Reduction. Once the feature embeddings are created, a [CLS] token (classification token) is appended to matrix T to form T_0. This matrix is then processed through multiple transformer layers (denoted by$F_1, F_2, \ldots, F_L$). Each Transformer Block performs the following operations:

$$T_i = F_i \bullet T_{i-1} \tag{6}$$

where i = 1, 2,..., L.

Finally, the [CLS] vector is extracted from the output of the Transformer encoder layer and used as the input for downstream prediction tasks. This is implemented as follows:

$$\hat{y} = Linear\left(ReLU\left(LayerNorm\left(T_L^{[CLS]}\right)\right)\right) \tag{7}$$

where $T_L^{[CLS]}$ denotes the learned [CLS] vector from the L-th layer of the Transformer encoder, representing a global representation of the input sequence, and corresponds to the final prediction output.

Linear Dimensionality Reduction in Self-Attention. The Transformer is Built upon the Idea of Multi-Head Self-Attention (MHA), and Each Head is Defined as:

$$\overline{head_i} = Attention\left(QW_i^Q,\ KW_i^k,\ VW_i^V\right) = \underbrace{softmax\left(\frac{QW_i^Q\left(KW_i^k\right)^T}{\sqrt{d^K}}\right)}_{P} VW_i^V \tag{8}$$

where $W_i^Q, W_i^k \in \mathbb{R}^{d_m \times d_k}, W_i^V \in \mathbb{R}^{d_m \times d_v}$ are learned matrices and d_k, d_v are the hidden dimensions of the projection subspaces. For the rest of this paper, we will not differentiate between $d_k$andd_v and just use d. The self-attention defined in (2) refers to a context mapping matrix $P \in \mathbb{R}^{n \times n}$. The Transformer uses P to capture the input context for a given token, based on a combination of all tokens in the sequence. However, computing P is expensive. It requires multiplying two n × d matrices, which is O(n^2) in time complexity. The self-attention refers to a context mapping $P \in \mathbb{R}^{n \times n}$ matrix, which is a low rank according to Wang et al. [18], the transformer uses P to capture the input context for a given token, based on a combination of all tokens in the sequence. The linear self-attention (Fig. 2) adds two linear projection matrices $E_i, F_i \in \mathbb{R}^{n \times k}$ when computing key and value. First, the original $(n \times d)$ dimensional key and value layers KW_i^k, VW_i^V are projected onto $(k \times d)$ dimensional projected key and value layers. Subsequently, $(n \times k)$ dimensional context mapping matrix $\overline{P}$ are computed by using scaled dot-product attention.

$$\overline{head_i} = Attention\left(QW_i^Q, E_iKW_i^k, F_iVW_i^V\right) = \underbrace{softmax\left(\frac{QW_i^Q\left(E_iKW_i^k\right)^T}{\sqrt{d^K}}\right)}_{\bar{P}:n \times k} \underbrace{F_iVW_i^V}_{k \times d} \tag{9}$$

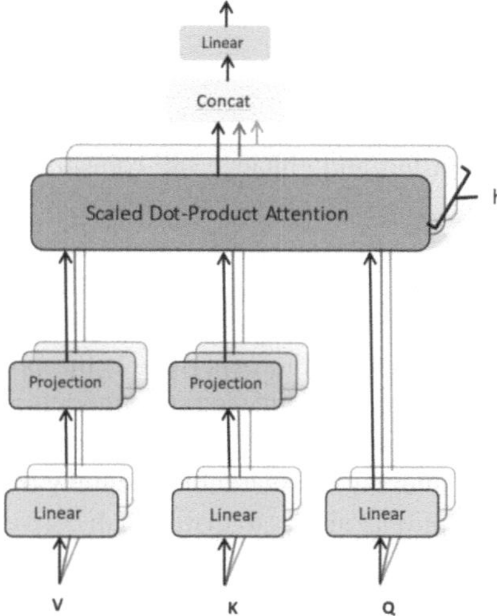

Fig. 2. Multihead linear self-attention

We compute context embeddings for each $head_i$ using $\overline{P}F_iVW_i^V$. If projected dimension k is very small, such that $k \ll n$, then it can significantly reduce the memory and space consumption. Finally, it reduces the overall self-attention time complexity from $O(n^2)$ to $O(n)$.

3 Experiment

3.1 Model Parameter Settings

To evaluate whether the proposed model maintains high predictive performance, comparative experiments on RCC prediction were conducted using the FT-Transformer, traditional DL model Transformer, and one representative shallow ML model, XGBoost (XGB), under the same dataset and task settings. The key parameter configurations of these baseline models are listed in Table 1.

Table 1. Model parameter settings

Model	Hyperparameter
XGBoost	n_estimators = 100, max_depth = [2, 3], gamma = [0, 0.5, 1]
Transformer	dim = 16, heads = 4, num_layers = 6, dim_feedforward = 128, dim_out = 1
FT-Transformer	dim = 16, depth = 3, heads = 4, dim_out = 1, attn_dro-out = 0.2, ff_dropout = 0.2
LFT-Transformer	dim = 16, depth = 3, heads = 4, dim_k = 6, dim_out = 1, attn_dropout = 0.2, ff_dropout = 0.2

4 Results

4.1 Experimental Setting

To mitigate the risk of overfitting and enhance the robustness and generalizability of model evaluation, a five-fold cross-validation strategy was employed during training and validation. This paper used a diverse set of evaluation metrics to comprehensively assess the performance of the proposed model. These metrics included accuracy, AUC, and F1-score. These metrics provide a comprehensive view of the model performance across different prediction aspects. In the experiment, the proposed model delivered outstanding results over other typical machine learning models and deep learning models in predicting process, as shown in Table 2. The model performed exceptionally well across several key metrics, achieving a remarkable accuracy of 98.19% and an AUC of 96.37%, highlighting its exceptional ability to distinguish between positive and negative cases. This balance was further underscored by an F1-score of 83.89%, indicating the effectiveness of the model in identifying actual positive cases.

Table 2. Evaluation metrics across different models

	Accuracy	F1	AUC
XGBoost	0.8476	0.3238	0.6508
Transformer	0.9320	0.7776	0.9638
FT-Transformer	0.9020	0.8352	0.9355
LFT-Transformer	0.9819	0.9520	0.9637

4.2 Time Complexity Analysis

To prove the linear dimensionality reduction is effective in RCC prediction, we plot the inference speed of the proposed LFT-Transformer and FT-Transformer versus different sequence length, while holding the total number of tokens fixed. The sequence lengths are in ascending order as follows: 1024, 2048, 4096, 8192, 16384, 32768, 65536.

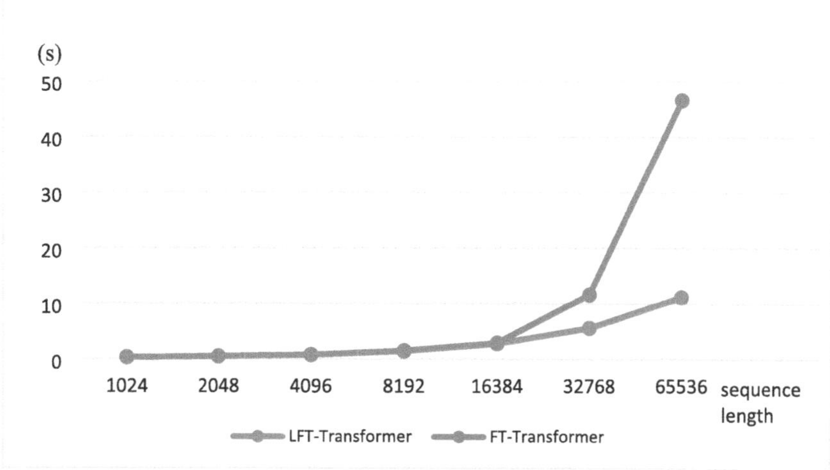

Fig. 3. Time complexity comparison between LFT-Transformer and FT-Transformer

As shown in Fig. 3, the results clearly show that the time complexity has been reduced from $O(n^2)$ to $O(n)$ aligning precisely with theoretical expectations. We observed that when the sequence length is less than 8192, the performance disparity between LFT-Transformer and FT-Transformer is not significant. This implies that FT-Transformer can still deliver satisfactory results when dealing with low-dimensional features. However, as the sequence length increases, a notable trend emerges. FT-Transformer starts to slow down, and when the sequence length reaches 65536, its performance drops sharply. In contrast, LFT-Transformer maintains a relatively stable speed and demonstrates significantly faster processing for long sequences. This advantage is particularly valuable when handling large volumes of structured tabular data, as it can effectively reduce computation time.

5 Conclusion

When dealing with high-dimensional sparse, highly heterogeneous features, and uneven distribution of positive and negative samples in tabular medical data, traditional machine learning models often suffer from insufficient generalization ability and limited prediction performance. This study proposes the LFT-Transformer for the task of predicting RCC. It significantly outperforms traditional baseline models in multiple evaluation metrics such as accuracy, AUC, and F1 score, verifying its strong modeling capability in handling complex tabular medical data.

These findings vividly highlight the immense potential of the LFT-Transformer, positioning it as a highly dependable tool for bolstering early prediction of RCC and elevating patient prognoses. With its capabilities, it stands poised to empower healthcare providers by significantly slashing the time taken for diagnosis and enhancing the precision of RCC screening procedures. Ultimately, this translates into improved patient outcomes and more efficient resource allocation within clinical environments.

Acknowledgments. This study was supported by Beijing Natural Science Foundation (Grant No. 422202).

References

1. Gao, l., Song, H., Song, Z., Wang, H., Xue, C., Yang, Y.: Development of a centrosome amplification-associated signature in kidney renal clear cell carcinoma based on multiple machine learning models. Comput. Biol. Chem. **115**, 1476–9271 (2025)
2. Maqsood, F., Wang, Z., Ali, M.M., Qiu, B., Mahmood, T., Sarwar, R.: An efficient enhanced feature framework for grading of renal cell carcinoma using Histopathological Images. Appl. Intell. **55**(3), 196 (2025)
3. Zhu, H., Zhao, S., Zuo, C., Ren, F.: FDG PET/CT and CT findings of renal cell carcinoma with sarcomatoid differentiation. Am. J. Roentgenol. **215**(3), 645–651 (2020)
4. Ursprung, S., et al.: Radiomics of computed tomography and magnetic resonance imaging in renal cell carcinoma-a systematic review and meta-analysis. Eur. Radiol. **30**(6), 3558–3566 (2020)
5. Dubey, C., Shukla, N., Kumar, D., Singh, A.K., Dwivedi, V.K.: Breast cancer modeling and prediction combining machine learning and artificial neural network approaches. In: International Conference on Computing, Communication, and Intelligent Systems (ICCCIS), Greater Noida, India, pp. 119–124 (2022)
6. Ayad, S., Al-Jamimi, H.A., Kheir, A.E.: Integrating advanced techniques: RFE-SVM feature engineering and nelder-mead optimized XGBoost for accurate lung cancer prediction. IEEE Access **13**, 29589–29600 (2025)
7. Goyal, A., Shrivastava, R.K., Agarwal, M., Joshi, N.: Enhanced prediction of lung cancer using machine learning. In: 2024 7th International Conference on Contemporary Computing and Informatics (IC3I), Greater Noida, India, pp. 1478–1483 (2024)
8. Lin, J., et al.: The development of a prediction model based on random survival forest for the postoperative prognosis of pancreatic cancer: a SEER-based study. Cancers **14**(19), 4667 (2022)
9. Wang, C., et al.: Data-driven risk stratification and precision management of pulmonary nodules detected on chest computed tomography. Nat. Med. **30**(11), 3184–3195 (2024)
10. Shirae, S., Debsarkar, S.S., Kawanaka, H., Aronow, B., Prasath, V.B.S.: Multimodal ensemble fusion deep learning using histopathological images and clinical data for glioma subtype classification. IEEE Access **13**, 57780–57797 (2025)
11. Du, W., Cao, Z., Song, T., Li, Y., Liang, Y.: A feature selection method based on multiple kernel learning with expression profiles of different types. BioData Mining **10**(1), 1–16 (2017)
12. Li, J., et al.: Mesothelin expression prediction in pancreatic cancer based on multimodal stochastic configuration networks. Med. Biol. Eng. Compu. **63**(4), 1117–1129 (2025)
13. Islam, U., Al-Atawi, A.A., Alwageed, H.S., Mehmood, G., Khan, F., Innab, N.: Detection of renal cell hydronephrosis in ultrasound kidney images: a study on the efficacy of deep convolutional neural networks. PeerJ. Comput. Sci. **10**, e1797 (2024)
14. Xie, J., et al.: A deep learning approach for early prediction of breast cancer neoadjuvant chemotherapy response on multistage bimodal ultrasound images. BMC Med. Imaging **25**(1), 26 (2025)
15. Mahootiha, M., Qadir, H.A., Bergsland, J., Balasingham, I.: Multimodal deep learning for personalized renal cell carcinoma prognosis: integrating CT imaging and clinical data. Comput. Methods Programs Biomed. **244**, 107978 (2024)

16. Gorishniy, Y., Rubachev, I., Khrulkov, V., Babenko, A.: Revisiting deep learning models for tabular data. In: Proceedings of the 35th International Conference on Neural Information Processing Systems (NeurIPS 2021), no. 1447, pp. 18932–18943 (2021)
17. Singh, D., Singh, B.: Investigating the impact of data normalization on classification performance. Appl. Soft Comput. **97**, 105524 (2020)
18. Wang, S., Li, B.Z., Khabsa, M., Fang, H., Ma, H.: Linformer: self-attention with linear complexity (2020)

An Interpretable Framework Based on Knowledge Distillation for the Hypertension Early Warning Model

Yumiao Chang[1], Shaofu Lin[1], and Jianhui Chen[2](✉)

[1] College of Computer Science, Beijing University of Technology, Beijing 100124, China
[2] School of Information Science and Technology, Beijing University of Technology, Beijing 100124, China
chenjianhui@bjut.edu.cn

Abstract. For any machine learning or deep learning model, explainability is of paramount importance. As data complexity increases, deep learning models renowned for their outstanding performance have been applied to a wide range of tasks. However, these models remain typical "black boxes" whose predictions are difficult to interpret. To address this limitation, this study proposes a progressive framework that integrates feature engineering with knowledge distillation for interpreting deep learning-based hypertension prediction models. Statistical relevance testing are performed to select target-associated variables, and numeric variables are first partitioned with a supervised decision tree to obtain interval-based, clinically legible features with interpretable thresholds. On this basis, FT-Transformer is adopted as the teacher to generate soft labels that capture nonlinear structure for distillation. Finally, a globally interpretable linear model is trained on the transformed features and soft labels, preserving accuracy while delivering quantitative, interval-level risk attribution. Experiments on the public MIMIC-III demonstrate that our method significantly outperforms traditional interpretable models and machine learning baselines. Although AUC and accuracy slightly lag behind deep learning models, our approach delivers intuitive feature interpretations while maintaining competitive performance.

Keywords: Interpretability · Deep learning · Feature engineering · Hypertension early warning · MIMIC-III

1 Introduction

Hypertension is a common, preventable, and controllable chronic condition that substantially contributes to cardiovascular events and mortality. Early stages are often asymptomatic and easily overlooked. Early warning and risk stratification based on routine examinations and electronic health records (EHR) can help identify high-risk individuals in primary care and follow-up settings, support lifestyle interventions and medication review, and reduce downstream complications and costs [1]. Therefore, in practical clinical settings, there is an urgent need for a hypertension warning model that demonstrates

A. Lombardi et al. (Eds.): BI 2025, LNAI 16348, pp. 26–37, 2026.
https://doi.org/10.1007/978-981-95-9578-5_3

reliable discriminatory power and can be interpreted in a straightforward and convenient manner within clinical workflows. Though the predictive accuracy based on structured EHRs has been enhanced, the widespread adoption of early warning for hypertension remains restricted [2]. Decision pathways are not transparent, leaving the documentation of threshold effects, interval risks, and interactions inadequate. Data heterogeneity and temporal drift weaken the cross-scenario generalizability of the models. Moreover, reproducible and transferable workflows for explanation are in short supply. To facilitate routine clinical use, models that can preserve predictive accuracy while providing transparent interval-level risk attribution are in demand.

Deep learning has achieved state-of-the-art performance across vision, language, reinforcement learning, and recommendation tasks [3–6], and it delivers strong accuracy in medical prediction as well. Yet the opaque "black-box" nature of deep networks limits clinical trust and deployment, making interpretability a central requirement. Recent work seeks to enhance interpretability without materially sacrificing accuracy, especially for safety-critical healthcare applications. For example, attention-based models highlight risk-relevant features and can be checked against clinical guidance [7, 8]. Nevertheless, prevailing post-hoc and attention-based techniques remain sensitive to architectures and training data, may misalign with domain knowledge, often yield ambiguous or biased explanations, and add complexity that can hinder real-time use [9].To reconcile accuracy with transparency, we propose a progressive framework that (i) performs statistical relevance testing to select target-associated variables, (ii) applies decision-tree–based supervised discretization to create semantically meaningful intervals, and (iii) distills a deep teacher's decision patterns into an interpretable surrogate. On a hypertension early-warning task with MIMIC-III data, this approach maintains competitive predictive performance while substantially improving model transparency.

The remainder of this paper is organized as follows: Sect. 2 reviews related work; Sect. 3 details our methodology; Sect. 4 describes the experimental design and result analysis; and Sect. 5 makes a conclusion.

2 Related Works

The prevalence of hypertension remains persistently high, while the control rate stays at a relatively low level, with notable regional disparities. This situation renders hypertension management a priority area in population health management. Based on 2019 global data, the prevalence of hypertension among adults aged 30–79 was approximately 32% for women and 34% for men. However, treatment and target control rates remain low, highlighting the significant public health value of shifting focus to early screening, early warning, and stratified interventions. As data dimensions and longitudinal patient information expand, deep learning applications in hypertension early warning systems are increasingly prevalent. Time-series models like LSTM leverage longitudinal EHRs to capture temporal dependencies and variable interactions. Attention-based architectures for tabular data demonstrate competitive performance across multiple tasks. Nevertheless, the clinical adoption of these models remains restricted by interpretability gaps. Post - hoc explanations can provide feature attribution, but they are subject to controversies regarding stability and consistency [10]. In high - risk decision scenarios, there is an increasing demand for endogenous interpretability or traceable decision pathways [11].

Early explainable models primarily employed post-hoc explanations. SHAP assigns additive contribution scores grounded in cooperative game theory, supporting global and local views [12]. LIME fits local surrogate models around individual predictions to provide model-agnostic rationales [13]. These tools have been used to quantify environmental and clinical risk factors and to improve user understanding and system credibility [14, 15]. However, post-hoc outputs can vary with model architecture and data distribution, may deviate from clinical priors, and do not reliably indicate the direction of feature influence under distribution shift limitations that motivate closer integration with domain knowledge.

Built-in interpretability is also one of the key directions in current research on explain ability. Attention mechanisms expose feature salience and have been used for clinical outcome prediction and sequence-to-sequence alignment [8, 16]. Recent EHR models further leverage structured/self-attention to reveal pattern-level risk drivers while improving predictive performance [17]. Still, attention weights are not causal attributions; explanations can be unstable across runs, and additional modules may increase computational burden, challenging deployment in time-sensitive settings.

Toward accurate and transparent tabular modeling. For structured data, discretization and feature engineering can encode nonlinearity while preserving interpretability [18]. Modern tabular deep learners such as FT-Transformer provide strong teachers for knowledge distillation into simpler students [19]. Based on the aforementioned observations, this study proposes a progressive interpretability framework. Our work combines (1) statistical screening (Mann–Whitney U and chi-square tests), (2) supervised discretization via decision trees, and (3) soft-label distillation into a linear surrogate, yielding interval-level risk semantics and weight-based global explanations—with competitive accuracy on early hypertension warning.

3 Methodology

3.1 A Progressive Interpretability Framework

Building on Liu et al.[20], this study presents a structured interpretability framework that distills a deep network into an interpretable linear surrogate. The framework consists of three stages: (i) feature engineering based on statistical testing methods, (ii) feature transformation based on decision trees; and (iii) knowledge distillation using soft labels. This design preserves global, weight-based explanations while retaining competitive accuracy. The overall architecture is shown in Fig. 1.

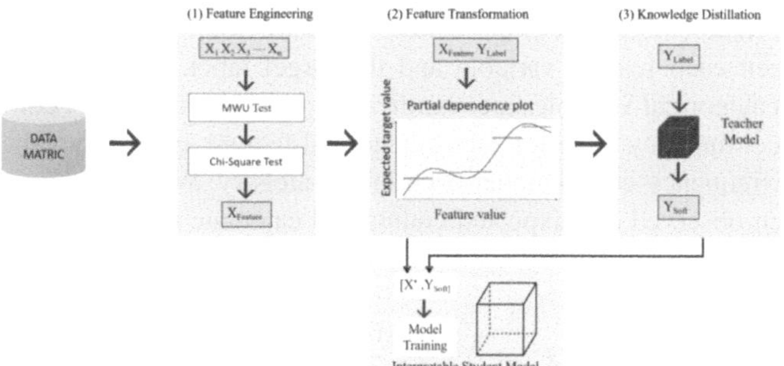

Fig. 1. Overall Framework Diagram

3.2 Feature Engineering Based on Statistical Testing Methods

In structured data modeling, the original categorical and numerical features often contain many redundant, non-discriminative, or multicollinear variables. If these are fed directly into a model, they can negatively affect predictive performance. To enhance both discrimination and interpretability, we begin with a preliminary significance screening of the raw features. For continuous features, we employ the nonparametric Mann Whitney *U* test to assess whether a given feature *x* shows a significant distribution difference between the two target-variable categories. Specifically, let x form sample sets X_1 and X_2 for the two classes, with sizes n_1 and n_2, respectively. We first merge X_1 and X_2 and sort all observations in ascending order, then assign each observation a rank. Based on these ranks, we compute the rank sum for samples in X_1 and define the U statistic as shown in Eq. (1):

$$U = R_1 - \frac{n_1(n_1 + 1)}{2} \tag{1}$$

where R_1 denotes the ranksum of the sample set X_1, which is the total of the ranks assigned to all observations in X_1 after merging X_1 and X_2 and sorting them in ascending order.

The statistic U reflects its relative position in the overall ranking. If *U* is significantly greater or smaller than its expected value, it indicates a significant difference in the variable's distribution between the two sample classes. Under the null hypothesis of no difference, we compute the expected value and standard deviation of *U* to evaluate the significance of a continuous feature, and then standardize *U* to obtain the *Z* score, as shown in Eq. (2):

$$Z = \frac{U - \mu_U}{\sigma_U} \tag{2}$$

where μ_U is the expected value of U, and σ_U is its standard deviation. The standardized statistic *Z* follows an approximate standard normal distribution, from which the two sided *P* value can be calculated. We set the significance level at $\alpha = 0.05$; when $p < \alpha$, the feature is deemed to exhibit a statistically significant distribution difference between the two classes and is therefore retained for subsequent model training.

For categorical features, we employ the Chi-square test to assess the statistical association between each feature variable and the target label. This method determines whether two categorical variables are significantly dependent. We first construct a two-dimensional contingency table for each categorical feature against the label, recording the observed frequency counts under each label category. We then compute the deviations between observed and expected counts and calculate the Chi-square statistic as shown in Eq. (3):

$$\chi^2 = \sum_{i=1}^{r}\sum_{j=1}^{c}\frac{(O_{ij} - E_{ij})^2}{E_{ij}} \tag{3}$$

where O_{ij} denotes the observed frequency in row i, column j, and E_{ij} is the expected frequency under the independence assumption. r and c represent the totals for row i and column j, respectively. To evaluate statistical significance, we compute the P value corresponding to the Chi-square statistic and set a significance level α. When $p < \alpha$, we reject the null hypothesis of independence, indicating that the categorical feature exhibits a significant difference across target-variable classes and should therefore be retained as a valid input.

3.3 Feature Transformation Based on Decision Trees

In actual data, features often exhibit complex nonlinear relationships with the target variable, making it difficult for a linear model to accurately capture feature effects. However, by appropriately transforming structured features, a linear model can also handle nonlinearities. Previous work has used decision-tree–based minimum-entropy partitioning [14] to discretize features and convert continuous values into meaningful expectations. In this study, we apply decision-tree–based transformation to all continuous numerical features. Specifically, let the original continuous feature be x and the target variable be y. We train a univariate classification tree using y as the supervisory signal to obtain an optimal set of interval splits $\{I_1, I_2, ..., I_m\}$, where each split boundary reflects a key turning point in the joint distribution of x and y. Then define the feature-transformation mapping as shown in Eq. (4):

$$x' = \mathbb{E}[y \mid x \in I_k] \tag{4}$$

where x' is the transformed feature value, ($\mathbb{E}[y|x \in I_k]$) represents the conditional expectation of the target variable y given that the original continuous feature x falls into the interval I_k.

The essence of this mapping is to replace each original feature value with the corresponding conditional expectation of y over interval I_k, thus representing the nonlinear structure by a set of statistically stable numeric values. The transformed feature x' reflects the average predicted trend of y when a sample falls into a given interval. To further enhance interpretability, we introduce an offset relative to the global mean, as follows:

$$x^* = \mathbb{E}[y \mid x \in I_k] - \mathbb{E}[y] \tag{5}$$

if $x^* > 0$, the interval into which the feature value falls has a higher expected target value than the overall sample mean and can be regarded as a "risk interval"; conversely, if $x^* < 0$, it indicates a "protective interval" associated with a lower probability of the event. After this feature-engineering process, the transformed features serve as a solid foundation for subsequent interpretable model training.

3.4 Knowledge Distillation Using the FT-Transformer to Generate Soft Labels

To alleviate the conflict between model interpretability and performance, we introduce a knowledge distillation mechanism. In this study, we incorporate the FT-Transformer [15] as the teacher model and leverage its high-order representation capabilities to optimize a structurally transparent linear student model, enabling it to approximate the teacher model's performance while preserving interpretability. The FT-Transformer maps numerical and categorical features into vectors and concatenates them into a sequence, then applies the standard Transformer self-attention module to capture high-order feature interactions, demonstrating strong performance on structured-data tasks. Specifically, we train the teacher model on the set $\{X_i, y_i\}$ constructed from the feature-engineering pipeline described above as input. We map each input feature through a tokenizer to a unified embedding e_i, $e_i = \varphi_i(x_i)$, for $i = 1,2, ..., n$. Where $\varphi_i(x_i)$ denotes the embedding function for the i-th feature; for numerical features, $\varphi_i(x_i)$ is an identity or linear projection, and for categorical features, $\varphi_i(x_i)$ is a lookup embedding. Next, we prepend a trainable global classification token cls_0 to these embeddings so that it participates in attention alongside all feature tokens. Formally, we define the input matrix to the Transformer as in Eq. (6):

$$Z_0 = [t; e_1; e_2; ...; e_n] \in \mathbb{R}^{(n+1)\times d} \tag{6}$$

where $cls_0 \in \mathbb{R}^d$ is a trainable vector and n is the number of features. This matrix is then fed into an L-layer Transformer encoder, which computes multi-head self-attention over the sequence to build contextualized feature representations.To produce a prediction, we extract the output corresponding to cls_0, denoted h_{cls}, apply layer normalization and a ReLU activation, and then project to a scalar logit, as shown in Eq. (7):

$$\hat{y} = w^\top \cdot \mathrm{ReLU}(\mathrm{LayerNorm}(h_{cls})) + b, \hat{y} \in \mathbb{R} \tag{7}$$

where $\hat{y}$ is the raw prediction score for a sample. We convert $\hat{y}$ into a probability p using the sigmoid function, as in Eq. (8):

$$p = \sigma(\hat{y}) = \frac{1}{1 + \exp(-\hat{y})} \tag{8}$$

Finally, we construct a two dimensional soft label vector based on Eq. (10), and combine these soft labels with the transformed features to form the new training dataset $\{x^*, y_{soft}\}$:

$$y_{soft} = [1 - p, \ p] \in \mathbb{R}^2 \tag{9}$$

Then, we train a logistic regression model on the new dataset, using Eq. (11) as the objective function to accommodate soft-label training:

$$\mathcal{L}(\theta) = -\frac{1}{N}\sum_{i=1}^{N}\left[y_{soft}\log(f_\theta(x_i^*)) + (1 - y_{soft})\log(1 - f_\theta(x_i^*))\right] \tag{10}$$

where $f_\theta(x_i^*)$ denotes the prediction of the logistic model with parameters $\theta = [w, b]$ on the transformed sample x_i^*; y_{soft} is the soft label generated by the teacher model; and *N* is the total number of samples. Modifying the objective function in this way does not alter the features or the model architecture, so interpretability remains intact. Finally, by adopting this progressive training scheme, we construct a simple, transparent model whose interpretable features and weight coefficients explain the decision process, thereby enhancing the overall explainability of the deep learning model.

4 Result

4.1 Dataset and Experiment Setup

The early-warning task was formulated as binary classification of incident hypertension using tabular records from MIMIC-III. Guided by the 2023 Chinese Guidelines for Hypertension Prevention and Treatment, 20 clinically pertinent attributes (17 numeric, 3 categorical) related to blood-pressure fluctuation, heart rate abnormality, obesity, lifestyle irregularity, and age were assembled as candidate predictors. Categorical missingness was imputed by mode, and short gaps in continuous variables were filled by nearest-neighbor interpolation.

Feature screening used the Mann–Whitney U test for numeric variables and chi-square tests for categorical variables at $\alpha = 0.05$; non-significant variables were removed (Table 1). In this cohort, mean arterial blood pressure and life pattern did not pass screening and were excluded, yielding a leaner and more interpretable set.

Table 1. Results of significance tests for screened features ($\alpha = 0.05$).

Feature	Test Type	P-value	Result
MBP	U test	0.075	NO
Life Pattern	x^2 test	0.088	NO

To encode nonlinear effects with explicit thresholds, numeric predictors underwent decision-tree–guided supervised discretization. As shown in Fig. 2. As an illustrative example, respiratory rate showed a clearly nonlinear partial dependence (XGBoost PDP) [21], with risk jumps at specific cut points (Fig. 2a–b). Discretized intervals were mapped to the conditional expectation deviation of the outcome, producing interval-level semantics with signed magnitude. Table 2 summarizes the transformed values for the respiratory rate feature.

Table 2. Details of Respiratory-Rate Feature Transformation

Respiratory Rate	Transformed Feature Value	Predicted Hypertension Probability
0–19	−0.0235	0.6394
19–31	0.0279	0.6758
31–43	−0.0747	0.5627
45–60	0.0061	0.6463

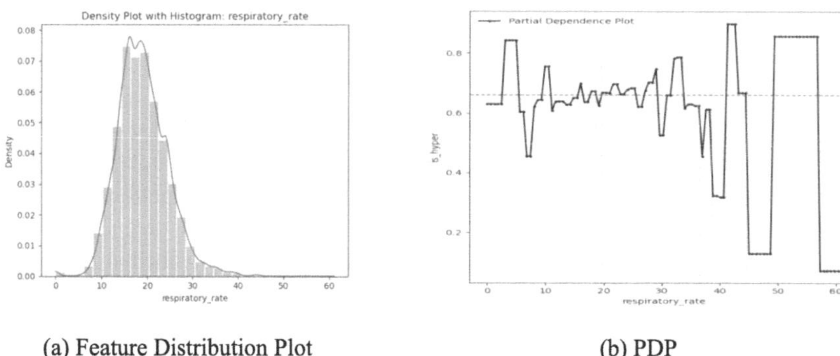

(a) Feature Distribution Plot (b) PDP

Fig. 2. An illustrative Example of Feature Transformation

All models were implemented in PyTorch 2.4.1 on a workstation with an NVIDIA RTX 4060 GPU. An FT-Transformer (FTT) served as the teacher to generate soft labels for knowledge distillation.The learning rate was set to 1e-5, the batch size was set to 64, 50 epochs are run, and Adam was used as the optimizer. Performance was assessed with stratified five-fold cross-validation over the full cohort. Metrics are reported as the mean across folds.

4.2 Comparative Experiments

This paper assess model efficacy using four complementary metrics: AUROC, AUPRC, F1-score, and Brier score. AUROC and AUPRC quantify the model's discriminative ranking capacity, whereas F1-score and Brier score jointly capture predictive accuracy and calibration quality, thus affording a holistic evaluation.

To systematically evaluate the effectiveness of our proposed framework on the hypertension risk prediction task, we designed six comparative experiments involving five classical machine learning models and the deep learning model FT-Transformer under a unified training configuration and evaluation protocol. The five machine learning baselines include Logistic Regression (LR) [22], Support Vector Machine (SVM) [23], Random Forest (RF) [24], k Nearest Neighbors (KNN) [25], and Decision Tree (DT), representing a range of expressive capacities. As reported in Table 3, our interpretable framework surpasses conventional approaches such as LR across all measures, notably achieving an AUROC of 0.6962 and an AUPRC of 0.8146, which attests to its robust predictive capability.

Table 3. Results of the model performance comparison

	AUROC↑	AUPRC↑	F1↑	Brier↓
DT	0.6151	0.7233	0.7973	0.2154
KNN	0.5852	0.7124	0.6633	0.2814
SVM	0.6133	0.726	0.7964	0.2079
RF	0.6594	0.7946	0.8048	0.2088
LR	0.6021	0.7286	0.7916	0.2193
Ours	**0.6962**	**0.8146**	0.794	0.1997
FTT	**0.8598**	**0.9261**	**0.8475**	**0.1434**

Although our method trails the FT-Transformer with relative reductions of approximately 16.4% in AUROC, 11.1% in AUPRC, and 5.4% in F1-score, along with a 5.6% increase in Brier score, it uniquely provides clear, quantitative attributions of each feature's contribution, which is essential in high-risk clinical settings. Furthermore, integration of soft label distillation enhances the surrogate model's predictive performance while fully preserving the transparency of its decision logic.

4.3 Weight Analysis

Feature weights from interpretable models clarify each variable's contribution. We analyze their magnitude and stability for hypertension early-warning. Figure 3 lists all features sorted by absolute weight. Positive/negative weights indicate promoting/suppressing effects on predicted hypertension risk; larger absolute values imply stronger influence. "High blood oxygen saturation" has the largest negative weight, while "age" has the largest positive weight. In our model, age, heart rhythm, low SpO_2, bradycardia, central venous pressure, tachypnea, elevated arterial pressure, tachycardia, systolic/diastolic blood pressure, body weight, body temperature, respiratory pattern, and respiratory rate receive positive weights, indicating that increases or abnormalities raise predicted risk. Mechanistically, age relates to vascular stiffness; low SpO_2, high respiratory rate, and higher weight reflect impaired cardiopulmonary reserve, ventilatory dysfunction, and metabolic syndrome; elevated SBP/DBP/MAP denote higher hemodynamic load—core indices for hypertension identification and stratification.

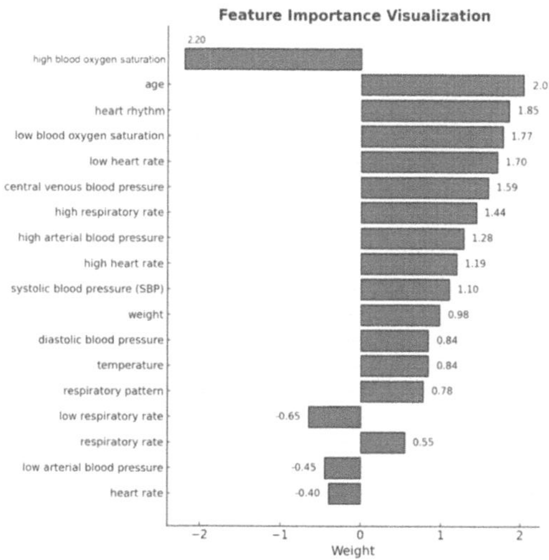

Fig. 3. Visualization of the Best Model's Weights

Negative-weight features include high blood oxygen saturation, low respiratory rate, low arterial blood pressure, and heart rate. These signs generally indicate adequate oxygenation, cardiopulmonary stability without compensatory hyperventilation, and overall lower hemodynamic load—thus a reduced hypertension risk. A negative weight on heart rate suggests that lower resting rates reflect favorable metabolic/autonomic status and correspond to lower risk. Overall, weight assignments align with established medical knowledge and support rapid identification of high-risk patients and individualized interventions.

5 Conclusion

This paper proposes a progressively interpretable framework that couples decision-tree–derived feature transformations with knowledge distillation to make deep models more transparent. Experiments show balanced gains in accuracy, stability, and interpretability. Interval-aware transformations sharpen sensitivity to critical value ranges, while soft-label supervision narrows the gap between the surrogate and the source model. Nonetheless, some transformed features lack clear semantics, and the staged training pipeline may cap ultimate performance. Future work will pursue an end-to-end interpretable architecture that jointly optimizes transformation, distillation, and surrogate learning.

Acknowledgments. The work is supported by Beijing Natural Science Foundation (No. 4222022).

References

1. Parikh, N.I., et al.: A risk score for predicting near-term incidence of hypertension: the framingham heart study. Ann. Intern. Med. **148**, 102–110 (2008). https://doi.org/10.7326/0003-4819-148-2-200801150-00005
2. Kanegae, H., Suzuki, K., Fukatani, K., Ito, T., Harada, N., Kario, K.: Highly precise risk prediction model for new-onset hypertension using artificial intelligence techniques. J. Clin. Hypertens. **22**, 445–450 (2020). https://doi.org/10.1111/jch.13759
3. LeCun, Y., Bengio, Y., Hinton, G.: Deep learning. Nature **521**, 436–444 (2015). https://doi.org/10.1038/nature14539
4. Schwartz, E., Giryes, R., Bronstein, A.M.: DeepISP: toward learning an end-to-end image processing pipeline. IEEE Trans. Image Process. **28**, 912–923 (2019). https://doi.org/10.1109/TIP.2018.2872858
5. Otter, D.W., Medina, J.R., Kalita, J.K.: A survey of the usages of deep learning for natural language processing. IEEE Trans. Neural Netw. Learn. Syst. **32**, 604–624 (2021). https://doi.org/10.1109/TNNLS.2020.2979670
6. Wiering, M., Van Otterlo, M. (eds.): Reinforcement Learning: State-of-the-Art. Springer, Heidelberg (2012). https://doi.org/10.1007/978-3-642-27645-3
7. Sha, Y., Wang, M.D.: Interpretable predictions of clinical outcomes with an attention-based recurrent neural network. In: Proceedings of the 8th ACM International Conference on Bioinformatics, Computational Biology, and Health Informatics, pp. 233–240. ACM, Boston (2017). https://doi.org/10.1145/3107411.3107445
8. Chen, P., Dong, W., Wang, J., Lu, X., Kaymak, U., Huang, Z.: Interpretable clinical prediction via attention-based neural network. BMC Med. Inform. Decis. Mak. **20**, 131 (2020). https://doi.org/10.1186/s12911-020-1110-7
9. Peleg, M., et al.: Comparing computer-interpretable guideline models: a case-study approach. J. Am. Med. Inform. Assoc. **10**, 52–68 (2003). https://doi.org/10.1197/jamia.M1135
10. Slack, D., Hilgard, S., Jia, E., Singh, S., Lakkaraju, H.: Fooling LIME and SHAP: adversarial attacks on post hoc explanation methods. In: Proceedings of the AAAI/ACM Conference on AI, Ethics, and Society, pp. 180–186. ACM, New York (2020). https://doi.org/10.1145/3375627.3375830
11. Rudin, C.: Stop explaining black box machine learning models for high stakes decisions and use interpretable models instead. Nat Mach Intell. **1**, 206–215 (2019). https://doi.org/10.1038/s42256-019-0048-x
12. Lundberg, S., Lee, S.-I.: A Unified approach to interpreting model predictions (2017). https://arxiv.org/abs/1705.07874
13. Ribeiro, M.T., Singh, S., Guestrin, C.: "Why should i trust you?": Explaining the predictions of any classifier (2016). https://arxiv.org/abs/1602.04938, https://doi.org/10.48550/ARXIV.1602.04938
14. Wang, C., Feng, L., Qi, Y.: Explainable deep learning predictions for illness risk of mental disorders in Nanjing, China. Environ. Res. **202**, 111740 (2021). https://doi.org/10.1016/j.envres.2021.111740
15. Rao, S., Mehta, S., Kulkarni, S., Dalvi, H., Katre, N., Narvekar, M.: A study of LIME and SHAP model explainers for autonomous disease predictions. In: 2022 IEEE Bombay Section Signature Conference (IBSSC), pp. 1–6. IEEE, Mumbai (2022). https://doi.org/10.1109/IBSSC56953.2022.10037324
16. Bahdanau, D., Cho, K., Bengio, Y.: Neural machine translation by jointly learning to align and translate (2014). https://arxiv.org/abs/1409.0473, https://doi.org/10.48550/ARXIV.1409.0473

17. Kamal, S.A., Yin, C., Qian, B., Zhang, P.: An interpretable risk prediction model for healthcare with pattern attention. BMC Med. Inform. Decis. Mak. **20**, 307 (2020). https://doi.org/10.1186/s12911-020-01331-7
18. Dougherty, J., Kohavi, R., Sahami, M.: Supervised and unsupervised discretization of continuous features. In: Machine Learning Proceedings 1995, pp. 194–202. Elsevier (1995). https://doi.org/10.1016/B978-1-55860-377-6.50032-3
19. Gorishniy, Y., Rubachev, I., Khrulkov, V., Babenko, A.: Revisiting deep learning models for tabular data (2021). https://arxiv.org/abs/2106.11959, https://doi.org/10.48550/ARXIV.2106.11959
20. Liu, M., Guo, C., Xu, L.: An interpretable automated feature engineering framework for improving logistic regression. Appl. Soft Comput. **153**, 111269 (2024). https://doi.org/10.1016/j.asoc.2024.111269
21. Chen, T., Guestrin, C.: XGBoost: a scalable tree boosting system. In: Proceedings of the 22nd ACM SIGKDD International Conference on Knowledge Discovery and Data Mining, pp. 785–794. ACM, San Francisco (2016). https://doi.org/10.1145/2939672.2939785
22. Dreiseitl, S., Ohno-Machado, L.: Logistic regression and artificial neural network classification models: a methodology review. J. Biomed. Inform. **35**, 352–359 (2002). https://doi.org/10.1016/S1532-0464(03)00034-0
23. Hearst, M.A., Dumais, S.T., Osuna, E., Platt, J., Scholkopf, B.: Support vector machines. IEEE Intell. Syst. Their Appl. **13**, 18–28 (1998). https://doi.org/10.1109/5254.708428
24. Breiman, L.: Random forests. Mach. Learn. **45**, 5–32 (2001). https://doi.org/10.1023/A:1010933404324
25. Cover, T., Hart, P.: Nearest neighbor pattern classification. IEEE Trans. Inform. Theory. **13**, 21–27 (1967). https://doi.org/10.1109/TIT.1967.1053964

Exploration of Chronic Disease Pre-triage System Based on LLM and RGA

Xuerui Cheng[1], Yu Zheng[2], Rui Han[2], and Hongxia Xu[2(✉)]

[1] The Grainger College of Engineering, University of Illinois Urbana-Champaign, Champaign, USA

[2] School of Information Science and Technology, Beijing University of Technology, Beijing, China

xhxccl@bjut.edu.cn

Abstract. Aiming at the problems that early screening of chronic diseases relies too much on doctors' experience, the utilization of patients' health data is not comprehensive, and the traditional deep learning model lacks clinical interpretability and traceability, this paper explores the application of large language model and retrieval enhancement generation technology in the classification of chronic diseases. Time alignment and semantic links are performed on multimodal data such as patient lifestyle, health records, electronic medical records, laboratory indicators, and medical images through data preprocessing. Based on clinical guidelines and medical literature, a domain vector knowledge base is constructed, and prompt word engineering and RAG technology are integrated to dynamically retrieve authoritative medical literature, providing context for large language model reasoning, realizing collaborative optimization of multimodal data fusion and dynamic knowledge incremental updating, and breaking through the limitations of traditional large models resulted from poor domain data quality and static knowledge storage. The experiments show that the accuracy of chronic diseases classification can be improved to more than 91% by fine-tuning the large language model and RAG technology, which provides a technical support for intelligent pre-triage of chronic diseases.

Keywords: large language model · multimodal data fusion · retrieval enhancement generation · classification of chronic diseases · knowledge base

1 Introduction

According to the WHO's World Health Statistics Report 2025, non-communicable diseases have become the main cause of death among people under 70, posing significant challenges to global health system. The trend of chronic diseases is different in different countries and regions. The prevalence and management of chronic diseases vary across regions: developed countries generally have lower rates due to mature prevention systems, whereas developing regions face higher rates owing to limited resources and insufficient health awareness. Therefore, employing intelligent methods for automatic classification and staging of chronic diseases is crucial to enhance early screening,

A. Lombardi et al. (Eds.): BI 2025, LNAI 16348, pp. 38–47, 2026.
https://doi.org/10.1007/978-981-95-9578-5_4

improve diagnostic accuracy, and reduce mortality, thereby alleviating the healthcare burden caused by regional disparities.

Chronic diseases are characterized by prolonged duration, slow development and low cure rate, making classification and staging essential for personalized treatment. However, early symptoms are often subtle or overlapping across diseases, and current assessments rely heavily on clinicians' experience, leading to inefficiency, subjectivity, and underutilization of patient data. Recent advances in large language models (LLMs) have demonstrated potential in medical applications such as clinical decision support, patient communication, and information retrieval [1]. While LLMs can generate medical insights from large corpora, they face limitations in chronic disease management. Firstly, the diagnosis of chronic diseases needs to be combined with multimodal data, such as living habits, behavior patterns, medical history and medical imaging. It is difficult for large models to understand and effectively integrate complex medical logic. Secondly, the development of chronic diseases is a long-term process, with decades of time series data, and the large model has limited ability to model long-term dependence. In addition, personalized precision treatment also needs to conduct accurate quantitative analysis. Large models have certain limitations in dealing with numbers.

To address these challenges, this study introduces a retrieval-augmented generation (RAG) framework combined with LLMs for early classification and staging of chronic diseases based on patient health data. The proposed approach aims to support hospital pre-triage, reduce the strain on healthcare resources, and promote personalized health management.

2 Background and Related Works

In recent years, general large language models, such as LLaMA [2], GPT-4 [3], etc., have been continuously developed. They are generally based on the Transformer architecture through pre-training on massive text data, with strong natural language understanding and generation capabilities, and even complex task reasoning capabilities. In the field of chronic disease management, large language models have also been explored and applied. For example, in the general chronic disease management platform, IBM Watson Health integrates multi-disease data, such as diabetes, cancer, etc., provides decision support, and shortens the doctor's decision-making time by 40%, but there is a partial risk of misdiagnosis, which requires manual review [4]. Ali Health 'Doctor You' builds a chronic disease risk early warning system based on the Damo Hospital model, covering hypertension, diabetes, etc., and the recognition rate of high-risk patients is increased by 25% [5]. In terms of classification and prediction of certain types of chronic diseases, DeepMind recently developed MedGemma, a collection of medical vision-language models with the ability of advanced medical understanding and reasoning on images and text. MedGemma achieved 15.5–18.1% improvements on chest X-ray finding classification compared to the base models [6]. Stanford University and Cedars-Sinai Medical Center used the Transformer model to analyze 12-lead ECG waveforms and predict the probability of CKD in each stage of chronic kidney disease. The predicted AUC index of the model for people under 60 years old reached 0.843 [7]. Tencent Imaging combines LLM and radiomics to provide personalized follow-up advice for patients after lung cancer surgery. The model reduces 30% of unnecessary reexaminations and reduces medical costs [8].

However, the large language model still has difficulties in knowledge updating and illusion problems, so researchers have proposed various knowledge enhancement methods. Among them, retrieval-augmented generation [9] is a universal and effective method, which allows the model to call external tools or databases when generating answers to obtain more accurate and real-time information, thereby improving the accuracy and reliability of large language model output. By applying large language model and RAG technology to the early classifying and staging of chronic diseases, this paper effectively uses the professional knowledge of chronic diseases and the personal health information of patients, makes up for the knowledge blind area of the general LLM, and improves the professionalism and interpretability of the classification of chronic diseases.

3 Objective and System Architecture

This paper proposes an LLM + RAG system for early classification and staging of chronic diseases. As shown in Fig. 1, the architecture consists of three layers: The data layer stores both structured and unstructured chronic disease knowledge and patient records. The processing layer conducts semantic retrieval and text generation to perform knowledge-driven classification and staging. The application layer supports pre-triage, personalized health management, and clinical decision assistance, facilitating interaction between physicians and patients. The main modules are as follows:

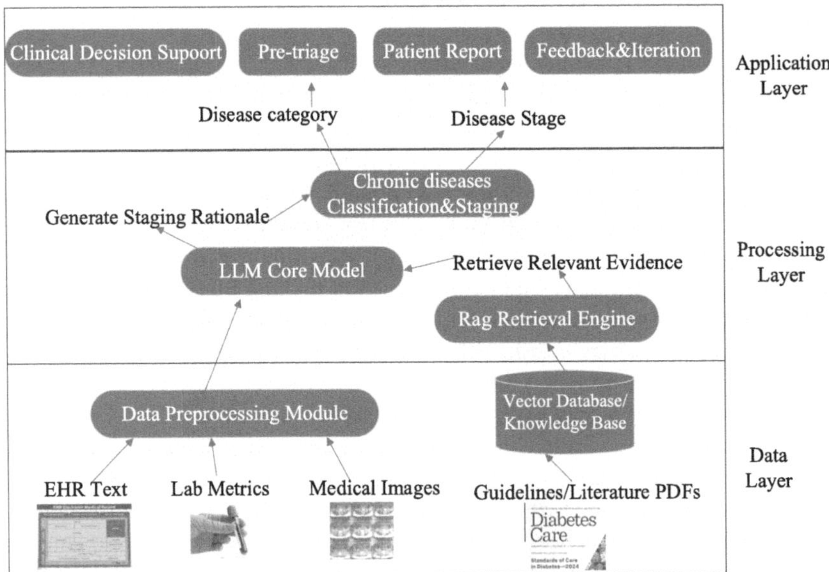

Fig. 1. The System Framework

1. Data input and preprocessing

   The system integrates multimodal data sources, including structured data, unstructured texts, and external knowledge. Unlike conventional multimodal preprocessing methods, a heterogeneous data fusion architecture and a multi-dimensional cross-modal alignment mechanism are provided, features are extracted by adopting different frameworks for structured data, unstructured data and medical images, and multi-modal alignment is carried out from multiple dimensions of time and semantic space, so that the unified vectorization quality of the multi-modal data is improved.
2. Construction of vector knowledge base

   It is constructed through knowledge embedding and dynamic updating. Classification rules from clinical guidelines and medical literature are encoded into vectors using biomedical embedding models such as *BioBERT*. To ensure interoperability between medical terminology and general language, ontology alignment is applied to handle synonyms and abbreviations, minimizing retrieval loss. Encoded knowledge is stored in high-performance vector databases such as *FAISS* or *Pinecone*, with hierarchical indexing by disease category, guideline version, and evidence level to enable fine-grained retrieval. The system supports automatic incremental updates, continuously embedding new knowledge from clinical guidelines or *PubMed* literature, while vector deduplication and clustering prevent redundancy during updates.
3. RAG retrieval engine

   A cross-lingual alignment models such as mBERT and XLM-R fine-tuned on biomedical corpora are employed to support bilingual medical question answering. A hybrid retrieval strategy combining knowledge graph filtering and vector search is adopted: ontology-based structural filtering first narrows candidate documents, followed by vector retrieval for refined selection, enhancing the interpretability of medical reasoning. Moreover, context-aware retrieval dynamically adjusts retrieval weights based on patient attributes, enabling more personalized and relevant results.
4. LLM reasoning and classification

   The part comprises three components: prompt construction, model selection, and output control. In the input stage, a structured prompt integrates patient attributes with relevant guideline excerpts as contextual input to enhance reasoning controllability and interpretability. For model selection, domain-specific LLMs with medical pre-training and instruction tuning, such as *ClinicalGPT*, *Med-PaLM*, and *BioMedLM*, serve as base models to ensure precise medical semantic understanding. In the output control stage, constrained generation is applied to produce structured results consistent with a predefined JSON Schema, ensuring outputs contain explicit classification and staging labels, evidence levels, and cited guideline sources.
5. Feedback and Iteration

   To enhance reliability and iterative optimization, a LoRA-based fine-tuning and human feedback loop is designed. With the base model frozen, LoRA updates only a small set of low-rank parameters, significantly reducing computation and storage overhead. Fine-tuning data sources include clinician-labeled error cases, historical reasoning errors, and newly released disease-specific guidelines. The objective is to mitigate reasoning bias in boundary or complex comorbidity cases by intensively retraining on misclassified samples. Through a human-in-the-loop mechanism, clinicians review and correct model outputs, and the system automatically integrates these corrections into the training pool, periodically triggering fine-tuning. This incremental LoRA adaptation enables continuous learning, allowing the model to incorporate new medical knowledge and expert feedback without catastrophic forgetting, thus maintaining a dynamic and optimized framework for chronic disease classification.

4 Methods and Implementation

4.1 Multimodal Data Preprocessing

Unlike traditional text-based LLM + RAG systems, the proposed chronic disease classification system employs a heterogeneous data fusion architecture with multi-dimensional cross-modal alignment. Structured data are converted into time series and processed using a Bi-LSTM + Transformer hybrid with time-aware multi-head attention to capture long-term trends and short-term fluctuations. Unstructured text is processed with NLP to extract temporal event associations and "symptom–time–drug" triples, providing features for disease progression modeling. Medical images are segmented using U-Net + + with attention mechanisms for precise tissue structure identification. For temporal alignment, clinical events serve as anchors, and the DTW algorithm aligns irregular follow-up and continuous monitoring data, improving prediction accuracy by 28.6% over fixed time windows. For semantic alignment, a shared medical concept embedding space maps textual symptoms and imaging features, and cross-modal attention links symptoms to corresponding image regions automatically.

4.2 Basic Model Selection

In the task of chronic disease classifying and staging, the optional basic model needs to have strong natural language processing, multi-modal fusion ability, and can adapt to the professionalism and complexity of the medical field. The basic model selection can be divided into two ways, one is to select the general large model, and then use the medical domain knowledge to fine-tune; the second is to directly select a large model for medical use. The former, such as PubMedBERT based on medical literature pre-training [10], is good at processing text information of electronic medical records, and multi-modal model Med-CLIP that supports text and medical image alignment [11], which is suitable for long-term monitoring of chronic diseases. The latter includes Google Health's Med-PaLM2 [12], NVIDIA 's GatorTron [13], and Chinese-oriented HuatuoGPT [14]. The selection of the model needs to take into account the data modality, deployment cost, medical and language adaptability.

4.3 RAG Semantic Retrieval Optimization

The proposed RAG framework integrates a chronic disease knowledge base to enable accurate classification and staging of chronic diseases. The system combines static medical knowledge with dynamic retrieval and adaptive updating to address the time lag inherent in traditional LLM-based reasoning.

1. Medical knowledge base construction: The knowledge base incorporates medical standards, clinical guidelines, and hospital internal data. It supports real-time updates, allowing newly published knowledge to be continuously integrated and mitigating the staleness of static large language models.
2. Semantic retrieval: Each knowledge document *di* is pre-encoded into a dense vector representation $v_{di}=E(di)$, where $E(\cdot)$denotes the domain embedding function. A clinical case *p* is encoded as $v_p=E(p)$. Retrieval is performed through cosine similarity in the vector space:

$$sim(v_p, v_{di}) = \frac{v_p \cdot v_{di}}{\|v_p\| \|v_{di}\|}, i \in [1, n] \tag{1}$$

   The top-k most relevant documents are retrieved as $\{d_1,d_2,\ldots,d_k\}$.
3. Classification generation: For each retrieved document di, the model predicts the probability distribution $P\,(\,a \mid p,\, di\,)$ of the answer based on the combination of case *p* and document *di*. The final prediction integrates evidence across retrieved documents:

$$\mathrm{P(a|p)} = \sum_{i=1}^{k} \mathrm{P(di|p)} \cdot \mathrm{P(a|p, di)} \tag{2}$$

4. Dynamic knowledge update: To adapt to evolving clinical guidelines, the system incorporates a Vector Deduplication and Clustering strategy for continuous update of the knowledge base.

   Step1 Incremental Embedding Update

   New documents *dnew* , such as new hospital policies and updated chronic disease classification clauses, are encoded into vectors by the domain embedding model f_θ.

$$\mathrm{v_{new}} = \mathrm{f}_\theta(\mathrm{d_{new}}),\ \mathrm{v_{new}} \in \mathrm{R^d} \tag{3}$$

   Where f_θ may be fine-tuned BioBERT or ClinicalBERT.

   Step2 Vector Deduplication and Clustering

   Similarity with existing entries is computed via formula 1.

- If sim $\geq$ 0.95: the entry is discarded as a duplicate.
- If 0.85 $\leq$ sim $<$ 0.95: it is merged while retaining metadata provenance.

  Remaining vectors are grouped into K clusters:

$$\{\mathrm{C_1, C_2, \ldots, C_K}\} = \mathrm{g(V_{new}),\ g} \in \{\mathrm{HDBSCAN, K\text{-}Means}\} \tag{4}$$

   Step4 Hierarchical Index Refresh

   A two-layer index is reconstructed. Layer 1: Establish coarse-grained IVF index by disease category; Layer 2: Build a fine-grained HNSW index within the cluster to ensure efficient approximate nearest neighbor retrieval.

5 Results and Evaluation

The data of nutritional status, health behavior and chronic diseases of Chinese residents were tracked for a long time by the China Health and Nutrition Survey (CHNS) data set, covering the survey data from 1989 to 2015, including demographics, dietary indicators, lifestyle, physical examination indicators and so on. For this dataset, existing studies have used machine learning [15, 16], interpretable machine learning [17], and large language models [18] to predict and analyze risk factors for chronic diseases, such as diabetes, hypertension, obesity, etc. Table 1 compares the predicting performance indicators for diabetes of several typical models based on the CHNS dataset. There are 8,277 individuals including 590 pre-diabetes patients and 7687 non-pre-diabetes patients in the dataset.

Table 1. Experimental results of each comparison model on CHNS

Method	Accuracy	Sensitivity	Specificity	AUC	F1-score
RF	0.79	0.83	0.79	0.91	0.37
XGBoost	0.84	0.89	0.84	0.93	0.45
MLP	0.74	0.62	0.74	0.74	0.25
LSTM	0.79	0.75	0.78	0.78	0.36
BioBERT	0.84	0.80	0.79	0.80	0.40
chatGPT4.0	0.87	0.83	0.79	0.83	0.43
ChatGLM3(pure)	0.86	0.80	0.78	0.82	0.42
ChatGLM3+RAG	0.91	0.85	0.80	0.88	0.45

From the results in Table 1, XGBoost achieves the best performance (AUC = 0.93), benefiting from its robustness to heterogeneous features and missing values. In contrast, deep learning models such as MLP and LSTM perform less favorably due to the limited sample size and temporal sparsity of the CHNS dataset. By applying CHNS-specific terminology adaptation and LoRA fine-tuning, the pure ChatGLM3 model achieves performance close to GPT-4.0 (Accuracy = 0.86, AUC = 0.82). The ChatGLM3 + RAG configuration further improves recall and F1 metrics (Accuracy = 0.91, Sensitivity = 0.85, AUC = 0.88). Its advantage stems from retrieving contextual evidence, such as entries from PubMed, Chinese chronic disease guidelines, or similar case summaries and clinical threshold notes, to support reasoning in borderline or rare-feature cases. This retrieval mechanism mitigates LLM overconfidence and enhances discriminative performance.

For multimodal evaluation, we additionally conducted experiments on the UK Biobank, one of the world's largest multimodal health cohorts, encompassing approximately 500,000 participants with genomic, biochemical, imaging, EHR, and wearable activity data. We selected about 80,000 participants without baseline diabetes, among whom approximately 4,500 were later diagnosed with type 2 diabetes.

From the results presented in Table 2, all models exhibit substantially better performance on the UK Biobank dataset than on CHNS, owing to its richer data modalities, larger sample size, and higher feature informativeness. XGBoost remains strong in handling structured features (AUC = 0.96), yet lacks cross-modal fusion capability. Benefiting from imaging and wearable modalities, the deep learning model MLP achieves significantly higher performance than in the CHNS experiments. The pure ChatGLM3 model

Table 2. Experimental results of each comparison model on UK Biobank (multimodal)

Method	Accuracy	Sensitivity	Specificity	AUC	F1-score
XGBoost	0.92	0.82	0.93	0.96	0.62
MLP	0.90	0.77	0.91	0.92	0.56
ChatGLM3(pure)	0.91	0.80	0.91	0.94	0.59
ChatGLM3+RAG	0.94	0.86	0.93	0.97	0.68

performs comparably to XGBoost (AUC = 0.94). However, its sensitivity is slightly lower, likely due to the model's tendency toward prediction averaging. When multimodal features are fully available, the RAG-enhanced ChatGLM3 shows greater improvements, particularly for borderline cases, such as participants with impaired glucose tolerance but without a confirmed diagnosis, achieving higher sensitivity.

All experiments were conducted on a platform equipped with NVIDIA RTX L40 (48 GB) GPU, CUDA 12.1, Python 3.11, and Ubuntu 24.04. The retriever employed the Sentence-Transformers/all-mpnet-base-v2 model with a 768-dimensional embedding space, retrieving the top k = 5 most similar documents. The LLM backbone was ChatGLM3-6B, with a maximum context window of 2048–4096 tokens. For LoRA fine-tuning, hyperparameters were set as follows: rank = 8, $\alpha = 32$, dropout = 0.05, learning rate = 1e−4, batch size = 16, epochs = 3. The AdamW optimizer and Binary Cross-Entropy loss were adopted during fine-tuning.

To assess clinical utility, the ChatGLM3 + RAG system was deployed for pre-triage in a local general hospital, processing 1,500 incoming patients over a 3-month period. Patient inputs included demographics, comorbidities, laboratory results, and prior visit records. Average time per triage decision reduced from 8 min by manual to 2.5 min using LLM + RAG-assisted recommendations, but LLM occasionally generated overly cautious recommendations for rare conditions, indicating a need for further calibration with hospital-specific protocols.

6 Conclusion

'Early detection, early intervention and accurate management' is the core of early classification and staging of chronic diseases. Through AI technology to assist the classification and staging of chronic diseases, targeted interventions can be formulated for patients to delay disease progression and improve prognosis. It can also reduce the medical burden and balance regional medical resources, which is of great significance in the field of chronic disease management and public health. This paper proposes an early classification and staging system for chronic diseases based on large language model and RAG technology. The system has the following advantages: First, it makes full use of the text understanding ability and generation ability of large language model, and eliminates the data standardization and manual feature extraction steps required by traditional machine learning. It can directly analyze electronic medical records and physical examination records, and can compensate for data loss through pre-training knowledge, which is more suitable for non-standardized data in primary hospitals. The second is to use the multi-modal fusion ability of the large language model, which can analyze the numerical value, text and image jointly, without modeling separately, and support cross-modal reasoning, and directly output the classification and staging report related to the image and text. The third is to combine RAG technology to improve the accuracy and clinical compliance of the classification and staging results of chronic diseases. It can not only dynamically retrieve the latest authoritative chronic disease knowledge base, but also make the LLM generation results come with the source of retrieval references and reduce the risk of hallucinations. Therefore, the combined application of LLM and RAG in the intelligent classification of chronic diseases not only breaks the static knowledge limitations of LLM, but also reduces the computational costs of using LLM alone. It is particularly suitable for early chronic disease screening in primary hospitals with limited medical resources.

References

1. Kai, H., Rui, M., Qika, L., et al.: A survey of large language models for healthcare: from data, technology, and applications to accountability and ethics. arXiv preprint arXiv:2310.05694 (2023)
2. Touvron, H., Lavril, T., Izacard,. G, et al.: LLaMA: open and efficient foundation language models. arXiv preprint arXiv:2302.13971 (2023)
3. Achiam, J., Adler, S., Agarwal, S., et al.: GPT-4 technical report. arXiv preprint arXiv:2303.08774 (2023)
4. Adrián, C.C., Suejb, M., et al.: Using cognitive computing for learning parallel programming: an IBM watson solution. Procedia Comput. Sci. **108**, 2121–2130 (2017)
5. AI Application in Healthcare Industry White Paper. Aliyun (2025)
6. Google Research and Google DeepMind. MedGemma Technical Report. arXiv preprint arXiv: 2507.05201v1 [cs.AI] (2025)
7. Holmstrom, L., Christensen, M., Yuan, N., et al. Deep learning-based electrocardiographic screening for chronic kidney disease. Commun. Med. (2023)
8. Medical imaging cloud application and network security capabilities Evaluation White Paper. Tencent Research Institute (2021)
9. Gao, Y., Xiong, Y., Gao, X., et al.: Retrieval-augmented generation for large language models: a survey. arXiv preprint arXiv:2312.10997 (2023)
10. Gu, Y., Tinn, R., Cheng, H., et al.: Domain-specific language model pretraining for biomedical natural language processing. ACM Trans. Comput. Healthc. **3**(1), 1–23 (2021)
11. Wang, Z., Z., Agarwal, D., et al.: Med-CLIP: contrastive learning for medical image and text. arXiv preprint arXiv:2210.10163 (2022)
12. Singhai, K., Yu, T., Juraj, G.: Towards expert-level medical question answering with large language models. Nat. Med. **31**, 943–950 (2025)
13. Yang, X., Chen, A., PourNejatian, N., et al.: A large language model for electronic health records. NPJ Digit. Med. (2022)
14. Zhang, H., Chen, J., Jiang, F., et al.: HuatuoGPT: towards taming language model to be a doctor. In: Findings of the Association for Computational Linguistics: EMNLP 2023, pp. 10859–10885. Association for Computational Linguistics, Singapore (2023)
15. Zhang, M., Xia, X., Wang, Q., et al.: Application of machine learning algorithms in predicting new onset hypertension: a study based on the China health and nutrition survey. Environ. Health Prevent. Med. **30** (2025). https://doi.org/10.1265/ehpm.24-00270

16. Xue, J., Ren, X., Xu, Y., et al.: Procedia Comput. Sci. **162**, 835–841 (2019)
17. Li, X., Ding, F., Zhang, L., et al.: Interpretable machine learning method to predict the risk of pre-diabetes using a national-wide cross-sectional data: evidence from CHNS. BMC Public Health **25**, 1145 (2025). https://doi.org/10.1186/s12889-025-22419-7
18. Huang, Y., Wu, R., He, J., et al.: Evaluating ChatGPT-4.0's data analytic proficiency in epidemiological studies: a comparative analysis with SAS, SPSS, and R. J. Glob. Health **14**, 04070 (2024). https://doi.org/10.7189/jogh.14.04070

Robustness of the ilr Approach in Likert Scales W-Shaped Data Analysis

René Lehmann[1,2(✉)] and Bodo Vogt[2]

[1] FOM University of Applied Science, Leimkugelstraße 6, 45141 Essen, Germany
rene.lehmann@fom.de

[2] Otto von Guericke University, Universitätsplatz 2, 39106 Magdeburg, Germany
{rene1.lehmann,bodo.vogt}@ovgu.de

https://www.fom.de, https://www.emwifo.ovgu.de/en/

Abstract. Accurate psychometric profiling and the selection of appropriate therapeutic interventions are essential components of any psychotherapeutic treatment. Developing a precise psychological profile not only benefits the patient but also saves time and reduces costs. Likert scales produce compositional data, as each level of agreement with an item assertion corresponds to a corresponding level of disagreement. By utilizing an isometric log-ratio (ilr) transformation, the bivariate information can be converted to a real-valued interval scale, resulting in unbiased statistical outcomes that enhance the statistical power of the Pearson correlation significance test, provided that the central limit theorem (CLT) holds true for statistics. However, in practical applications, the CLT depends on factors such as the number of components (i.e., items) and the distributional shape of the (ilr transformed) data generating process (DGP). Through simulations, we demonstrate that the ilr approach remains effective even when the CLT assumptions are violated. This indicates that the ilr method is robust in scenarios with few components and extremely shaped DGPs, thereby boosting the statistical power of correlation tests. Using the ilr approach sample sizes can be reduced while maintaining the statistical power and saving sampling costs. W-shaped DGPs can occur if individuals are indifferent or favor extreme values, e.g., concerning the acceptance or rejection of life-prolonging measures in hospital or the death penalty. The findings of this study extend previous research, highlighting the versatility and reliability of the ilr approach in analyzing psychometric data. The results support the medical treatments of patients as well as the improvement of health information systems. This has implications for psychometric health economics (e.g., grant funding and QALY index values), patient well-being, grant allocation decisions, economic planning, and overall profitability.

Keywords: bipolar Likert scale · isometric log-ratio transformation · correlation · statistical power · W-shaped distribution

A. Lombardi et al. (Eds.): BI 2025, LNAI 16348, pp. 48–66, 2026.
https://doi.org/10.1007/978-981-95-9578-5_5

1 Introduction and Literature Review

Likert scales (LS) are commonly employed in psychology and medical psychometrics [1,2] to establish standards and develop psychological profiles of patients. From a scientific perspective, it is crucial to obtain reliable insights into the relationships and effects among latent variables, as well as the magnitude of therapeutic interventions [3]. The effectiveness of treatment and its outcomes rely heavily on these standards and the patient's psychological profile. Inadequate data analysis can lead to biased standards, which may distort psychological assessments and medical diagnoses. Consequently, borderline cases in medicine might be incorrectly classified as positive or negative. Additionally, poor psychological profiling increases the risk of misdiagnoses, undermines treatment plans, jeopardizes patient well-being, and may result in higher healthcare costs. Therefore, it is essential to utilize statistical methods that offer high statistical power [4].

Improving patient well-being helps uphold medical ethical standards. The success of treatment outcomes depends on accurate standards and precise psychological profiling of patients. Additionally, artificial intelligence models from brain informatics can assist in diagnosis and the formulation of treatment plans [5]. In psychometric big data analysis, the focus is primarily on identifying patterns and associations rather than establishing causal relationships, such as exploring the connection between psychological measures and workplace hazards [6]. Psychological big data is essential for validating predictive models by applying a model created from one dataset to a different dataset or hold-out sample [7]. The analysis of individual psychometric data and large datasets both supports the development of standards and the evaluation of psychotherapeutic treatment effectiveness. This process often combines techniques like individual psychometric profiling and machine learning algorithms [8,9]. However, the use of big data techniques can lead to the detection of false or misleading correlations [10]. As a result, psychological evaluations that rely heavily on correlation-based methods like partial least squares structural equation modeling (PLS-SEM) [11] may be less effective, potentially increasing costs and reducing the efficacy of healthcare interventions.

The effectiveness of psychotherapeutic interventions and behavior prediction depends on precisely identifying individuals' personality traits, attitudes, and preferences. Accurate and unbiased psychometric profiling can aid in choosing suitable healthcare strategies, resulting in cost reductions and improved time efficiency, which positively impact the quality-adjusted life years (QALY) metric and can support funding opportunities. In health psychology, assessing therapeutic success typically involves considering the associations between latent variable outcomes and evaluating relationships, e.g., via correlations [12] or correlation-based methods (e.g., linear regression or SEM) [11]. Enhancing statistical power generally requires increasing the effect size (e.g., through optimized treatment plans or the use of improved and unbiased measures of effect size), which in turn raises the QALY index values and can lead to increased grant funding. Moreover, demanding larger power can cause an increase in sampling costs, because statistical power also depends on sample size. Enhancing the statistical power through improved statistical analysis helps achieve a desired level of power without increasing the sample size, thereby lowering sampling costs.

Individual psychometric values are often represented as the means or sums of item responses on a bipolar LS [13]. The central limit theorem (CLT) in statistics, along with its different versions that account for non-i.i.d. random variables and other generalizations [14], ensures that the means and sums of (arbitrarily transformed) item response values approach a normal distribution asymptotically [15]. Regarding [14] the CLT seems to apply if the number of summands is not less than 30. Psychometric questionnaires often consist of a limited number of items. For example, the BFI-10 uses two items per trait to assess the Big Five personality traits [16]. As a result, deriving item response means from a small number of items can hinder the application of the CLT.

In the context of large datasets, various forms of stochastic distributions are possible, leading to an expectation of a W-shaped distribution favoring extreme values and centered values of item response means. As an example think of the individual attitudes towards life-prolonging measures in the hospital. While many people support these or are even obligated to implement them by the Hippocratic Oath, others reject life-prolonging measures or are completely indifferent. The topic appears to be highly polarizing from an ethical perspective (leading to extreme attitudes), but it also requires a certain level of expertise to form a well-informed opinion (possibly leading to an indifferent position). Therefore, it seems plausible to expect a W-shaped distribution of individual attitudes towards this health-economically, psychologically, and medically relevant issue.

Recently, [17] uncovered the compositional structure inherent in data derived from bipolar scales. As highlighted by [18–21], analyzing compositional data presents unique challenges due to the Aitchison metric that underpins it. The space of compositional data, known as the Simplex, is fundamentally non-linear, which makes traditional linear association measures like Pearson's correlation coefficient and standard linear regression methods unsuitable [18,22,23]. Additionally, linear regression techniques such as moderator and mediator analyses that rely on (partial) correlations can introduce bias when applied to compositional data [24].

Ignoring the Simplex can lead to biases in statistical analyses, affecting areas like hypothesis testing and the estimation of psychometric benchmarks [19,25]. To address the bias inherent in association measures such as Pearson's correlation, [17] introduced the isometric log-ratio (ilr) transformation. This method yields interval-scaled real-valued data and produces unbiased outcomes.

The ilr approach can support psychotherapeutic treatment at various points. On the one hand, it can be used in the context of scale development. When exploring the factorial structure of a construct, inter-item correlations and factor loadings play a central role. If these are distorted, the factorial structure may be inaccurately captured [17]. Additionally, scale validation - particularly when examining convergent or discriminant validity - also considers correlations, but between different constructs. These correlations can provide supplementary information during the development of new therapies as well as the refinement of existing approaches. For example, considering strongly positively or negatively correlated constructs allows for adjunctive or indirect treatment of psychological disorders. Furthermore, improved correlation analysis can identify new associations between psychological constructs or reveal false positive correlations, which can enhance adjunctive or indirect therapy strategies. Such improvements directly impact the quality of psychological treatments and, consequently, patient well-being, QALY index values, and funding opportunities.

[26] provided empirical evidence that the statistical power of unpaired two-sample t-tests is enhanced by the ilr approach, leading to an increase in meaningful significant findings and a reduction in spurious ones. Furthermore, patterns in participants' response behaviors are more readily identified using the ilr method [27]. [28] and [29] showed that the shaped of the underlying data-generating process (DGP) affects the order of normal approximation of items response means. That is, small numbers of items and an arbitrarily shaped DGP can reduce the normal approximation of means. Assuming a normally, skewed, bimodal or heavy-tailed DGP of item response means, studies by [17,30–32] demonstrate that the ilr approach improves the statistical power of the correlation t-test emphasizing its universality. While [21] provide evidence that the ilr approach enhances the statistical power of both paired and unpaired two-sample t-tests, [33] demonstrated that statistical power can decline when the DGP becomes more extreme, especially in the case of heavy-tailed distributions. Therefore, it is essential to consider the correlation test also in more extreme scenarios than previously examined in order to rule out the possibility of a loss in statistical power, which could diminish the benefits associated with the ilr transformation regarding patient well-being, grant funding, and QALY index values.

Consider the hypothesis test for zero correlation, $H_0 : \varrho = 0$, using Student's t-distribution, where ϱ represents the true correlation coefficient [34]. Through simulation studies, we show that the ilr approach produces favorable outcomes even when the CLT assumptions are violated and the DGP exhibits a W-shaped distribution. Compared to traditional methods, this approach enhances the statistical power of the commonly used correlation test based on Student's t-distribution, leading to more dependable data-driven conclusions.

2 Materials and Methods

To thoroughly understand the different types of measurement scales, it is important to distinguish between statements (i.e., items within a questionnaire) and their corresponding response scale (RS), as well as a LS - a collection of items represented by the sum or mean of their responses - and the scale of interest (SOI), which may be a trait or attitude encompassing the full range of possible expressions. The RS measures the degree of agreement (OMA) or disagreement (OMD) a person has with a statement. It is common practice to assign numerical values (e.g., 1 to 5) to verbal responses (such as "not at all" to "very much")

[35,36]. The LS functions as a model of the SOI, helping to estimate the magnitude of a personality trait or attitude (OMT) [13]. In the following context, unless otherwise specified, the term "construct" denotes a psychological construct.

2.1 Bipolar Constructs and Psychometric Scales

Psychometric scales provide assessments of individual levels for various constructs. For example, consider the Big Five trait of openness. Questionnaire items - such as those in the BFI-10 inventory by [16,37] - target specific facets of this construct. By aggregating responses to these items (for instance, calculating their mean), an individual's estimate of the underlying trait (OMT) can be obtained. However, due to incomplete knowledge, uncertainties across different contexts, and environmental complexity [38–40], psychometric scales may not fully capture all expressions of a person's construct. This suggests the existence of a certain limit of quantification (LOQ) [17]. An illustrative example is provided in Fig. 1.

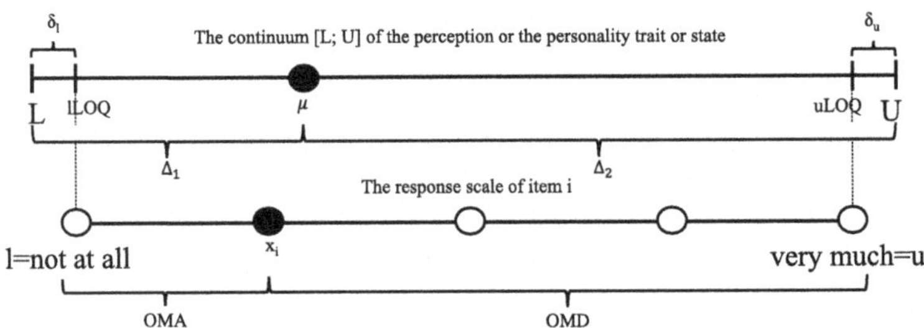

Fig. 1. Illustration of the different types of scales used in psychometrics. The continuum [L; U] represents the TS. The lower scale represents the RS. Figure according to [17].

The continuum ([L; U]) encompasses all possible individual expressions of a construct, ranging from a minimum value (L) (for example, complete non-openness to anything) to a maximum value (U) (such as openness to everything). An individual's underlying trait level (denoted as μ) - the OMT - resides within these bounds. Additionally, the complements Δ_1 and Δ_2 both represent the OMT, with their sum satisfying $\Delta_1 + \Delta_2 = U - L$. For instance, if we set $L = 0$, $U = 100$, and $\mu = 70$, then $\Delta_1 = 70$ and $\Delta_2 = 30$.

A psychometric scale consists of multiple items indexed by $i = 1, \ldots, I$, each associated with a RS that ranges from "not at all" to "very much" with lower and upper limits denoted as l and u. Since these items may not capture all facets of the construct, the RS's lower and upper bounds can differ from L and U, representing the lower ($lLOQ$) and upper ($uLOQ$) quantification limits. The regions beyond these limits - edges of the construct scale not addressed by the items or their RS - are called δ_l and δ_u.

Any response x_i to an item reflects both the OMA and OMD toward that statement. For example, if $l = lLOQ = 2.5$, $u = uLOQ = 97.5$, with $\mu = 60$, and a response $x_i = 50$, this indicates an OMA of 50 and an OMD of 50. The regions $\delta_l = [0, 2.5)$ and $\delta_u = (97.5, 100]$ represent unmeasured areas beyond the quantification limits. In this case, the response $x_i = 50$ provides an estimate for the unknown true trait level $\mu = 60$, and the pair $(50, 50)^T$ - comprising the respondent's OMA and OMD - constitutes a bivariate compositional data point.

2.2 The Compositional Structure in Brief

According to [17], the parameters $L, U \in \mathbb{R}$ can be chosen arbitrarily as long as $L < U$. In the following, we set $L = 0$ and $U = 100$. Without loss of generality, consider a RS $r = \{r_1, \ldots, r_{k+1}\} = \{1, \ldots, k+1\}$, with $k \in \mathbb{N}$. For example, this could be the discrete scale $\{1, 2, 3, 4, 5\}$ with $k + 1 = 5$ five categories ranging from "not at all" (1) to "very much" (5).

Let $pLOQ \in (0, 1)$ quantify the LOQ. Assuming symmetric bounds for the $lLOQ$ and $uLOQ$ we have $lLOQ = 100 \cdot pLOQ/2$ and $uLOQ = 100(1 - pLOQ/2)$. Consequently, the edge regions are also symmetric with $|\delta_l| = |\delta_u| = pLOQ/2$.

Let $x' \in \{r_1, \ldots, r_{k+1}\}$ be an observed response value. The following steps transform any response value x' onto the trait scale within the interval $(0, 100)$, taking into account the value of $pLOQ$. Let $K = k + 1$ and $pLOQ \in (0; 1)$ being the LOQ. Consider the stepwidth $sw = (100 - pLOQ)/(K - 1)$ (e.g., $sw = (100 - 5)/(5 - 1) = 23.75$). For $j = 1, \ldots, K$ compute $x_j^* = p/2 + (j - 1)sw$. Then, $RS^* = \{x_1^*, \ldots, x_K^*\}$ represents the equidistant RS^* with $p/2 = x_1^* < x_2^* < \ldots < x_K^* = 100 - p/2$ (e.g., $RS^* = \{2.5, 26.25, 50, 73.75, 97.5\}$). In this example, $x^* \in (lLOQ; uLOQ) = (2.5; 97.5)$ reflects the transformed OMA and $100 - x^*$ represents the transformed OMD.

According to [19] the compositional data space can be defined as $\mathcal{S} := \{x = (x_1, \ldots, x_D)^T \in \mathbb{R}^D \mid \sum_{i=1}^{D} x_i = \kappa \in \mathbb{R},\ x_i > 0\, \forall\, i = 1, \ldots, D\}$. Choosing $D = 2$ and $\kappa = 100$ $x = (x^*, 100 - x^*)^T \in \mathbb{R}^2$ fulfills the definition of compositional data [17,41–43]. An illustration of the Simplex of bipolar scales data is presented in Fig. 2.

2.3 Ilr and Inverse Ilr Transformation

Any compositional data point is inherently related to the Aitchison metric [19]. However, most conventional statistical methods - such as calculating arithmetic means, Pearson correlation, (multiple) linear regression, and t-tests - are based on the Euclidean metric. The ilr transformation converts compositional data into an interval-scale form that underpins the Euclidean metric [44]. Using the ilr and its inverse, data and statistical results (e.g., mean values) can be easily transformed back and forth between the compositional and Euclidean spaces. In the present case of a $D = 2$ dimensional Simplex the ilr transformation is defined as $ilr((x^*, 100 - x^*)^T) = z_1$ with

$$z_1 = \sqrt{0.5} \ln \frac{x^*}{100 - x^*}. \tag{1}$$

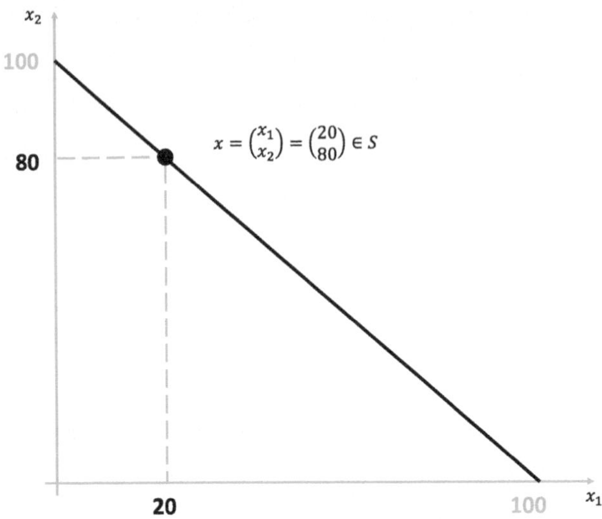

Fig. 2. The black line illustrates the Simplex of bipolar scales data. x_1 (x_2) represents the OMA (OMD) towards the item assertion, respectively. The exemplary point $x = (20, 80)^T$ illustrates an OMA of 20 and an OMD of 80. Figure according to [30].

For instance, the ilr transforms the $RS^* = \{2.5, 26.25, 50, 73.75, 97.5\}$ to $RS^{ilr} = \{-2.59, -0.73, 0, 0.73, 2.59\}$. Please note that the bounds of the RS^{ilr} depend on $pLOQ$, since the bounds of RS^* are also determined by $pLOQ$. As $pLOQ \in (0, 1)$ approaches zero, the bounds of RS^* become closer to 0 and 100, respectively. Consequently, we observe that $\lim_{pLOQ \to 0} \frac{r_1^*}{r_{k+1}^*} = 0$, $\lim_{pLOQ \to 0} \frac{r_{k+1}^*}{r_1^*} = \infty$ and $\lim_{pLOQ \to 0} \ln \frac{r_1^*}{r_{k+1}^*} = -\infty$, $\lim_{pLOQ \to 0} \ln \frac{r_{k+1}^*}{r_1^*} = \infty$, i.e., the spread of the RS^{ilr} increases as $pLOQ \to 0$.

The inverse ilr back-transforms any $z \in \mathbb{R}^{D-1}$ to a compositional data point $x \in \mathcal{S}$. In the present case of $D = 2$ it is defined as follows:

$$x^* = 100 \cdot \frac{e^{y_1}}{e^{y_1} + e^{y_2}} \text{ with } y_1 = \sqrt{0.5} z_1 \text{ and } y_2 = -\sqrt{0.5} z_1. \tag{2}$$

And the compositional data point is given by $x = (x^*, 100 - x^*)^T$. For example, applying the inverse ilr transformation to the RS^{ilr} yields the RS^*.

The evaluation procedure of compositional data can be described as follows:

1. Obtain interval-scaled data through the ilr transformation.
2. Analyse the interval-scaled data using any appropriate statistical procedure (e.g., Shapiro-Wilk test, t-test, linear regression, Pearson correlation etc.) and interpret.
3. If necessary: back-transform the results to the Simplex (e.g., apply the invilr to the arithmetic mean of ilr transformed data) and interpret.

2.4 Simulation Study on Correlations

We explore various combinations of parameters that generate different DGPs. The parameters considered include the number of items (I), the number of individuals (N), the length of the RS ($K = k + 1$), the value of the LOQ ($pLOQ$), and the correlation coefficient (ϱ).

Simulation Parameters. Since the sign of the correlation coefficient only indicates the direction rather than the strength of the association, it is sufficient to consider positive values $\varrho \in \{j \cdot 0.05 \mid j = 1, \ldots, 19\}$. We examine different values of $pLOQ \in \{0.05, 0.1, 0.2\}$ because the LOQ varies across different LSs. Symmetric values for the lower and upper LOQ bounds are assumed. Consequently, the boundary regions are also symmetric, with $|\delta_l| = |\delta_u| = pLOQ/2$. To investigate violations of the CLT, we follow the proposal of [31] and focus on LSs with a small number of items: $I \in \{2, 4, 6\}$. According to [32] the number of responses $K = k + 1$ in the RS may influence subsequent analysis results; we select $K \in \{5, 6, 7\}$; varying the sample size $N \in \{25, 50, 100\}$, we assess how the number of individuals impacts the statistical power of the correlation test.

Implementation of the Simulation. Consider two hypothetical personality traits, T_1 and T_2 (for example, T_1 could represent openness, and T_2 might reflect risk disposition). Let ζ_1 and ζ_2 denote the magnitudes of these traits for a test individual within the ilr-transformed space. Correspondingly, let z_1 and z_2 be the means of the ilr-transformed item responses. We interpret z_i as realizations of random variables Z_i, meaning that z_i serve as estimates of ζ_i ($i = 1, 2$).

Define ϱ as the correlation between Z_1 and Z_2, and σ_1 as the standard deviation of Z_1, based on the underlying DGP. To model the relationship between these traits, we set $Z_2 = \beta_0 + \beta_1 Z_1 + \varepsilon$ where ε is a normally distributed error term with mean zero ($E[\varepsilon] = 0 = \mu_\varepsilon$) and variance $\sigma_\varepsilon^2 \in \mathbb{R}$. The variables Z_1) and ε are assumed to be stochastically independent. From $Cov(Z_1, Z_2) = Cov(Z_1, \beta_0 + \beta_1 Z_1 + \varepsilon) = \beta_1 Var(Z_1) = \beta_1 \sigma_1^2$ it follows that $\beta_1 = \frac{Cov(Z_1,Z_2)}{\sigma_1^2} = \frac{Cov(Z_1,Z_2)}{\sigma_1\sigma_2}\frac{\sigma_2}{\sigma_1} = \varrho\frac{\sigma_2}{\sigma_1}$ [15]. Furthermore, we have $\sigma_2^2 := Var(Z_2) = Var(\beta_0 + \beta_1 \cdot Z_1 + \varepsilon) = \beta_1^2\sigma_1^2 + \sigma_\varepsilon^2$.

$$\beta_1^2 = \varrho^2 \frac{\sigma_2^2}{\sigma_1^2} = \varrho^2 \frac{\beta_1^2\sigma_1^2 + \sigma_\varepsilon^2}{\sigma_1^2} = \varrho^2\beta_1^2 + \varrho^2\frac{\sigma_\varepsilon^2}{\sigma_1^2} \tag{3}$$

$$\Leftrightarrow \beta_1^2(1 - \varrho^2) = \varrho^2\frac{\sigma_\varepsilon^2}{\sigma_1^2} \Leftrightarrow \beta_1^2 = \frac{\varrho^2}{1 - \varrho^2}\frac{\sigma_\varepsilon^2}{\sigma_1^2} \tag{4}$$

$$\Leftrightarrow \beta_1 = \frac{\varrho\sigma_\varepsilon}{\sigma_1\sqrt{1 - \varrho^2}} \Leftrightarrow \sigma_\varepsilon = \beta_1\sigma_1\frac{\sqrt{1 - \varrho^2}}{\varrho} \tag{5}$$

Choose any regression coefficient β_1 and any deserved correlation ϱ. Using the relationship in Eq. (5) the variance σ_ε^2 of the normally distributed error variable can be derived. Therefore, β_1 can be chosen as desired. Obviously, the value of the intercept β_0 neither affects the correlation ϱ nor the variance σ_ε^2. Therefore, without loss of generality we choose $\beta_1 = 1$ and $\beta_0 = 0$ and set $\sigma_\varepsilon = \sigma_1 \frac{\sqrt{1-\varrho^2}}{\varrho}$. The calculation of Z_2 simplifies to

$$Z_2 = Z_1 + \varepsilon. \tag{6}$$

The inversion method is used to generate N random Z_1 values, say $z_{11}, \ldots, z_{1N}$, interpreted as item response means according to a predefined DGP based on a specific combination of the number of items, the LOQ, and the number of response categories.

Let F be the cumulative distribution function (CDF) of a DGP. Consider the generalized inverse CDF, say $F^{-1}(u) = \inf\{x |\; F(x) \geq u\}$ with $u \in [0;1]$. Let U be a continuous and uniformly distributed random variable with CDF

$$F_U(u) = \begin{cases} 0, & u < 0 \\ u, & u \in [0;1] \\ 1, & u > 1 \end{cases}. \tag{7}$$

The DGPs are defined according to the following procedure. As an illustration consider a LS consisting of $I = 2$ items and $K = 5$ responses with $pLOQ = 0.05$. The original RS denotes $\{1, \ldots, 5\}$ while the ilr transformed RS equals $\{-2.59, -0.73, 0, 0.73, 2.59\}$.

1. Consider the ordered set of possible means $PM_{I,K,pLOQ}$ of I ilr transformed item responses with $PM_{I,K,pLOQ} = \{pm_1, \ldots, pm_r\}$ ($pm_i < pm_{i+1}\ \forall\ i \in \{1, \ldots, r-1\}$, $r \in \mathbb{N}$). In the above example we have $I = 2$, $K = 5$, $r = 13$ and $PM_{2,5,0.05} = \{\pm 2.59, \pm 1.66, \pm 1.30, \pm 0.93, \pm 0.73, \pm 0.37, 0\}$.
2. Mimic a W-shape. Locate the two minima of the W at the possible means corresponding to the rounded values of $0.25 \cdot r$ and $0.75 \cdot r$. Name the corresponding indices $Min_1, Min_2 \in \{1, \ldots, r\}$. In the above example we have the minima located at the 4th and 10th possible mean (i.e., $Min_1 = 4$ and $Min_2 = 10$) and the possible means denote $pm_4 = pm_{Min_1} = -0.93$ and $pm_{10} = pm_{Min_2} = 0.93$.
3. Consider the center of the W. The center is unique if and only if r is uneven. Otherwise, there exist two central positions. Name the corresponding index $CENTER$ (r even) or $CENTER_1$ and $CENTER_2$ (r uneven). In the above example, the center is located at $CENTER = 7$ and the corresponding possible mean equals $pm_7 = pm_{CENTER} = 0$.
4. Consider the corresponding probability density $PD = \{PD_1, \ldots, PD_r\}$. Set all $PD_i = 0$ ($i \in \{1, \ldots, r\}$).
5. Set the probability density values $PD_1 = PD_r = 1/r$. In the above example we have $PD_1 = PD_{13} = 1/13 = 3/39$.
6. If r is uneven set $PD_{CENTER} = 0.75 PD_1$. Otherwise, set $PD_{CENTER_1} = PD_{CENTER_2} = 0.75 PD_1$. In the above example we have $PD_{CENTER} = PD_7 = 0.75 \cdot 1/13 = \frac{3}{52}$.

7. Set $d = PD_1/(Min_1 - 1)$ Starting from the left maximum (right maximum) of the W, iteratively allocate the probabilities of the ascending (descending) possible means by setting $PD_{next} = PD_{previous} - d$ until $Min_1 - 1$ (Min_2+1) is reached. In the above example we have $Min_1 = 4$ and $d = \frac{1}{13}/3 = \frac{1}{39}$. Thus, $\{PD_1, \ldots, PD_{Min_1}, \ldots, PD_{CENTER}, \ldots, PD_{Min_2}, \ldots, PD_{13}\}$ $= \{\frac{3}{39}, \frac{2}{39}, \frac{1}{39}, 0, 0, 0, \frac{3}{52}, 0, 0, 0, \frac{1}{39}, \frac{2}{39}, \frac{3}{39}\}$.
8. Set $d = PD_{CENTER}/(CENTER - Min_1)$ Starting from the center (or the left and right center, respectively) of the W, iteratively allocate the probabilities of the descending (ascending) possible means by setting $PD_{next} = PD_{previous} - d$ until the index $Min_1 + 1$ (Min_2-1) is reached. In the above example we have $CENTER = 7$, $Min_1 = 4$ and $d = 0.75\frac{1}{13}/3 = \frac{1}{52}$. Thus, $\{PD_1, \ldots, PD_{Min_1}, \ldots, PD_{CENTER}, \ldots, PD_{Min_2}, \ldots, PD_{13}\}$ $= \{\frac{3}{39}, \frac{2}{39}, \frac{1}{39}, 0, \frac{1}{52}, \frac{2}{52}, \frac{3}{52}, \frac{2}{52}, \frac{1}{52}, 0, \frac{1}{39}, \frac{2}{39}, \frac{3}{39}\}$.
9. Let $S = \sum_{j \in PD} PD_j$ be the sum of all probability density values of the initial set. Define the final probability density $P = \{P_1, \ldots, P_r\}$ as $P_j = PD_j/S$ with $PD_j \in PD$. An illustration is presented in Fig. 3.

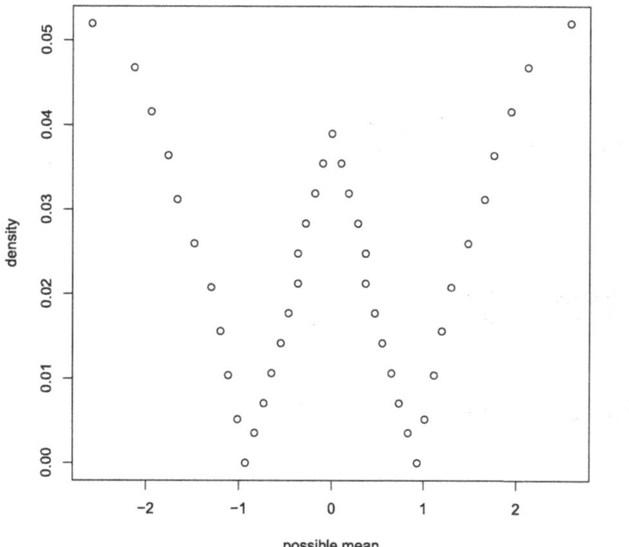

Fig. 3. Illustration of a W-shaped DGP. The item response means are derived from $I = 2$ items using the $RS^{ilr} = \{-2.59, -0.73, 0, 0.73, 2.59\}$.

Using the R function `runif` random values $u \in [0; 1]$ are generated [45]. Then, $F^{-1}(u)$ yields randomly generated item response means of Z_1. The simulation is applied $B = 1000$ times to each combination of parameters (i.e., $pLOQ$, I, N, K, ϱ) yielding 1,539 scenarios and an overall number of 1,539,000 simulation runs (Fig. 4).

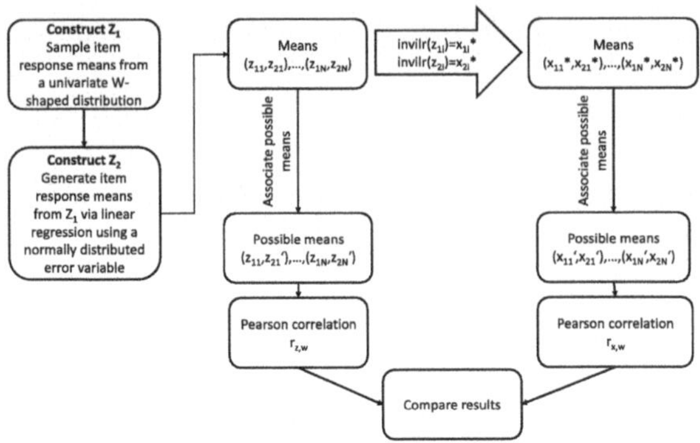

Fig. 4. The simulation process. Figure similar to [31].

Associating Simulated Data to Possible Data. Calculating means of a finite number of item responses yields a discrete set of possible means. The set of possible item response means in the ilr data space $PM_{I,K,pLOQ}$ depends on the number of items I, the number of responses K and the value of the LOQ $pLOQ$. For example, if $K = 5$ and $pLOQ = 0.05$ the ilr RS denotes $\{-2.59, -0.73, 0, 0.73, 2.59\}$. Using using $I = 2$ items the set of possible means is given by $PM_{2,5,0.05} = \{-2.59, -1.66, -1.30, -0.93, -0.73, -0.37, 0, 0.37, 0.73, 0.93, 1.30, 1.66, 2.59\}$. The simulation of z_2 values does not yield data in the set $PM_{I,N,pLOQ}$ because of the random error variable, see Eq. 6. To obtain realistic values any simulated mean z_2 is replaced with its nearest possible item response mean in $PM_{I,N,pLOQ}$ according to the Euclidean metric.

Concerning the original $RS = \{1, \ldots, K\}$ the set of possible item response means of a LS with I items and K responses denotes $PM^{orig}_{I,K} = \{1 + \frac{j}{I} \| j = 0, \ldots, (K-1) \cdot I\}$. The inverse ilr is used to transform any simulated random value z_i $(i = 1, 2)$ towards the original RS. Replace the inverse ilr tranformed value with its nearest possible mean according to the Euclidean metric. Although the Aitchison metric should be used on the original RS, the Euclidean metric is used to obtain the nearest possible mean. This approach is necessary because in common practice means and correlations are calculated without considering the compositional structure of the response data. The intention of the simulation is to show the effects of disregarding the compositional structure on the statistical analysis.

The estimated statistical power of the correlation test of $H_0 : \varrho = 0$ is given by the proportion of rejected null-hypotheses in 1000 simulation runs. For each scenario We obtain two estimates: one for the ilr data and one for the non-ilr data. The difference of the statistical powers Δ indicates the superiority or inferiority of the ilr approach.

3 Results of the Simulation Study and Conclusions

The results of the simulation study are illustrated in Fig. 5a–5c. Splines are created using the `splinefun` function of the R statistic software package, applying the `fmm` method of [46]. We compute the reduction in sample size using the mean increase of statistical power derived from the `splinefun` function (see Fig. 7 and Table 1). The results are summarized as follows:

1. The ilr approach tends to increase the statistical power of the correlation test. The maximal loss of statistical power equals 0.012 and the maximal gain in statistical power equals 0.064 ($\Delta \in (-0.012, 0.064)$, see Fig. 5a).
2. The maximal mean increase of statistical power is observed for $\varrho \in (0.25; 0.45)$ (Fig. 5a–5b).
3. $\Delta > 0$ is observed for all numbers of items $I \in \{2, 4, 6\}$ and the Δ-curves are practically identical. That is, we observe the same change in statistical power irrespective of the value of I (Fig. 6a).
4. As $pLOQ$ increases Δ decreases (Fig. 5c).
5. The value of K does not affect the Δ-curve (Fig. 6b).
6. As the number of individuals N increases the Δ-curve is shifted to the left (Fig. 6c).
7. For $|\varrho| \geq 0.15$, savings in sample size associated with the 25th percentile, the mean, and the 75th percentile of the Δ values are positive. Therefore, from this point onward, a reduction in sample size can be expected. For $|\varrho| < 0.15$, the anticipated savings in sample size are positive, provided that the ilr-induced power change Δ in individual cases is at least equal to the average Δ observed in the simulations.
8. Especially for ϱ close to zero, slight losses in statistical power may occur. These are associated with a potential increase in sample size (see the negative values in Table 1).

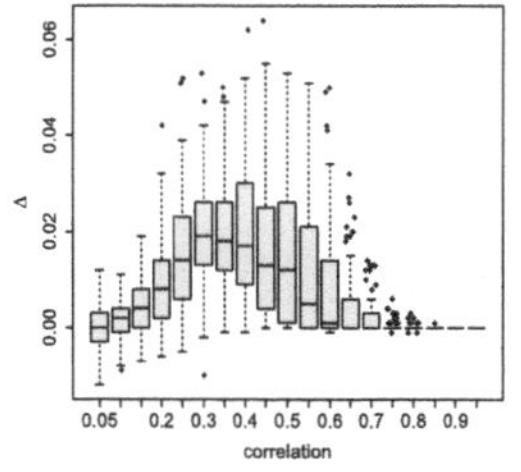

(a) Boxplots of Δ for different correlations ϱ.

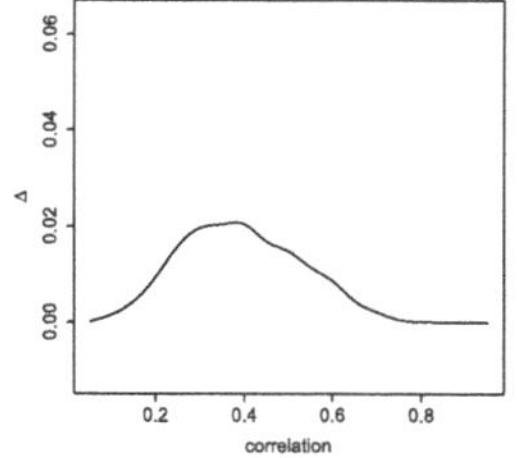

(b) Spline of Δ for different correlations ϱ.

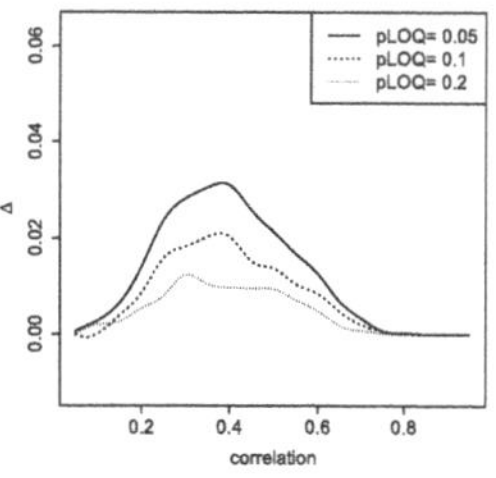

(c) Δ with respect to the LOQ $pLOQ$.

Fig. 5. Δ of rejection of $H_0: \ \varrho = 0$ (part 1)

A reduction of the sample size is observed as long as the absolute value of the correlation is not larger than 0.6 (see Fig. 7 and Table 1). Enlarging the

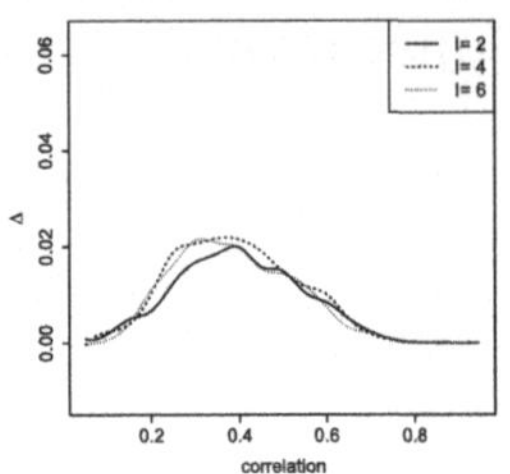

(a) Δ with respect to the number of items I.

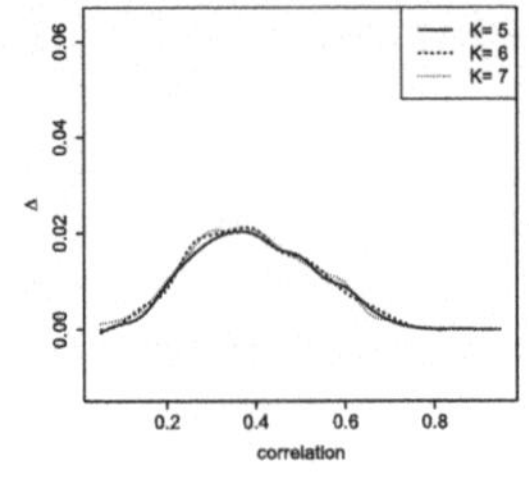

(b) Δ with respect to the number of responses K.

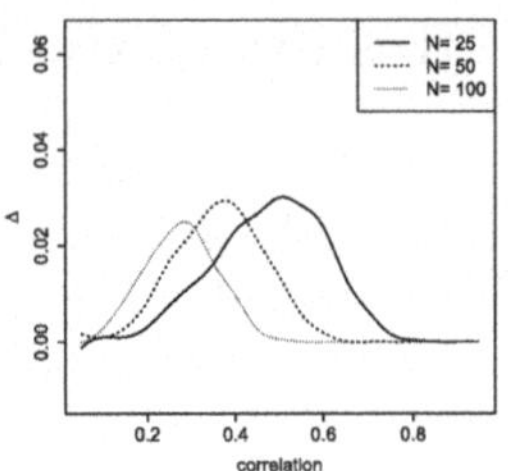

(c) Δ with respect to the number of individuals N.

Fig. 6. Δ of rejection of $H_0: \ \varrho = 0$ (part 2)

demanded power raises the saving in sample size and the decrease is largest for small to moderate effect sizes $\varrho \leq 0.35$.

Table 1. Ilr-induced reduction of sample size according to the demanded power (0.8, 0.85, 0.9, 0.95) and correlation ϱ. The first/second/third number correspond to assumptions about changes in Δ based on the 25th percentile/the arithmetic mean/the 75th percentile of all Δ values associated with ϱ.

ϱ	0.8	0.85	0.9	0.95
±0.05	−24/1/24	−31/1/31	−44/2/44	−86/3/82
±0.1	−2/3/8	−3/4/10	−4/5/14	−7/11/26
±0.15	0/4/7	0/5/9	0/7/13	0/12/22
±0.2	1/5/7	1/6/8	2/8/12	4/15/21
±0.25	2/5/7	2/6/8	4/9/12	6/15/21
±0.3	3/4/6	3/5/6	4/7/9	8/12/15
±0.35	1/2/3	2/4/5	3/5/6	6/9/11
±0.4	1/2/3	2/3/4	2/4/5	3/7/9
±0.45	0/1/2	1/2/3	0/2/3	1/4/6
±0.5	0/1/2	0/1/2	1/2/3	0/3/5
±0.55	0/0/1	0/1/1	0/1/2	0/2/4
±0.6	0/0/0	0/0/0	0/1/1	0/1/2
$\geq$ |±0.65|	0/0/0	0/0/0	0/0/0	0/0/0

4 Discussion and Limitations

The choice of the reduction factor 0.75 used in the calculation of the height of the inner top of the W may seem arbitrary at first. In fact, it provides an initial

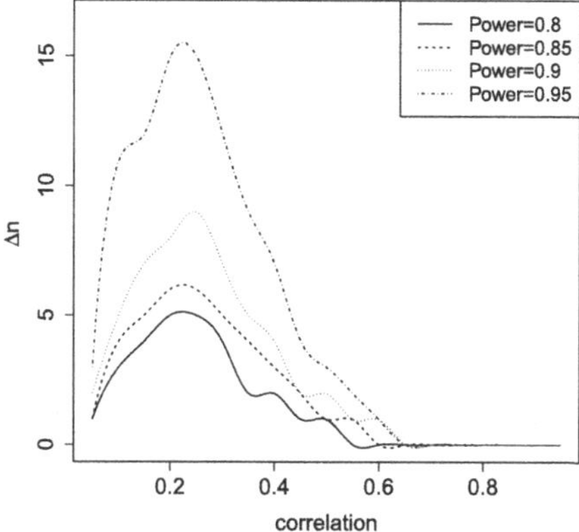

Fig. 7. Ilr-induced average saving of sample size according to different statistical powers and correlations.

approach to the issue. It rather represents a middle ground between the different forms of W-shaped distributions, as already investigated by [28, 29] who showed that the intensity of the shape of a DGP has less influence than the type of the shaped. The influence of the W-shape on Δ therefore represents an adjacent research area.

The ilr approach offers a greater number of potential item means, enabling a more nuanced quantification of a construct. The higher the measurement resolution, the better small differences in attitudes, opinions, or personality traits among individuals can be distinguished. This enhances measurement precision and, consequently, increases statistical power making it easier to quantify the strength of associations or show a significance.

In our simulation, we implicitly assume that the set of possible item response means for Z_1 and Z_2 are identical - meaning that both LSs have the same number of items and RSs. It is well established that the number of response options K in an $RS = \{1, \ldots, K\}$ (where $k \in \mathbb{N}$) does not affect the validity of a psychometric scale [47], although increasing K can improve measurement reliability [48]. Therefore, assuming equal RSs is generally not problematic, as this equality can be easily achieved by assigning the same RS to both LSs.

Regarding the implicit assumption of equal numbers of items, it should be noted that this is not necessarily the case. In fact, the number of items influences the set of possible mean responses. For example, consider the sets of possible means for $I \in 2, 4$ with $pLOQ = 0.05$ and $K = 4$. The values in $PM_{4,4,0.05}$ are more densely distributed than those in $PM_{2,4,0.05}$, indicating a finer granularity in the support of the DGP. However, this increased granularity only has a moderate impact on the shape of the DGP. The maximum (minimum) distance between two values is $max_{2,4,0.05} = 2.59 - 1.53 = 1.06$ (and $min_{2,4,0.05} = 0.46 - 0 = 0.46$), while for the other set it is $max_{4,4,0.05} = 2.59 - 2.06 = 0.53$ and $min_{4,4,0.05} = 0.230 - 0.230 = 0$. In this sense, a LS with a higher number of items provides a numerically more precise measurement than one with fewer items.

Increasing K also results in a finer granularity of the DGP and expands the set of possible item means. However, the relative qualitative benefit diminishes with each increase in K or I, as it primarily subdivides the value range (here, the interval $(-2.59; 2.59)$) more finely. When two constructs are operationalized using at least $I \geq 2$ items and a RS with $K \geq 4$, the possible item means tend to be closely clustered. Consequently, whether equal numbers of items are assumed in the simulation becomes of minor importance.

Furthermore, increasing I and/or K significantly raises the total number of possible item means, regardless of whether the ilr approach is employed. As a result, the qualitative advantage of increased measurement granularity provided by the ilr approach tends to diminish in relevance. Specifically, increasing K broadens the central part of the W-shaped DGP - that is, the range of values with high probability expands, effectively widening the top in the center. In practical terms, values in the center (and at the edges) of the set $PM_{I,K,pLOQ}$ become less (or more) likely to be observed.

This leads to denser clusters of possible means-particularly in the center of the distribution-which are less frequently observed. These two effects - denser clustering and reduced likelihood of extreme values - may explain why increasing K and/or I has little impact on statistical power. This observation aligns with findings from [17,30–32], which show that both $K \geq 4$ and $I \geq 2$ have minimal influence on gains in statistical power.

An increase in $pLOQ$ shortens the ilr RS. As a result, the same number of possible item means are spread over a smaller range, causing construct values to become more concentrated. They move closer together, reducing their distinguishability from one another. This effect is more pronounced in the ilr data space, which contains a greater number of possible item means. While in the untransformed data space all item means are equally spaced, the distances between neighboring item means vary in the ilr data space. Sometimes, these distances can be very close to zero. This leads to a clustering or "clumping" effect, making it more difficult to identify structures within the data and relationships between constructs. Consequently, the measure Δ decreases as $pLOQ$ increases.

Large (small) correlations ϱ close to 1 (near 0) are detected with high (low) probability; that is, the probability of rejecting the null hypothesis $H_0 : \varrho = 0$ approaches 1 (or 0). This holds true regardless of whether the ilr approach is used. Consequently, Δ is close to zero when ϱ is near 1 or near 0. Increasing the sample size enhances statistical power [12], which results in a leftward shift of the Δ curve. However, the increase in power appears smaller than reported in [17], possibly because we explicitly exclude the normal approximation here. Although the correlation test is relatively robust to violations of normality [49, 50], its power diminishes when normality assumptions are violated. As a result, the test loses statistical power in both scenarios - whether with or without ilr transformation. For example, if power decreases by 10% in each case, then Δ also decreases by approximately 10%, since $0.9 \cdot Power^{ilr} - 0.9 \cdot Power^{traditional} =$

$0.9(Power^{ilr} - Power^{traditional}) = 0.9\Delta$. This explains the relatively lower values for Δ.

A limitation of the simulation is its finite set of scenarios; many other practically relevant situations exist - such as different degrees of steepness, varying numbers of scale items $I \in \mathbb{N}$, response options $K = k + 1 \in \mathbb{N}$, or non-symmetric limits of quantification (δ_l and δ_u). Further research is needed to explore the effects of non-symmetric LOQ and alternative distribution shapes (e.g., J-shaped DGPs).

So far, the results appear to be plausible and align with the findings of [17,21,23,26–32], which emphasize the broad applicability of the ilr approach. The ilr method enhances the statistical analysis of psychometric data used in medical decision-making and the development of standards. These findings are applicable across various fields that utilize LS, including health psychology (e.g., measuring and assessing personality traits, predicting human behavior, validating psychometric scales through correlation analysis), neurology (e.g., examining the relationship between cognition and intelligence measures), health economics (e.g., evaluating treatment efficacy, derivation of QALY index values), and econometrics (e.g., analyzing customer attitudes and preferences). Future applications from a statistical perspective include regression-based machine learning techniques and exploring how arbitrarily shaped DGPs influence the effects of the ilr approach on correlation tests. The ilr method can also be employed to obtain unbiased parameter estimates in linear regression models, as well as in multivariate analyses such as (co-)variance analysis (AN(C)OVA and MANOVA) and mediator analyses. Additionally, it is relevant for other areas relying on correlations, means, and standard deviations - such as partial least squares path modeling and factor analysis.

Author contributions. RL wrote the manuscript, did the programming and developed the Tables and Figures. BV wrote the manuscript.

Funding. Not applicable.

Data Availability Statement. Not applicable.

Declarations

Conflict of Interest/Competing Interests. The authors declare no conflict of interests or competing interests.

Ethics Approval and Consent to Participate. Not applicable.

Materials Availability. Not applicable.

Code Availability. R-codes available upon request.

References

1. Edmondson, D., Edwards, Y., Boyer, S.: Likert scales: a marketing perspective. Int. J. Bus. Mark. Decis. Sci. **5**, 73–85 (2012)
2. Sullivan, G., Artino, A.: Analyzing and interpreting data from Likert-type scales. J. Grad. Med. Educ. **5**, 541–542 (2013)
3. Button, K., et al.: Confidence and precision increase with high statistical power. Nat. Rev. Neurosci. **14**, 585 (2013)
4. Button, K., et al.: Power failure: why small sample size undermines the reliability of neuroscience. Nat. Rev. Neurosci. **14**, 365–376 (2013)
5. Muetunda, F., Sabry, S., Jamil, M., Pais, S., Dias, G., Cordeiro, J.: AI-assisted diagnosing, monitoring and treatment of mental disorders: a survey. ACM Trans. Comput. Healthc. **5**, 1–24 (2024)
6. Kang, L., Wu, C., Wang, B.: Principles, approaches and challenges of applying big data in safety psychology research. Front. Psychol. **10** (2019)
7. Tariq, M.U., Babar, M., Poulin, M., Khattak, A.S., Alshehri, M.D., Kaleem, S.: Human behavior analysis using intelligent big data analytics. Front. Psychol. **12** (2021)
8. Cheung, M., Jak, S.: Analyzing big data in psychology: a split/analyze/meta-analyze approach. Front. Psychol. **7** (2016)
9. Cheung, M., Jak, S.: Challenges of big data analyses and applications in psychology. Zeitschrift Für Psychol. **226**, 209–211 (2018)
10. Fan, J., Han, F., Liu, H.: Challenges of big data analysis. Natl. Sci. Rev. **1**, 293–314 (2014)
11. Hair, J., Hult, G., Ringle, C., Sarstedt, M., Danks, N., Ray, S.: Partial Least Squares Structural Equation Modeling ((PLS)-(SEM)) Using R. Springer (2021)
12. Cohen, J.: Statistical Power Analysis for the Behavioral Sciences. Routledge (2013)
13. Likert, R.: A technique for the measurement of attitudes. Arch. Psychol. **22**, 5–55 (1932)
14. Fischer, H.: A History of the Central Limit Theorem. Springer (2011)
15. Davidson, J.: Econometric Theory. Blackwell Publishing (2001)
16. Rammstedt, B., John, O.: Measuring personality in one minute or less: a 10-item short version of the big five inventory in English and German. J. Res. Pers. **41**, 203–212 (2007)
17. Lehmann, R., Vogt, B.: Reconsidering bipolar scales data as compositional data improves psychometric healthcare data analytics. In: Proceedings Of The 56th Hawaii International Conference on System Sciences, pp. 2380–2389 (2023)
18. Aitchison, J.: The Statistical Analysis of Compositional Data. Chapman (1986)
19. Filzmoser, P., Hron, K., Reimann, C.: Univariate statistical analysis of environmental (compositional) data: problems and possibilities. Sci. Total Environ. **407**, 6100–6108 (2009)
20. Lehmann, R.: A new approach for assessing the state of environment using isometric log-ratio transformation and outlier detection for computation of mean PCDD/F patterns in biota. Environ. Monit. Assess. **187**, 4149 (2014)
21. Lehmann, R., Vogt, B.: Increasing the power of two-sample T-tests in health psychology using a compositional data approach. Brain Inform. 333–347 (2023)
22. Aitchison, J.: The Statistical Analysis of Compositional Data. Blackburn Press (2003)
23. Lehmann, R., Vogt, B.: Compositional data statistics improves smart tourism data analytics: profound managerial decisions through reduced statistical bias and

increased power (accepted for publication). In: Proceedings of the 57th Hawaii International Conference on System Sciences (2024)
24. Pawlowsky-Glahn, V., Egozcue, J.: BLU estimators and compositional data. Math. Geol. **34**, 259–274 (2002)
25. Filzmoser, P., Hron, K.: Correlation analysis for compositional data. Math. Geosci. **41**, 905–919 (2009)
26. Lehmann, R., Vogt, B.: Empirical insights into the value of a novel compositional data approach for analyzing bipolar Likert scale data. In: Brain Informatics, pp. 351-361 (2025). https://doi.org/10.1007/978-981-96-3294-7_27
27. Lehmann, R., Bengart, P., Vogt, B.: Discovering careless response behavior in psychometric data. In: Proceedings of the 58th Hawaii International Conference on System Sciences (2025). https://doi.org/10.24251/hicss.2025.400
28. Lehmann, R., Vogt, B.: Shifting psychometric bipolar scales data towards the normal distribution (accepted for publication). In: Proceedings of the 57th Hawaii International Conference on System Sciences (2024)
29. Lehmann, R., Vogt, B.: Increasing normal approximation in psychometric health care data analyses using a compositional data approach (accepted for publication). In: Proceedings of the 57th Hawaii International Conference on System Sciences (2024)
30. Lehmann, R., Vogt, B.: Improving Likert scale big data analysis in psychometric health economics: reliability of the new compositional data approach. Brain Inform. **11** (2024). https://doi.org/10.1186/s40708-024-00232-z
31. Lehmann, R., Vogt, B.: Robustness of the compositional data approach in bipolar psychometric Likert scales big skewed data analysis. In: 2024 IEEE/WIC International Conference on Web Intelligence and Intelligent Agent Technology (WI-IAT), pp. 338–344 (2024). https://doi.org/10.1109/wi-iat62293.2024.00053
32. Lehmann, R., Vogt, B.: Robustness of the compositional data approach in bipolar psychometric Likert scales big bimodal data analysis. In: 2024 International Conference on Engineering and Emerging Technologies (ICEET), pp. 1–8 (2024). https://doi.org/10.1109/iceet65156.2024.10913870
33. Lehmann, R., Vogt, B.: Breakdown of the compositional data approach in psychometric Likert scale big data analysis: about the loss of statistical power of two-sample t-tests applied to heavy-tailed big data. Brain Inform. **12** (2025)
34. Soper, H., Young, A., Cave, B., Lee, A., Pearson, K.: On the distribution of the correlation coefficient in small samples. Appendix II to the papers of "student" and R.A. Fisher. A co-operative study. Biometrika **11**, 328–413 (1917)
35. Pennycook, G., Epstein, Z., Mosleh, M., Arechar, A., Eckles, D., Rand, D.: Shifting attention to accuracy can reduce misinformation online. Nature **592**, 590–595 (2021)
36. Murphy, J., et al.: Psychological characteristics associated with COVID-19 vaccine hesitancy and resistance in Ireland and the United Kingdom. Nat. Commun. **12** (2021)
37. Rammstedt, B., Kemper, C., Klein, M., Beierlein, C., Kovaleva, A.: Big Five Inventory (BFI-10). Zusammenstellung Sozialwissenschaftlicher Items Und Skalen (ZIS) (2014)
38. Romano, A., Mosso, C., Merlone, U.: The role of incomplete information and others' choice in reducing traffic: a pilot study. Front. Psychol. **7**, 135 (2016)
39. Loke, W.: The effects of framing and incomplete information on judgments. J. Econ. Psychol. **10**, 329–341 (1989)
40. James, J., Wood, G.: The effects of incomplete information on the formation of attitudes toward behavioral alternatives. J. Pers. Soc. Psychol. **54**, 580–591 (1988)

41. Aitchison, J., Mateu-Figueras, G., Ng, K.: Characterization of distributional forms for compositional data and associated distributional tests. Math. Geol. **35**, 667–680 (2003)
42. Aitchison, J.: A concise guide to compositional data analysis. Department of Statistics University of Glasgow (2003)
43. Aitchison, J., Egozcue, J.: Compositional data analysis: where are we and where should we be heading? Math. Geol. **37**, 829–850 (2005)
44. Filzmoser, P., Garrett, R., Reimann, C.: Multivariate outlier detection in exploration geochemistry. Comput. Geosci. **31**, 579–587 (2005)
45. R Core Team R: A Language and Environment for Statistical Computing (2020). https://www.R-project.org/
46. Forsythe, G., Malcolm, M., Moler, C.: Computer Methods for Mathematical Computations. Wiley (1977)
47. Weijters, B., Baumgartner, H.: Misresponse to reversed and negated items in surveys: a review. J. Mark. Res. **49**, 737–747 (2012)
48. Preston, C., Colman, A.: Optimal number of response categories in rating scales: reliability, validity, discriminating power, and respondent preferences. Acta Physiol. (Oxf) **104**, 1–15 (2000)
49. Carifio, J., Perla, R.T.: Common misunderstandings, misconceptions, persistent myths and urban legends about Likert scales and Likert response formats and their antidotes. J. Soc. Sci. **3**, 106–116 (2007)
50. Carifio, L., Perla, R.: Resolving the 50 year debate around using and misusing Likert scales. Med. Educ. **42**, 1150–1152 (2008)

The 4th Workshop on Environmental Adaptation and Mental Health

Altered Resting-State Brain Activity in MDD and Schizophrenia: An ALE Meta-Analysis

Yufei Chang, Junwen Mo, Yilin Meng, and Yang Yang(✉)

Department of Psychology, Beijing Forestry University, Beijing 100000, China
hi.yangyang@hotmail.com

Abstract. This study used Activation Likelihood Estimation (ALE) meta-analysis to investigate resting-state functional abnormalities in major depressive disorder (MDD) and schizophrenia (SZ). 41 MDD and 35 SZ studies employing ALFF and ReHo were included. Compared with healthy controls (HC), MDD patients showed increased ALFF in the Right Thalamus and Left globus pallidus, and decreased ALFF in the Temporal, Cingulate, and Posterior Cingulate regions. ReHo was elevated in Parietal and limbic areas. SZ showed increased ALFF in the Striatum and Subcallosal Gyrus, and decreased ALFF in visual, somatosensory, and Cerebellar regions, with ReHo increases in the Striatum and decreases in the Insula, Superior Temporal Gyrus, and Anterior Cingulate Cortex. Direct comparisons indicated greater temporal–limbic activity in MDD patients and higher visual–somatosensory activity in SZ patients. No overlapping regions emerged in the conjunction analysis, suggesting distinct neural mechanisms for the two disorders.

Keywords: Major Depressive Disorder · Schizophrenia · Activation Likelihood Estimation

1 Introduction

Mental disorders are a major cause of disability in adolescents, affecting lifelong development. Globally, about 252 million adolescents suffer from mental disorders, with major depressive disorder (MDD) and schizophrenia (SZ) exerting particularly severe effects on psychological development [1]. Around 25% of SZ patients attempt suicide, and a substantial proportion of deaths are related to depressive symptoms [2]. Although numerous neuroimaging studies have examined MDD and SZ separately, systematic comparisons of their resting-state brain function remain limited. MDD is a chronic mood disorder associated with cognitive and emotional dysfunctions that impair adolescents' academic performance, social interaction, and quality of life [3]. SZ is a severe psychiatric illness with high disability rates [9] and prominent emotional, cognitive, and behavioral disturbances [10]. Depressive symptoms are common in SZ, further worsening prognosis and quality of life [11]. Resting-state functional magnetic resonance imaging (rs-fMRI) has been widely used to explore spontaneous brain activity in mental

A. Lombardi et al. (Eds.): BI 2025, LNAI 16348, pp. 69–77, 2026.
https://doi.org/10.1007/978-981-95-9578-5_6

disorders. Patients with MDD show abnormalities in the Prefrontal Cortex (PFC), Cerebellum, Occipital lobe, and Amygdala (AMY) [4], while SZ involves dysfunction in the PFC, Parietal Lobe, Cingulate Gyrus (CG), Thalamus (THA), and Striatum [5]. Comparative studies further revealed differential alterations in amplitude of low-frequency fluctuation (ALFF) and VMHC between the two disorders, with SZ patients showing higher ALFF in the striatum and MDD patients showing lower VMHC in the Middle Frontal Gyrus (MFG) compared to HC [12]. Among rs-fMRI metrics, ALFF, fractional ALFF (fALFF), and regional homogeneity (ReHo) are commonly used to reflect activity intensity, noise resistance, and local synchronization, respectively. The combination of these indicators provides a comprehensive understanding of local spontaneous brain activity.

Most studies on MDD and SZ have small sample sizes and heterogeneous findings. Meta-analytic approaches can integrate these results to identify consistent activation patterns and clarify shared or distinct neural mechanisms [13]. Therefore, this study employed a coordinate-based ALE meta-analysis of ALFF and ReHo to explore neural differences and potential connections between MDD and SZ.

2 Method

This study followed the PRISMA (Preferred Reporting Items for Systematic Reviews and Meta-Analyses) guidelines to ensure methodological rigor, including systematic literature search, transparent analysis, and standardized reporting [6]. The workflow is illustrated in Fig. 1. A comprehensive search of PubMed, Web of Science, Wanfang, CNKI, and Google Scholar databases was performed for resting-state fMRI studies on MDD and SZ published before December 2023 in both English and Chinese. The keywords used in the depression group were: 1) resting OR regional homogeneity OR amplitude of low-frequency fluctuation OR fraction of amplitude of low-frequency fluctuation OR ReHo OR ALFF OR fALFF; 2) functional magnetic resonance imaging; 3)depressive disorder OR depressive disorders OR unipolar depression; The keywords used in the SC group are: 1) resting OR regional homogeneity OR amplitude of low-frequency fluctuation OR fraction of amplitude of low-frequency fluctuation OR ReHo OR ALFF OR fALFF; 2) Schizophrenia; 3) functional magnetic resonance imaging. Inclusion criteria were as follows: 1) empirical studies reporting between-group resting-state fMRI differences between patients and HC; 2) participants diagnosed with MDD or SZ according to DSM-IV/5 and with HAMD $\geq$ 17; 3) whole-brain analysis rather than ROI-only studies; 4) participants aged 18–55 years; and 5) spatial coordinates reported in standard space (Talairach or MNI). Exclusion criteria included reviews, meta-analyses, case reports, non-human studies, and theses. Coordinate-based meta-analysis was conducted using GingerALE 3.0.2 (http://www.brainmap.org) [7]. Talairach coordinates were converted to MNI space. ALE maps were generated using a cluster-level family-wise error (FWE) correction at $p < 0.05$ (cluster-forming threshold uncorrected $p < 0.05$, 1000 permutations). Conjunction and contrast analyses were performed to identify overlapping and disorder-specific alterations in MDD and SZ. The threshold for comparison analyses was $p < 0.05$ with 5000 permutations and a minimum cluster size of 300 mm3 [8].

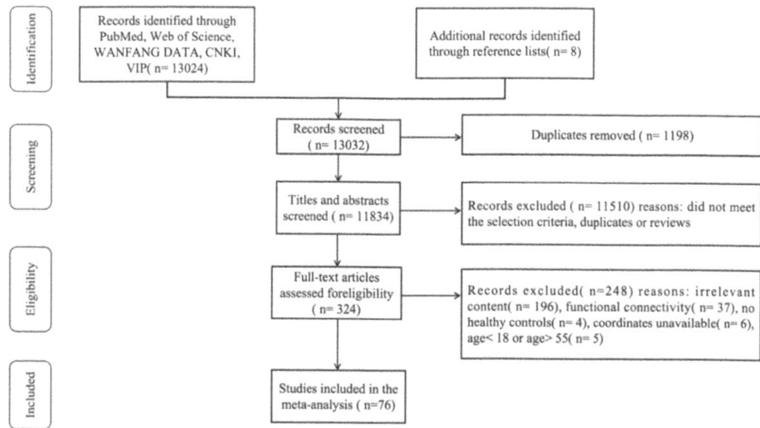

Fig. 1. Flowchart for Literature Screening

3 Result

Through keyword search, a total of 13,024 articles were retrieved in this study, including 1,958 articles on depression and 11,066 articles on schizophrenia. According to the above search criteria, 41 articles on depression and 35 articles on schizophrenia were finally included. Among them, depression included 3,232 subjects, reporting a total of 339 peak coordinates; schizophrenia included 4,733 subjects, reporting a total of 404 peak coordinates.

A single analysis was conducted on 41 studies that compared the activation coordinates of ALFF and ReHo in MDD patients and HC at rest. The ALFF results indicated that compared with the HC group, the MDD group had enhanced activation in the Right THA and Left Medial Globus Pallidus (MGP), and reduced activation in the Left Middle Temporal Gyrus (MTG), Superior Temporal Gyrus (STG), Posterior Cingulate Cortex (PCC) as well as the bilateral CG. The ReHo results showed that compared with the HC group, the MDD group had enhanced activation in the Left Superior Parietal Lobule (SPL), Precuneus (Pcu), Cuneus (Cun), Parahippocampal Gyrus (PHG), STG, and AMY. Based on 35 studies comparing SZ and HC at rest, ALFF analysis showed increased activation in bilateral Caudate (Cau), Right Lateral Globus Pallidus (LGP), CG, Putamen (Put) and Subcallosal Gyrus (SCG), and decreased activation in bilateral Cun and LG, Right PHG, Precentral Gyrus (PreCG), Culmen, Declive (Dec), Postcentral Gyrus (PostCG), and Pcu. ReHo analysis revealed enhanced activation in Left Put and bilateral Cau, but reduced activation in bilateral ACG, Left Transverse Temporal Gyrus (TTG), Insula (Ins), and STG in SZ compared with HC.

A meta-analysis directly comparing MDD and SZ revealed that MDD showed higher ALFF than SZ in the Left Ins, MTG, and STG, whereas patients with SZ showed higher ALFF than MDD in the Bilateral Culmen, LG, Right Cun, PostCG, PCC, PreCG, and Pcu. ReHo in MDD was higher than SZ in the Left PHG, HPC, and AMY, but lower than in SZ in the Bilateral Cau, Put, Left Globus Pallidus (GP) and Clau. Conjunction analysis of ALFF and ReHo between the two disorders yielded no significant overlap. Results are illustrated in Fig. 2, 3 and 4. The Table 1 in the article presents only a subset of the results, the complete findings are provided in the supplementary materials: https://doi.org/10.5281/zenodo.19564103.

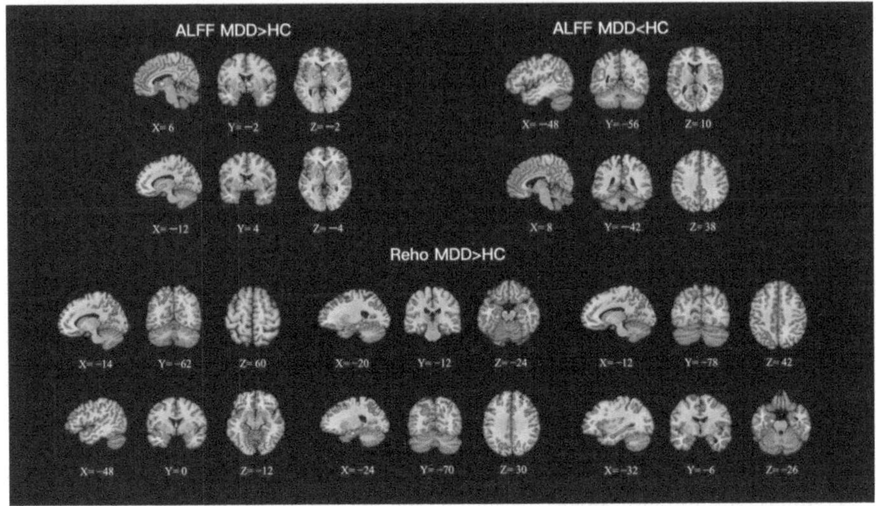

Fig. 2. ALFF and ReHo results from the comparison between MDD and HC.

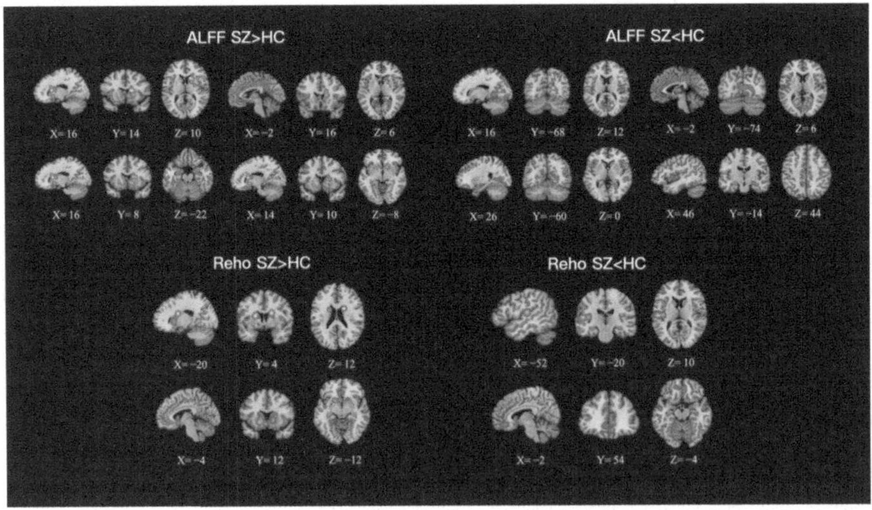

Fig. 3. ALFF and ReHo results from the comparison between SZ and HC.

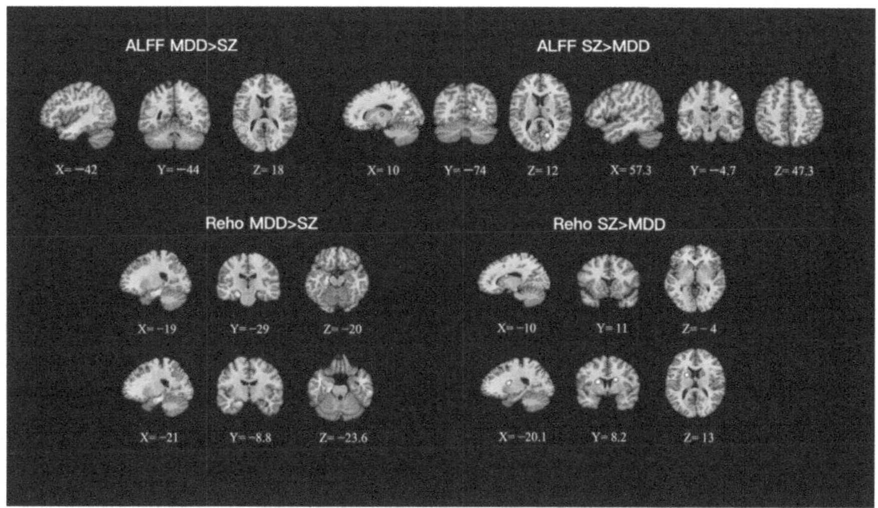

Fig. 4. ALFF and ReHo results from the comparison between MDD and SZ.

Table 1. Regions showing higher ALFF in MDD than SZ

Brain Area	L/R	BA	MNI coordinate			Z-Score
			x	y	z	
Middle Temporal Gyrus	L	37	–46.3	–61.1	7.3	2.5622
Middle Temporal Gyrus	L	19	–35	–58	20	1.8808
Superior Temporal Gyrus	L	22	–48	–56	20	2.1973
Superior Temporal Gyrus	L	39	–45.3	–51.9	13	2.0749
Middle Temporal Gyrus	L	39	–40	–66	22	1.9205
Middle Temporal Gyrus	L	21	–54	–46	12	1.8093
Insula	L	13	–42	–44	18	1.7369

4 Discussion

The ALFF meta-analysis showed lower activation in Left STG and MTG in MDD compared to HC, which may reflect impairments in auditory and language processing, social signal interpretation, and rumination [35]. ALFF was also decreased in Left PCC and Right CG, components of DMN that support self-processing, episodic memory, and emotion regulation [14], potentially associated with emotional rumination and negative self-bias in MDD patients [15]. ALFF was increased in Right THA and Left MGP in MDD. The Right THA is a sensory relay which may be associated with emotional irritability and alertness [36], while Left MGP, connected to motor output and the limbic system, may relate to sad emotion, reward, and motivation-driven behavior [16].

Overall, MDD shows decreased ALFF in DMN regions and increased thalamus–basal ganglia activity, reflecting emotion and motivation regulation abnormalities. ReHo was increased in multiple MDD regions, suggesting potential enhancement of local neural activity synchronization during emotion regulation and self-related cognition. Left Pcu and SPL, as core components of the DMN, may potentially underlie self-processing and introspection, contributing to rumination and negative emotion [17]. Increased ReHo in Left CUN may indicate visual–emotional integration abnormalities [18], the Left PHG and AMY may work together to sustain negative memories [19], and heightened Left STG activity may reflect increased sensitivity to social-emotional cues and negative language bias in MDD patients compared to HC [20].

The ALFF meta-analysis showed that SZ patients exhibited reduced activity in Bilateral CUN and LG in visual cortex, reflecting impaired spatial integration and visual attention, which is consistent with previous studies [22]. Right PHG, plays a crucial role in spatial memory and contextual recognition, its reduced ALFF may reflect alterations in these functions in patients with SZ. This finding aligns with previous studies [23]. Cerebellar Right Dec and Right Cul also decreased, supporting a role of cerebellum in cognition beyond motor coordination [24]. Right PreCG and Right PostCG reductions suggest sensory-motor pathway dysfunction, associated with motor retardation and perceptual deficits [25]. Right Pcu showed decreased ALFF, indicating inhibition in self-processing, autobiographical memory, and internal simulation [26]. In SZ > HC, ALFF was enhanced in Right Cau, Right Put, and Right LGP, reflecting basal ganglia circuit overactivation, possibly linked to cognitive and dopaminergic dysfunction [28]. Increased ALFF in Right CG and Right SCG suggests limbic-ACC circuit activation, related to emotional abnormalities and negative symptoms [28]. In SZ > HC, ReHo analysis showed increases in Left Put and bilateral Cau, indicating enhanced local synchrony in the basal ganglia, associated with dopamine regulation, reward relate processing, and executive function [27]. Compare to HC, SZ patients showed ReHo decreases in bilateral Anterior Cingulate Cortex (ACC), Left TTG, STG and Ins, which may reflect deficits in emotion monitoring, conflict resolution, auditory processing, and language comprehension, which may contribute to hallucinations and delusions [28].

After analyzing 41 MDD and 35 SZ studies, a comparative assessment was conducted to identify overlapping or distinct patterns of enhanced resting-state activation between the two disorders. Left MTG and STG, key regions for language integration, show greater ALFF in MDD patients, reflecting stronger introspection and rumination in speech compared to SZ patients [30]. Left Ins activity further suggests that relatively intact engagement in emotion regulation processes, contrasting with the disrupted insula function typically observed in SZ, and highlighting its role in distinguishing the two disorders [29]. In contrast, SZ > MDD results reveal enhanced ALFF in bilateral LG and Culmen, suggesting altered processing of visual-somatosensory information, while increased Right Cun and Pcu may reflect elevated posterior DMN activity, which indicating that SZ patients exhibit greater cognitive and emotional processing abnormalities [21]. ReHo analysis shows that MDD exhibits higher ReHo in Left PHG, HPC, and AMY, supporting stronger negative emotion processing, emotional regulation, and language-related episodic memory [37]. Compared to MDD patients, SZ patients show increased ReHo in bilateral Cau, Put, and Left Clau, may reflect excessive response to external stimuli, executive dysfunction, and integration abnormalities associated with hallucinations and delusions [31].

Although SZ patients often presents depressive symptoms, with approximately 61% showing clinical depressive manifestations [33], conjunction analysis found no overlapping activated regions with MDD, suggesting that shared symptoms may arise from distinct neural mechanisms [34].

This study included only ReHo and ALFF/fALFF studies on MDD, excluding other neuroimaging methods such as FC, ICA, and VBM, which reduces potential confounding from mixed analysis techniques. Nevertheless, several limitations remain. First, although ALE controls false positives, false negatives cannot be fully avoided [32]. Second, heterogeneity in sample demographics and number of depressive episodes may introduce bias. Third, the cross-sectional design prevents causal inference, highlighting the need for longitudinal studies. Finally, all neuroimaging data are susceptible to artifacts such as respiratory rhythms or head movements, which may affect the results.

5 Conclusion

This study screened MDD and SZ articles, extracted data for ALE meta-analysis, and identified activation differences between both disorders and HC. Contrast and conjunction analyses further revealed distinct ALFF and ReHo differences between MDD patients and SZ patients, though no overlapping regions were found.

Acknowledgements. This work was funded by The National Social Science Fund of China (No. 23BSH136).

References

1. Ferrari, A.J., et al.: Global incidence, prevalence, years lived with disability (YLDs), disability-adjusted life-years (DALYs), and healthy life expectancy (HALE) for 371 diseases and injuries in 204 countries and territories and 811 subnational locations, 1990–2021: a systematic analysis for the Global Burden of Disease Study 2021. Lancet **403**(10440), 2133–2161 (2024)
2. Benedyk, A., et al.: Initial response to the COVID-19 pandemic on real-life well-being, social contact and roaming behavior in patients with schizophrenia, major depression and healthy controls: a longitudinal ecological momentary assessment study. Eur. Neuropsychopharmacol. **69**, 79–83 (2023)
3. Geng, J., et al.: Altered regional homogeneity in patients with somatic depression: a resting-state fMRI study. J. Affect. Disord. **246**, 498–505 (2019)
4. Nawaz, H., Shah, I., Ali, S.: The amygdala connectivity with depression and suicide ideation with suicide behavior: a meta-analysis of structural MRI, resting-state fMRI and task fMRI. Prog. Neuropsychopharmacol. Biol. Psychiatry **124**, 110736 (2023)
5. Yang, Y., Sun, Y., Zhang, Y., et al.: Abnormal patterns of regional homogeneity and functional connectivity across the adolescent first-episode, adult first-episode and adult chronic schizophrenia. Neuroimage Clin. **36**, 103198 (2022)
6. Page, M.J., et al.: The PRISMA 2020 statement: an updated guideline for reporting systematic reviews. Int. J. Surg. **88**, 105906 (2021)

7. Turkeltaub, P.E., Eden, G.F., Jones, K.M., Zeffiro, T.A.: Meta-analysis of the functional neuroanatomy of single word reading: method and validation. NeuroImage **16**(3, Part A), 765–780 (2002)
8. Ragland, J.D., Laird, A.R., Ranganath, C., Blumenfeld, R.S., Gonzales, S.M., Glahn, D.C.: Prefrontal activation deficits during episodic memory in schizophrenia. Am. J. Psychiatry **166**(8), 863–874 (2009)
9. Wiersma, D., et al.: Social disability in schizophrenia: its development and prediction over 15 years in incidence cohorts in six European centres. Psychol. Med. **30**(5), 1155–1167 (2000)
10. Alptekin, K., et al.: Disability in schizophrenia: clinical correlates and prediction over 1-year follow-up. Psychiatry Res. **135**(2), 103–111 (2005)
11. Li, W., et al.: Prevalence of comorbid depression in schizophrenia: a meta-analysis of observational studies. J. Affect. Disord. **273**, 524–531 (2020)
12. Chen, C., et al.: A comparative study of interhemispheric functional connectivity in major depression and schizophrenia. J. Affect. Disord. **347**, 293–298 (2024)
13. Wager, T.D., Lindquist, M.A., Nichols, T.E., Kober, H., Van Snellenberg, J.X.: Evaluating the consistency and specificity of neuroimaging data using meta-analysis. Neuroimage **45**(1), S210–S221 (2009)
14. Raichle, M.E.: The brain's default mode network. Annu. Rev. Neurosci. **38**(1), 433 (2015)
15. Wisco, B.E., Gilbert, K.E., Marroquín, B.: Maladaptive processing of maladaptive content: rumination as a mechanism linking cognitive biases to depressive symptoms. J. Exp. Psychopathol. **5**(3), 329–350 (2014)
16. Arias, J.A., et al.: The neuroscience of sadness: a multidisciplinary synthesis and collaborative review. Neurosci. Biobehav. Rev. **111**, 199–228 (2020)
17. Azarias, F.R., Almeida, G.H.D.R., de Melo, L.F., Rici, R.E.G., Maria, D.A.: The journey of the default mode network: development, function, and impact on mental health. Biology **14**(4), 395 (2025)
18. Runia, N., et al.: The neurobiology of treatment-resistant depression: a systematic review of neuroimaging studies. Neurosci. Biobehav. Rev. **132**, 433–448 (2022)
19. Dolcos, F., LaBar, K.S., Cabeza, R.: Interaction between the amygdala and the medial temporal lobe memory system predicts better memory for emotional events. Neuron **42**(5), 855–863 (2004)
20. Gou, X.Y., et al.: The conscious processing of emotion in depression disorder: a meta-analysis of neuroimaging studies. Front. Psych. **14**, 1099426 (2023)
21. Hoptman, M.J., et al.: Amplitude of low-frequency oscillations in schizophrenia: a resting state fMRI study. Schizophr. Res. **117**(1), 13–20 (2010)
22. Wang, P., et al.: Amplitude of low-frequency fluctuation (ALFF) may be associated with cognitive impairment in schizophrenia: a correlation study. BMC Psychiatry **19**(1), 30 (2019)
23. Peng, Y., et al.: Abnormal functional connectivity based on nodes of the default mode network in first-episode drug-naive early-onset schizophrenia. Psychiatry Res. **295**, 113578 (2021)
24. Zhou, H.Y., et al.: Altered topographical organization of grey matter structural network in early-onset schizophrenia. Psychiatry Res. Neuroimaging **316**, 111344 (2021)
25. Zhang, Y., et al.: Functional connectivity between sensory-motor subnetworks reflects the duration of untreated psychosis and predicts treatment outcome of first-episode drug-naive schizophrenia. Biol. Psychiatry: Cogn. Neurosci. Neuroimaging **4**(8), 697–705 (2019)
26. Whitfield-Gabrieli, S., Ford, J.M.: Default mode network activity and connectivity in psychopathology. Annu. Rev. Clin. Psychol. **8**(1), 49–76 (2012)
27. Tahmasian, M., et al.: Resting-state functional reorganization in Parkinson's disease: an activation likelihood estimation meta-analysis. Cortex **92**, 119–138 (2017)
28. Gong, J., et al.: Abnormalities of intrinsic regional brain activity in first-episode and chronic schizophrenia: a meta-analysis of resting-state functional MRI. J. Psychiatry Neurosci. **45**(1), 55–68 (2020)

29. Zhang, Y., Becker, B., Kendrick, K.M., Zhang, Q., Yao, S.: Self-navigating the "Island of Reil": a systematic review of real-time fMRI neurofeedback training of insula activity. Transl. Psychiatry **15**(1), 170 (2025)
30. Zhu, X., Zhu, Q., Shen, H., Liao, W., Yuan, F.: Rumination and default mode network subsystems connectivity in first-episode, drug – naïve young patients with major depressive disorder. Sci. Rep. **7**(1), 43105 (2017)
31. Cui, L.B., et al.: Putamen-related regional and network functional deficits in first-episode schizophrenia with auditory verbal hallucinations. Schizophr. Res. **173**(1–2), 13–22 (2016)
32. Radua, J., et al.: A new meta-analytic method for neuroimaging studies that combines reported peak coordinates and statistical parametric maps. Eur. Psychiatry **27**(8), 605–611 (2012)
33. Gozdzik-Zelazny, A., Borecki, L., Pokorski, M.: Depressive symptoms in schizophrenic patients. Eur. J. Med. Res. **16**(12), 549–552 (2011)
34. Lange, S.M.M., et al.: A comparison of depressive symptom profiles between current major depressive disorder and schizophrenia spectrum disorder. J. Psychiatr. Res. **135**, 143–151 (2021)
35. Wang, L., et al.: Amplitude of low-frequency oscillations in first-episode, treatment-naive patients with major depressive disorder: a resting-state functional MRI study. PLoS ONE **7**(10), e48658 (2012)
36. Venkataraman, A., Dias, B.G.: Expanding the canon: An inclusive neurobiology of thalamic and subthalamic fear circuits. Neuropharmacology **226**, 109380 (2023)
37. Andrews-Hanna, J.R., Smallwood, J., Spreng, R.N.: The default network and self-generated thought: Component processes, dynamic control, and clinical relevance. Ann. N. Y. Acad. Sci. **1316**(1), 29–52 (2014)

The International Workshop on Brain Information Mechanisms in Special Populations

NeuroLingua: An Interpretable Machine Learning Method for Bilingual Speech Reconstruction from Stereotactic EEG Signals

Ruicong Wang[1], Xueyi Zhang[1], Deyuan Peng[2], Duo Ma[1], Siqi Cai[3](✉), and Haizhou Li[1]

[1] School of Artificial Intelligence, School of Data Science, SRIBD, The Chinese University of Hong Kong, Shenzhen, China
ruicongwang@link.cuhk.edu.cn, {zhangxueyi,maduo,haizhouli}@cuhk.edu.cn
[2] Department of Neurosurgery, South China Hospital, Medical School, Shenzhen University, Shenzhen, China
[3] School of Intelligence Science and Engineering, Harbin Institute of Technology, Shenzhen, China
caisiqi@hit.edu.cn

Abstract. Recent studies in decoding neural signals for speech-related applications have shown considerable promise for advanced brain-computer interfaces (BCIs). However, most studies have focused on speech production, while auditory speech reconstruction remains a challenging task. This paper introduces *NeuroLingua*, a lightweight and interpretable machine learning framework for bilingual auditory speech reconstruction from stereotactic electroencephalography (sEEG) signals. While high-frequency sEEG features are often used exclusively, we propose to integrate both low- and high-frequency neural features that complement one another, and employ an extreme gradient boosting (XGBoost) regression model paired with Shapley additive explanations (SHAP) for enhanced interpretability. To evaluate *NeuroLingua*, we collected and analyzed a bilingual sEEG-audio dataset from epilepsy patients undergoing intracranial monitoring. We show that the proposed framework consistently outperforms conventional single-band approaches in speech reconstruction. Furthermore, the model allows us to identify the most informative neural channels for bilingual speech reconstruction tasks. This study advances the neural speech decoding studies that support the development of next-generation BCIs for assistive communication and rehabilitation in multilingual populations. Code is publicly available (https://github.com/seegdecoding/NeuroLingua).

Keywords: Brain-computer interface · Bilingual neural decoding · Speech reconstruction · Stereotactic electroencephalography · XGBoost

A. Lombardi et al. (Eds.): BI 2025, LNAI 16348, pp. 81–92, 2026.
https://doi.org/10.1007/978-981-95-9578-5_7

1 Introduction

Brain-computer interfaces (BCIs) establish direct communication pathways between the brain and external devices [12], offering significant potential to restore function for individuals with severe neurological impairments such as amyotrophic lateral sclerosis (ALS) or stroke [9,16]. Although research has made considerable advances in decoding neural signals related to speech production [17,20], the decoding of speech perception remains a considerable challenge. Understanding how the brain processes auditory speech is critical for developing BCIs for advanced bi-directional communication and neural rehabilitation [14].

Auditory speech reconstruction relies on diverse neural recording methods, each balancing signal quality and clinical feasibility. Stereotactic electroencephalography (sEEG) has emerged as a promising modality for this task, offering an optimal balance of high-resolution neural recordings and minimal surgical invasiveness. Unlike conventional electrocorticography (ECoG), sEEG electrodes are implanted through small burr holes, significantly reducing trauma [11]. Techniques such as 3D angiography, MRI guidance, and robot-assisted surgery have further enhanced its safety and precision, solidifying its role in speech decoding research [4].

With the advantages of sEEG, recent studies have explored the possibility of decoding neural signals for auditory speech reconstruction using deep learning [15,22]. However, these models often function as "black boxes", prioritizing predictive accuracy over interpretability and providing little insight into the underlying neural mechanisms [1,5,21]. Moreover, previous studies mainly focus on the high-gamma band (70–150 Hz) [6,8], overlooking valuable information encoded in low-frequency oscillations (<30 Hz) that are also fundamental to speech processing [19]. Finally, existing research is largely confined to monolingual contexts, creating a significant gap in our understanding of the neural dynamics that support multilingual speech perception.

To address these limitations, we propose *NeuroLingua*, a lightweight and interpretable machine learning framework for bilingual auditory speech decoding from sEEG signals. Our model integrates information from both low-frequency and high-gamma band signals to provide a more complete representation of the neural response to speech. We employ an Extreme Gradient Boosting (XGBoost) regressor as opposed to complex deep learning architectures for the former's effectiveness with small data and inherent interpretability. To ensure interpretability, we employ Shapley Additive exPlanations (SHAP) to quantify the contribution of individual neural channels, revealing the neural dynamics of speech perception. Finally, we validate the framework on a bilingual dataset, demonstrating its effectiveness across multiple languages.

The remainder of this paper is structured as follows. Section 2 describes the dataset and pre-processing pipeline. Section 3 details the architecture and implementation of the proposed *NeuroLingua* framework. Section 4 presents the experimental results. Section 5 discusses the key findings, with a particular focus on channel importance and the effect of channel number. Finally, Sect. 6 concludes the paper and outlines potential future directions.

2 Methodology and Materials

2.1 Participants

Two patients with epilepsy undergoing intracranial monitoring were enrolled in this study. The first participant (Subject 1) was a 34-year-old male, and the second participant (Subject 2) was a 26-year-old female. Both participants were native Chinese speakers with proficient English skills.

The study protocol was approved by the Ethics Committee of the South China Hospital of Shenzhen University (Approval No. HNLS20231229003-A). Written informed consent was obtained from both participants before the experiment. To ensure participants' safety and comfort, two experienced doctors monitored the procedure throughout the data collection process.

2.2 Neural Recordings

Both participants were implanted with sEEG electrode shafts, with locations determined based on clinical requirements. Subject 1 was implanted with 12 shafts in both hemispheres, and Subject 2 with 10 shafts in the right hemisphere. Each shaft contained 8 to 16 electrode contacts, yielding a total of 186 contacts for Subject 1 and 144 contacts for Subject 2.

To visualize electrode positions, we used LeGUI [7], an open-source MATLAB package based on the Statistical Parametric Mapping toolbox (SPM12) [3]. First, pre-implantation MRI scans were segmented. These MRI scans were then co-registered with post-implantation CT scans to determine the precise locations of electrode contacts. Detailed electrode positions are illustrated in Fig. 1, where contacts belonging to the same electrode shaft are in identical colors.

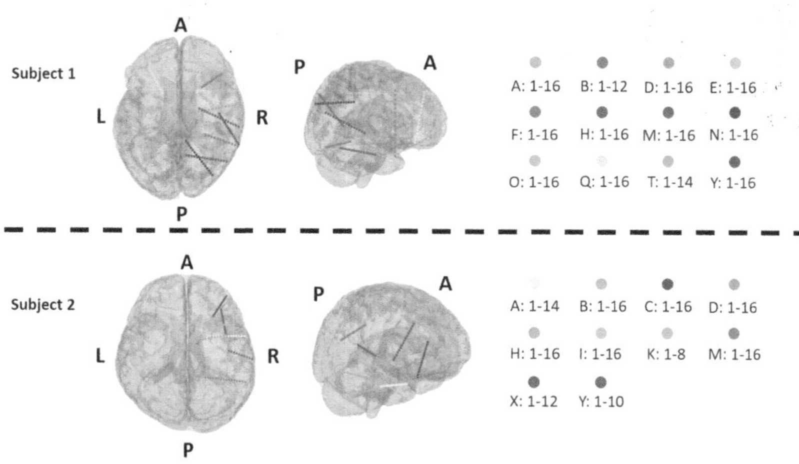

Fig. 1. sEEG electrode contact locations for each subject. Points of the same color represent contacts from the same electrode shafts. These locations are determined by co-registering pre-implantation MRI scans with post-implantation CT scans.

2.3 Experiment Protocol

Participants were presented with auditory stimuli consisting of English and Chinese words. The experiment consisted of 60 rounds in total. Each round began with a 5-second preparation interval, which included an instructional prompt and an auditory starting cue (a "ding"). Following this, participants were presented with a block of 20 English words and 20 Chinese words. The order of words was randomized within each block. Each auditory word stimulus had a fixed duration of 2 s. A rest period was provided after each round to mitigate fatigue and maintain engagement. In total, 1,200 words per language were recorded for each participant. The dataset, along with a comprehensive summary detailing its structure and composition, is publicly accessible[1].

2.4 Data Acquisition

sEEG recordings were obtained using platinum-iridium electrode shafts (model SDE-10/12/16, Sinovation Medical Technology, Beijing, China). Each shaft, with a diameter of 0.8 mm and an inter-contact spacing of 3.5 mm, contained 8 to 16 individual contacts. Neural signals were acquired using a Nihon Kohden EEG-1200 system (Nihon Kohden, Tokyo, Japan) at a sampling rate of 1,000 Hz.

As shown in Fig. 2, auditory stimuli were delivered via a loudspeaker connected to a central control computer, positioned in front of the participant. sEEG signals were amplified and digitized using a signal amplifier and acquisition system. Precise temporal synchronization between stimulus presentation and neural recording was achieved using a custom Python script, which generated and logged trigger markers directly into the continuous sEEG data stream.

2.5 Neural Signal Preprocessing

sEEG data were preprocessed by first excluding channels with pathological epileptiform activity, as identified in clinical reports. This resulted in the removal of 38 of 186 channels for Subject 1 and 22 of 144 channels for Subject 2. The remaining signals were then re-referenced to a bipolar montage to reduce common noise and artifacts [13]. We then isolated two frequency bands: high-gamma activity (HGA; 70150 Hz) and the low-frequency signal (LFS; 130 Hz). Finally, to mitigate the effects of non-stationarity, the HGA and LFS time series were standard normalized within each 2-s window.

2.6 Audio Signal Pre-processing

In this study, audio data were pre-processed using the LibROSA toolkit. All recordings were first resampled to a 16 kHz mono signal. We subsequently extracted two distinct feature representations: the Mel-spectrogram and the speech envelope. Mel-spectrograms were computed with a 64 ms Hann window,

[1] https://github.com/seegdecoding/NeuroLingua.

a 20 ms hop length, and 80 Mel bands to optimize the trade-off between temporal and spectral resolution. The speech envelope was derived by calculating the short-time energy across 20-ms frames with a 10-ms overlap, which was then low-pass filtered at 10 Hz to isolate its temporal modulations.

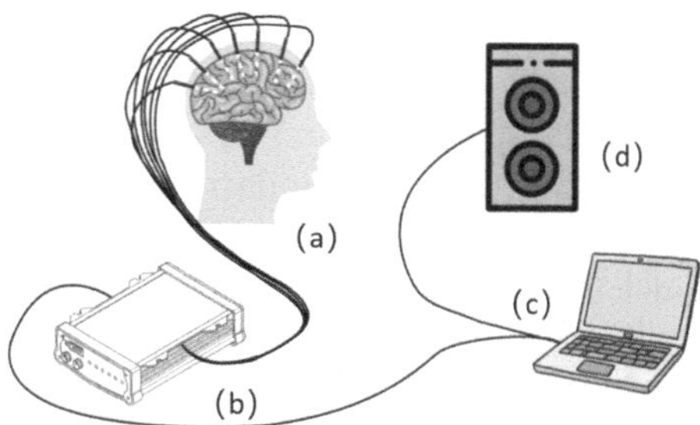

Fig. 2. Experiment setup for intracranial data collection. (a) sEEG recording electrodes. (b) Signal amplifier and acquisition system. (c) Data pipeline and experimental control center. (d) Loudspeaker for auditory stimulus delivery.

3 Method

3.1 Architecture

The overall architecture of *NeuroLingua* is designed to decode bilingual auditory speech from sEEG signals by integrating the complementary information inherent in distinct neural oscillations. Specifically, high-frequency (HGA) activity is expected to capture fine-grained spectral details of the auditory stimulus, while low-frequency signals (LFS) track its slower amplitude envelope fluctuations. As illustrated in Fig. 3, the proposed model processes pre-processed sEEG inputs through a pipeline comprising two main stages: parallel acoustic feature regression followed by similarity-based decoding.

Parallel Acoustic Feature Regression. The first stage transforms the preprocessed sEEG inputs into estimates of key auditory features using two regression modules operating in parallel.

The high-frequency neural dynamics, captured by the HGA component of the sEEG signal (X_{HGA}), are mapped to a time-frequency representation of speech. This mapping is performed by an Extreme Gradient Boosting (XGBoost) regressor (f_{HGA}), which is trained to predict an 80-bin mel-spectrogram from the neural data. The mapping function is defined as follows:

$$\hat{M} = f_{HGA}(X_{HGA}; \theta_1) \tag{1}$$

where $\hat{M}$ denotes the predicted mel-spectrogram and θ_1 represents the learned parameters of the regressor.

In parallel, another XGBoost regressor (f_{LFS}) processes the low-frequency neural signals (X_{LFS}) to predict the temporal envelope of the speech with a 10 Hz low-pass filter. This mapping is defined as:

$$\hat{E} = f_{LFS}(X_{LFS}; \theta_2) \tag{2}$$

where $\hat{E}$ is the predicted speech envelope, and θ_2 represents the learned parameters of the regressor.

Similarity-Based Decoding. In the similarity-based decoding, the model identifies the target word from a predefined vocabulary. For each candidate word k with ground-truth mel-spectrogram M_k and envelope E_k, a combined error metric is computed against the predictions ($\hat{M}$, $\hat{E}$). This metric is a weighted sum of the mean squared errors (MSE) of the spectral and temporal features:

$$MSE_{total}(k) = \alpha \cdot MSE_M(\hat{M}, M_k) + (1 - \alpha) \cdot MSE_E(\hat{E}, E_k) \tag{3}$$

where α is a hyperparameter that balances the contribution of both error terms. The candidate word associated with the smallest total error, min(MSEtotal(k)), is selected as the decoded output.

Overall, *NeuroLingua* provides an efficient framework for speech decoding from sEEG signals. Its dual-path architecture is motivated by the neurophysiological distinction between neural oscillations, allowing it to integrate HGA for spectral content and LFS for temporal dynamics.

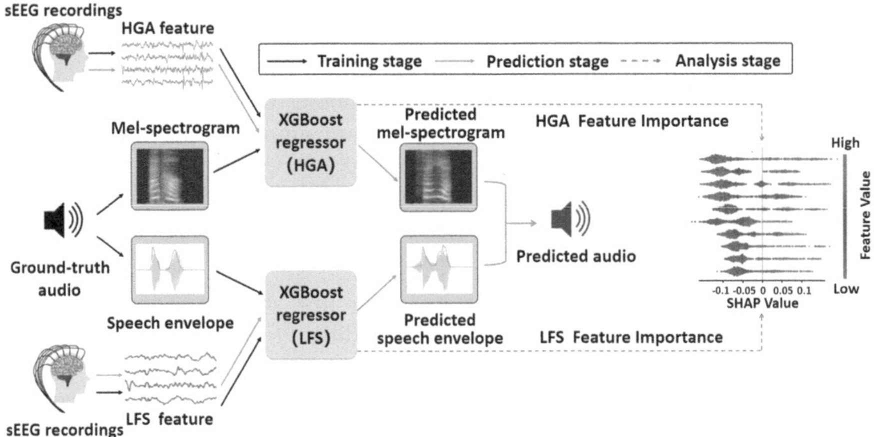

Fig. 3. Architecture of the *NeuroLingua* model. sEEG signals are processed to extract High-Gamma Activity (HGA) and Low-Frequency Signals (LFS). These features are then fed into two parallel XGBoost regressors to predict the mel-spectrogram and speech envelope of the auditory stimulus, respectively. A weighted combination of the MSE between these predictions and the ground-truth acoustic features of each candidate word is computed. The word associated with the minimal combined error is selected as the decoded speech output.

3.2 Implementation and Performance Evaluation

Training Details. The XGBoost regressors for both HGA-to-mel-spectrogram and LFS-to-envelope mappings were implemented using the XGBoost library in Python, with hyperparameter tuning via 5-fold cross-validation. Key parameters included a maximum tree depth of 5, with the number of boosting rounds with a maximum 1000 iterations. Regularization was applied using L1 regularization (λ) set to 0.1 and L2 regularization (γ) set to 0.01. The learning rate was set to 0.03, while a subsample ratio of 0.8 introduced stochasticity to improve generalization. The mean squared error (MSE) served as the objective function for both regression tasks, aligning to minimize discrepancies between predicted and ground-truth acoustic features. The weighting factor α in the combined MSE calculation was optimized via grid search over [0.1, 0.3, 0.5, 0.7, 0.9], with the best performance achieved at $\alpha = 0.7$ for both subjects.

Evaluation Metrics

Accuracy. Decoding accuracy was defined as the proportion of correctly predicted words relative to the total number of trials, calculated separately for Chinese, English, and Bilingual conditions. This metric quantifies the model's performance in decoding auditory speech from sEEG feature representations.

Pearson Correlation Coefficient. To evaluate the similarity between predicted and ground-truth mel-spectrograms, we used the Pearson Correlation Coefficient (PCC). Since mel-spectrograms are two-dimensional matrices with dimensions $T \times F$ (where T represents time steps and F denotes frequency bins), we first flattened each mel-spectrogram into a one-dimensional sequence. Then, for two flattened sequences $\hat{y} = [\hat{y}_1, \hat{y}_2, \ldots, \hat{y}_n]$ (predicted, with $n = T \times F$) and $y = [y_1, y_2, \ldots, y_n]$ (ground-truth), PCC is computed as:

$$\mathrm{PCC} = \frac{\sum_{i=1}^{n} \left(\hat{y}_i - \bar{\hat{y}}\right)\left(y_i - \bar{y}\right)}{\sqrt{\sum_{i=1}^{n} \left(\hat{y}_i - \bar{\hat{y}}\right)^2} \cdot \sqrt{\sum_{i=1}^{n} \left(y_i - \bar{y}\right)^2}} \tag{4}$$

where $\bar{\hat{y}}$ and $\bar{y}$ denote the means of the flattened predicted and ground-truth sequences, respectively. PCC ranges from -1 to 1, with values closer to 1 indicating a more similar relationship between the two mel-spectrograms. This metric effectively quantifies the model's ability to reconstruct both the spectral and temporal characteristics of the original mel-spectrogram.

4 Results

4.1 Auditory Speech Reconstruction

The performance of the *NeuroLingua* model in reconstructing auditory speech from sEEG signals was evaluated using two primary metrics: decoding accuracy and the PCC.

As summarized in Table 1, for monolingual decoding tasks involving 20 word categories, Subject 1 achieved accuracies of 43.96% for Chinese and 46.55% for English stimuli. Subject 2 exhibited marginally superior performance with 45.26% accuracy for Chinese and 48.27% for English words. The bilingual decoding task, which required discrimination among a combined set of 40 Chinese and English word categories, presented a greater challenge. Despite this increased complexity, the model maintained competitive performance, attaining decoding accuracies of 33.19% and 37.93% for the two subjects.

Table 1. Word decoding accuracy (%) of the *NeuroLingua* model. Performance is compared across three language conditions: Chinese, English, and Bilingual.

	Chinese	English	Average[a]	Bilingual
Subject 1	43.96%	46.55%	45.26%	33.19%
Subject 2	45.26%	48.27%	46.77%	37.93%
Average	44.61%	47.41%	46.01%	35.56%

[a] Average calculates the mean performance solely from the Chinese and English monolingual tasks.

Table 2. Pearson Correlation Coefficient (PCC) values of the *NeuroLingua* model for auditory speech reconstruction. Performance is compared across three language conditions: Chinese, English, and Bilingual.

	Chinese	English	Average[a]	Bilingual
Subject 1	0.906	0.911	0.909	0.871
Subject 2	0.913	0.924	0.919	0.884
Average	0.910	0.918	0.914	0.878

[a] Average calculates the mean PCC solely from the Chinese and English monolingual tasks.

Table 2 shows the similarity between predicted and ground-truth speech mel-spectrograms using PCC. Subject 1's PCC values were 0.906 for Chinese, 0.911 for English, and 0.871 for the bilingual task. Subject 2 demonstrated even higher performance, with values of 0.913 (Chinese), 0.924 (English), and 0.884 (bilingual). The consistently high PCC values indicate that *NeuroLingua* effectively captures the critical spectro-temporal features of speech, suggesting that the model has learned a robust mapping between sEEG signal patterns and the acoustic properties of speech.

4.2 Ablation Study

An ablation study was conducted to evaluate the contribution of LFS features to speech decoding performance. We compared decoding accuracy under two different neural feature conditions: (1) using HGA alone to reconstruct speech

Table 3. Speech decoding accuracy with and without LFS features.

Subject	Subject 1			Subject 2		
Features	Chinese	English	Bilingual	Chinese	English	Bilingual
without[a]	41.38%	42.67%	31.03%	41.81%	45.26%	34.05%
with[b]	43.96%	46.55%	33.19%	45.26%	48.27%	37.93%

[a] Without refers to HGA without the LFS feature.
[b] With refers to HGA with the LFS feature.

mel-spectrograms, and (2) using LFS and HGA features to reconstruct speech envelope and mel-spectrogram representations, respectively.

As summarized in Table 3, the inclusion of LFS features consistently enhanced decoding performance across both subjects and all linguistic tasks. For Subject 1, decoding accuracy on English words increased from 42.67% to 46.55%, while bilingual task performance improved from 31.03% to 33.19%. Subject 2 demonstrated similar improvements, with Chinese word decoding increasing from 41.81% to 45.26% and bilingual decoding accuracy rising from 34.05% to 37.93%. The consistent performance improvement across all conditions validates our hypothesis that temporal information encoded in LFS provides complementary information to the spectral representations captured by HGA features.

5 Discussion

5.1 Channel Importance

To move beyond decoding accuracy and identify the specific neural features that underpin model performance, we evaluated the contribution of individual sEEG channels using Shapley Additive exPlanations (SHAP) [18]. SHAP provides a model-agnostic measurement of feature importance by calculating the marginal contribution of each feature to the model's output across all possible feature combinations [2].

As illustrated in Fig. 4(a) and 4(b), a single electrode shaft was markedly more influential than all others in each subject. In Subject 1, the most important shaft traversed the right superior marginal gyrus and extended into the posterior insula. In Subject 2, the shaft with the highest SHAP values was located within the right operculum and the posterior long gyrus of the insula. Notably, the clustering of high-importance channels within these regions, which are known to be fundamental for speech perception [10], provides strong convergent evidence for the neuroscientific plausibility of the *NeuroLingua* model.

5.2 Effect of Channel Number on Decoding Performance

To investigate the impact of the number of electrode channels on decoding performance, we investigated the relationship between the number of electrodes and decoding accuracy. We ranked all channels for Subject 1 and Subject 2 by their feature importance, as derived from SHAP analysis, and incrementally constructed models using the top N channels, where N = 10, 20, 30, 40, 100, as shown in (Fig. 4c).

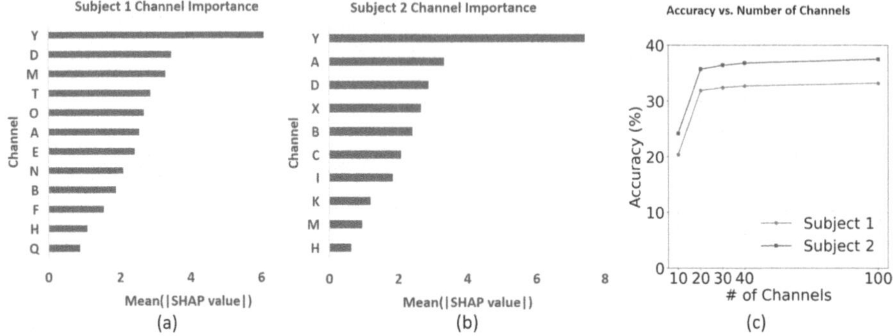

Fig. 4. The impact of channel selection on neural decoding. (a, b) Feature importance maps for Subject 1 and Subject 2, respectively, with channels ranked by mean absolute SHAP value. (c) Bilingual word decoding accuracy as a function of the number of channels used. Channels were added sequentially in descending order of feature importance. Performance saturates after approximately 20 channels for both subjects, indicating diminishing returns from additional electrodes.

Decoding accuracy demonstrated a strong, non-linear relationship with the number of channels. For Subject 1, decoding accuracy exhibited a significant increase when the number of channels was expanded from 10 to 20, rising from 20.4% to 31.9%. Subsequent channel additions yielded diminishing returns, with accuracy reaching 32.4%, 32.7%, and 33.2% for 30, 40, and 100 channels. A similar trend was observed for Subject 2, where accuracy increased sharply from 24.2% (10 channels) to 35.7% (20 channels), but subsequent additions resulted in less improvement (36.4%, 36.8%, and 37.5% for 30, 40, and 100 channels).

Together, these results support that the initial 10–20 channels contribute the most critical information for speech decoding. This has significant practical implications for speech BCIs, suggesting that focusing on this optimal subset can maximize efficiency by reducing complexity and setup effort without substantially compromising performance.

6 Conclusion and Future Work

This study presents *NeuroLingua*, an interpretable framework for reconstructing bilingual auditory speech from sEEG signals. By integrating high-gamma band and low-frequency signals via an XGBoost regressor, the model is capable of mapping neural activities to mel-spectrograms and speech envelopes, demonstrating robust performance in both Chinese and English.

Results indicate high decoding performance, with a mean accuracy of 44.61% for Chinese, 47.41% for English, and 35.56% under bilingual conditions. Reconstructed mel-spectrograms also exhibited high correlation with ground-truth audios. Ablation studies confirmed the necessity of integrating multiple frequency bands, as this approach significantly outperformed models relying solely on high-gamma activity. Neuroscientific plausibility was further supported by the spatial distribution of the most contributory electrodes, which were consistently clustered within brain regions known to be involved in speech perception. Finally, we demonstrated that a minimal subset of 20 channels can achieve performance comparable to that of a full electrode array, suggesting a viable path toward practical and minimally invasive BCIs.

While this study provides a framework for bilingual speech decoding, its findings are constrained by a small sample size. Future work could expand the datasets to enhance generalizability and extend the approach to other languages and paradigms to test the robustness of the decoded neural representations.

Acknowledgments. This study was funded by Shenzhen Science and Technology Program (Shenzhen Key Laboratory, Grant No. ZDSYS20230626091302006), Shenzhen Science and Technology Research Fund (Fundamental Research Key Project, Grant No. JCYJ20220818103001002), and Program for Guangdong Introducing Innovative and Entrepreneurial Teams (Grant No. 2023ZT10X044).

Disclosure of Interests. The authors have no competing interests to declare that are relevant to the content of this article.

References

1. Angrick, M., et al.: Real-time synthesis of imagined speech processes from minimally invasive recordings of neural activity. Commun. Biol. **4**(1), 1055 (2021)
2. Antwarg, L., Miller, R.M., Shapira, B., Rokach, L.: Explaining anomalies detected by autoencoders using shapley additive explanations. Expert Syst. Appl. **186**, 115736 (2021)
3. Ashburner, J., et al.: SPM12 manual. Wellcome Trust Centre for Neuroimaging, London, UK **2464**(4), 53 (2014)
4. Chaitanya, G., et al.: Robot-assisted stereoelectroencephalography exploration of the limbic thalamus in human focal epilepsy: implantation technique and complications in the first 24 patients. Neurosurg. Focus **48**(4), E2 (2020)
5. Chen, X., et al.: A neural speech decoding framework leveraging deep learning and speech synthesis. biorxiv (2023)
6. Chen, X., et al.: A neural speech decoding framework leveraging deep learning and speech synthesis. Nat. Mach. Intell. **6**(4), 467–480 (2024)
7. Davis, T.S., et al.: LeGUI: a fast and accurate graphical user interface for automated detection and anatomical localization of intracranial electrodes. Front. Neurosci. **15**, 769872 (2021)
8. Duraivel, S., et al.: High-resolution neural recordings improve the accuracy of speech decoding. Nat. Commun. **14**(1), 6938 (2023)

9. Gaur, P., Gupta, H., Chowdhury, A., McCreadie, K., Pachori, R.B., Wang, H.: A sliding window common spatial pattern for enhancing motor imagery classification in EEG-BCI. IEEE Trans. Instrum. Meas. **70**, 1–9 (2021)
10. Hartwigsen, G., Baumgaertner, A., Price, C.J., Koehnke, M., Ulmer, S., Siebner, H.R.: Phonological decisions require both the left and right supramarginal gyri. Proc. Natl. Acad. Sci. **107**(38), 16494–16499 (2010)
11. Herff, C., Krusienski, D.J., Kubben, P.: The potential of stereotactic-EEG for brain-computer interfaces: current progress and future directions. Front. Neurosci. **14**, 123 (2020)
12. Kawala-Sterniuk, A., et al.: Summary of over fifty years with brain-computer interfaces–a review. Brain Sci. **11**(1), 43 (2021)
13. Li, G., et al.: Optimal referencing for stereo-electroencephalographic (SEEG) recordings. Neuroimage **183**, 327–335 (2018)
14. Li, Y., et al.: Dissecting neural computations in the human auditory pathway using deep neural networks for speech. Nat. Neurosci. **26**(12), 2213–2225 (2023)
15. Mai, A., Riès, S., Ben-Haim, S., Shih, J.J., Gentner, T.Q.: Acoustic and language-specific sources for phonemic abstraction from speech. Nat. Commun. **15**(1), 677 (2024)
16. Mane, R., Chouhan, T., Guan, C.: BCI for stroke rehabilitation: motor and beyond. J. Neural Eng. **17**(4), 041001 (2020)
17. Metzger, S.L., et al.: A high-performance neuroprosthesis for speech decoding and avatar control. Nature **620**(7976), 1037–1046 (2023)
18. Nohara, Y., Matsumoto, K., Soejima, H., Nakashima, N.: Explanation of machine learning models using shapley additive explanation and application for real data in hospital. Comput. Methods Programs Biomed. **214**, 106584 (2022)
19. Poeppel, D., Assaneo, M.F.: Speech rhythms and their neural foundations. Nat. Rev. Neurosci. **21**(6), 322–334 (2020)
20. Silva, A.B., Littlejohn, K.T., Liu, J.R., Moses, D.A., Chang, E.F.: The speech neuroprosthesis. Nat. Rev. Neurosci. **25**(7), 473–492 (2024)
21. Verwoert, M., et al.: Dataset of speech production in intracranial electroencephalography. Sci. Data **9**(1), 434 (2022)
22. Wu, X., Wellington, S., Fu, Z., Zhang, D.: Speech decoding from stereo-electroencephalography (sEEG) signals using advanced deep learning methods. J. Neural Eng. **21**(3), 036055 (2024)

Virtual Reality vs. Real-World Learning: A Comprehensive Neurocognitive Analysis of Brain Activity and Cognitive Outcomes in Kinetic and Spatial Tasks

Param Barodia(✉), Abhijeet Satani, Heth D. Joshi, Bharath Banavath, and Krishna Thaker

Satani Research Centre, Ahmedabad, India
parambarodia26@gmail.com

Abstract. This comprehensive pilot study presents an in-depth neurocognitive comparison of learning and creative pursuits across immersive Virtual Reality (VR) environments, flat-screen desktop interfaces, and real-world physical settings, with particular emphasis on brain activity monitoring using advanced Electroencephalography (EEG) techniques. In terms of brain informatics and artificial intelligence applications, the study explores the neurological underpinnings of spatial cognition and kinetic learning tasks, analysing their different impact on learning efficacy and cognitive load.

Two different task categories: pottery (motor kinetic) and spatial thinking tasks were completed by nine healthy adults (ages 21–35) in three different environments: real world, a flat-screen desktop, and an immersive virtual reality environment utilizing Oculus Quest 2. EEG signals were acquired at 512 Hz using a 24-channel configuration following international 10–20 standards, with comprehensive preprocessing including notch filtering (50 Hz), band-pass filtering (0.1–50 Hz), Independent Component Analysis (ICA), and Common Average Referencing (CAR).

Behavioural assessments utilized psychometrically balanced multiple-choice examinations administered post-experiment for each learning environment. In VR-based spatial tasks, EEG spectral analysis revealed substantial elevations in theta (4–7 Hz) and alpha (8–12 Hz) activity, particularly in the parietal and occipital regions, indicating heightened visual engagement and cognitive load. On the other hand, pottery tasks in the real world showed more somatosensory activation and delta band activity, which means that sensorimotor feedback was more integrated.

Finding out, performance scores were much lower in VR settings (mean = 3.2/20) than in flat-screen delivery, (mean = 6.8/20). This means that cognitive stress or attention problems could be why more neuronal activation doesn't always lead to better learning outcomes. This study involves creating basic datasets for EEG-informed, neuroadaptive VR learning systems that can adapt in real time and keep track of cognitive states. This will directly help AI applications that use neuroscience to improve educational technologies.

Keywords: Brain Informatics · Virtual Reality · Electroencephalography · Cognitive Load · Spatial Learning · Motor Learning · Brain-Computer Interface · Neuroadaptive Systems

A. Lombardi et al. (Eds.): BI 2025, LNAI 16348, pp. 93–109, 2026.
https://doi.org/10.1007/978-981-95-9578-5_8

1 Introduction and Theoretical Framework

1.1 Background and Rationale

Virtual Reality has evolved as a powerful medium in modern education, simulation-based training, and cognitive rehabilitation, representing a crucial convergence between neuroscience and artificial intelligence applications. By creating immersive, interactive, and spatially enriched digital environments, VR enables learners to experience unprecedented levels of presence, agency, and contextual relevance that traditional instructional media frequently fails to deliver [1]. These distinctive affordances have catalysed widespread implementation across diverse fields, including surgical training, STEM education, architectural visualization, athletic preparation, and therapeutic cognitive interventions [2, 4–8].

While the immersive depth and engagement capacities of VR are unquestionable, its effectiveness in facilitating concrete cognitive learning outcomes, particularly if compared to real-world and traditional desktop learning environments, constitutes a significant empirical study necessitating exploration within the brain informatics framework [3, 9].

1.2 Cognitive Load Theory and Immersive Learning

An important limitation of VR-based learning environments is the cognitive strain created by immersive environments. Cognitive Load Theory (CLT) states that learning efficacy is maximized when extraneous cognitive load is reduced and germane load is effectively regulated. Immersive environments inherently present non-task-relevant stimuli, including unique user interface designs, perceptual discrepancies (such as lack of haptic feedback), and sensory overload, all of which may influence cognitive resources critical for memory encoding and information synthesis.

1.3 Embodied Cognition and Sensorimotor Integration

In conjunction with CLT concerns, Embodied Cognition Theory argues that cognition is essentially based on sensory interactions with environmental settings [15, 16]. As a result, real-world activities, especially those requiring tactile, proprioceptive, and vestibular inputs, may engage somatosensory circuits that are poorly emulated in existing VR systems. These embodied cues facilitate not just the acquisition of physical skills but also the establishment of semantic and procedural memory, particularly in scenarios involving tool use or spatial manipulation.

1.4 Brain Informatics and EEG-Based Cognitive Assessment

Despite increasing scholarly interest in the educational potential of virtual reality, a notable methodological deficiency persists: few research has utilized neurophysiological instruments to measure cognitive states during VR-based learning within a brain informatics perspective. Much of the current research relies on behavioural proxies (such as test scores and completion times) or self-reported metrics (including presence and engagement), both of which are prone to bias and do not accurately reflect the real-time brain mechanisms that underlie learning and attention.

Electroencephalography (EEG), with its millisecond-level temporal resolution and mobility, provides an optimal approach to address this gap. By capturing dynamic changes in electrical brain activity across key frequency bands—theta (4–7 Hz; linked to working memory and cognitive load), alpha (8–12 Hz; associated with attention and inhibition), beta (13–30 Hz; related to problem-solving and motor planning), and delta (0.5–4 Hz; connected to somatosensory processing and rhythmic action) EEG allows researchers to assess the impact of various learning modalities on neural processing in actual time.

1.5 Research Objectives and Contributions

This study fills the methodological gap by executing an in depth EEG analysis of neural and behavioural responses to educational tasks conducted in real-world, flat screen, and immersive VR settings. We investigate two learning contexts: (1) kinetic/motor skill acquisition through pottery making and (2) spatial cognitive development through 3D object manipulation and navigation. These activities were chosen for being reliant on sensory integration and sophisticated cognitive processes, rendering them suitable for brain informatics investigation.

This research advances the intersection of brain science and artificial intelligence by creating crucial datasets for the development of neuroadaptive learning systems that can adapt in real-time with respect to cognitive state monitoring.

2 Literature Review

2.1 Virtual Reality in Educational Neuroscience

The use of virtual reality in educational environments has significantly increased within the brain informatics community during the last two decades. Virtual reality facilitates the reproduction of real-world surroundings and abstract concepts, making it especially beneficial in fields demanding procedural expertise and spatial awareness. Meta-analytical research on virtual reality in education reveals considerable efficacy relative to conventional approaches in disciplines such as anatomy, mechanical engineering, and architectural design [11], with VR-enhanced instruction improving student motivation, engagement, as well as outcomes, especially when interactive components are encompassed.

Educational VR applications are classified into three main categories: (a) exploratory learning, (b) experiential learning, and (c) constructivist engagement. Experiential VR learning exhibits superior memory rates through embodied involvement and active engagement. Nonetheless, the efficacy of virtual reality fluctuates depending on task difficulty, cognitive domain, and an individual's experience with virtual settings [12].

2.2 Cognitive Load and Attentional Modulation in Immersive Environments

While immersive VR environments have been praised for their interaction and engagement, they may impose higher cognitive burden than conventional interfaces. Research demonstrates that although VR learners report increased enjoyment and presence, their learning outcomes can be inferior in complex topics due to divided attention. According to Sweller's Cognitive Load Theory, extraneous load introduced by novel interaction schemes or complex user interfaces may hinder memory encoding and schema acquisition [13].

Investigations measuring cognitive load using both subjective surveys and physiological metrics (pupil dilation, EEG) reveal that immersive VR environments may inhibit learning if not properly scaffolded, especially in younger learners or with cognitively demanding material [14]. Minimising UI complexity and coordinating information pacing with cognitive capabilities are suggested as design solutions within brain-inspired computing systems.

2.3 Embodied Cognition, Tactile Feedback, and Sensorimotor Learning

The notion of embodied cognition claims that the body significantly influences cognitive processes, learning, and memory formation. This hypothesis asserts that motor actions and tactile interactions enhance cognitive representations, especially in tasks related to object manipulation, spatial reasoning, or tool utilisation. Research indicates that multifaceted input, particularly touch and proprioception, improves item recognition and memory retention [17].

This is a constraint for contemporary VR systems: while they deliver high-quality visual and auditory experiences, they seldom emulate haptic, proprioceptive, or vestibular inputs with adequate accuracy. Research suggests that motor learning in virtual reality environments does not translate well to real-world scenarios, mostly due to the lack of realistic feedback. This study confirms that virtual reality can facilitate skill development but does not enable performance transfer without the enhancement of tactile or haptic feedback [4].

2.4 EEG as a Tool for Real-Time Cognitive Assessment in Brain Informatics

EEG provides non-invasive, high-temporal-resolution insights into cerebral activity in various cognitive domains, making it vital for brain informatics applications. Cognitive neuroscience studies utilize EEG to detect markers of attention, working memory, and cognitive stress. Brainwave bands are categorized based on functional relevance: theta (4–7 Hz) correlates with memory and cognitive load, alpha (8–12 Hz) with alertness and attention regulation, beta (13–30 Hz) with logical reasoning and motor planning, and gamma (>30 Hz) with integrative processing [18].

Recent research establishes direct links between EEG-based frontal theta activity and task difficulty [19]. Passive Brain-Computer Interfaces (BCIs) that dynamically adapt digital environments based on EEG-derived workload estimates represent cutting-edge applications in brain-inspired computing [20]. Such systems pave the way for adaptive learning platforms where difficulty adjusts in real time based on the learner's neural state.

2.5 EEG in VR-Specific Cognitive Load Research

Studies combining EEG with VR have produced mixed but promising results for brain informatics applications. Research demonstrates that spatial learning tasks in VR elicit hippocampal engagement comparable to real-world navigation, as measured through fMRI and EEG co-registration [21]. However, EEG data acquired during VR is often complicated by motion artefacts and electromagnetic interference from headsets [22]. Careful artefact rejection and preprocessing protocols are necessary for valid interpretation.

Nevertheless, studies demonstrate that EEG-based workload detection is feasible in VR with proper baseline and normalization procedures performed [23]. Frontal theta and parietal alpha are most sensitive to content difficulty and visual complexity in spatial learning tasks, providing valuable biomarkers for neuroadaptive system development.

3 Methodology

3.1 Participants and Recruitment

This pilot study recruited nine healthy adult participants (5 males, 4 females) between ages 21 and 35 ($M = 27.4$, $SD = 3.1$). All participants were right-handed except two, with normal or corrected-to-normal vision. Exclusion criteria included neurological disorders, psychiatric conditions, cardiovascular complications, or substance abuse history. Participants with prior formal experience in EEG recording or VR research were excluded to maintain internal validity of naïve cognitive response profiles.

Prior to participation, subjects completed a comprehensive pre-screening survey assessing digital fluency, spatial skills (via Santa Barbara Sense of Direction Scale), and previous VR exposure levels. This data was used for stratifying learning outcomes to post HOC analyses. Participants were recruited via academic mailing lists, university flyers, and Social Media outreach. Informed consent was obtained under procedures approved by the GMERS SOLA Ethical Review Board (Ref ID: 24387164/24-4-2022/AH).

3.2 Experimental Design Overview

The study employed a within-subjects, repeated-measures factorial design optimized for brain informatics analysis. Each participant engaged in two distinct task paradigms: (1) a motor-kinetic pottery task and (2) a multi-layered spatial reasoning task, under three environmental settings: real-world, flat-screen 2D simulation, and immersive VR. The six resulting experimental conditions were:

1. Real-world Pottery
2. Flat-screen Pottery
3. VR Pottery
4. Real-world Spatial Cognition
5. Flat-screen Spatial Cognition
6. VR Spatial Cognition

To minimize cognitive fatigue and order bias, conditions were distributed across two experimental days with randomized, counterbalanced order assignments. Each session lasted approximately 90 min, including breaks. Environmental factors (lighting, temperature, and noise) were controlled and standardized across all sessions. Task engagement duration was fixed at 15–20 min per condition, with within-condition breaks of 5 min and inter-condition breaks of 15–20 min.

3.3 Equipment and Technical Setup

3.3.1 EEG System Configuration

A 24-channel wireless EEG acquisition system was utilised, with electrodes positioned according to the International 10–20 system for optimal brain informatics data collection. Scalp impedance was maintained under 5 kΩ using conductive paste. Signals were digitised at 512 Hz with 24-bit resolution. Hardware notch filtering at 50 Hz eliminated line noise. EEG sensors were distributed with emphasis on frontal (F3, F4, Fz), central (C3, C4), parietal (P3, P4, Pz), and occipital (O1, O2) regions to capture task-relevant neural activity in attentional and spatial processing networks. Electrode placement was verified via photogrammetry prior to recording (Fig. 1).

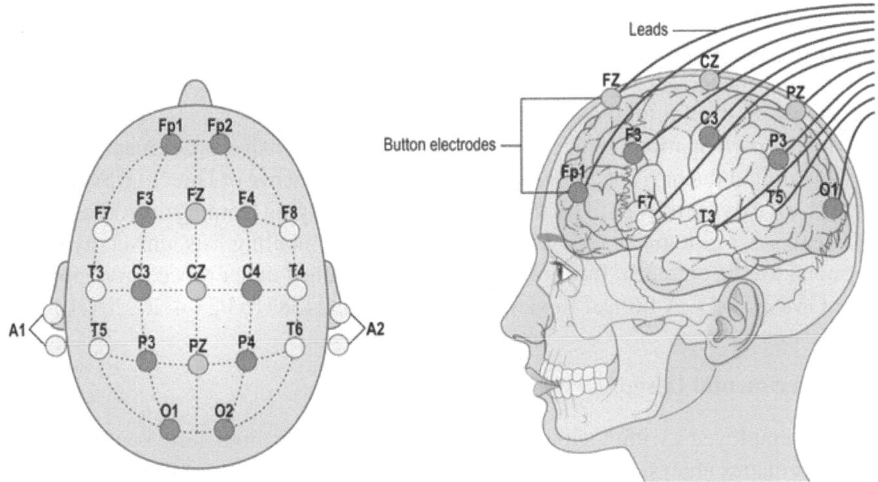

Fig. 1. Standardized electrode placement configuration in the International 10–20 System for electroencephalography (EEG) recording. (A) Superior view and (B) lateral view. Systematic positioning of recording electrodes across the scalp surface. The 10–20 system focuses on anatomical landmarks to establish standardized electrode placement.

3.3.2 Virtual Reality Environment

The Oculus Quest 2 delivered immersive VR experiences with software including "Pottery VR" (by Infinite Dreams) and a custom Unity3D-based spatial cognition module built with WebXR plugins. Visual resolution was set to 1832 × 1920 pixels per eye with a 90 Hz refresh rate. Hand controllers enabled 6DoF interaction, simulating clay manipulation and spatial object assembly. For enhanced ecological validity, haptic feedback was introduced through vibration modules embedded in controllers. Spatial tracking was validated to have sub-centimetre drift tolerance via built-in guardian system calibration.

3.3.3 Flat-Screen Setup

Flat-screen conditions were executed on a 27-inch ZEBRONICS Curved 75Hz 80Cm (32") Standard peripherals (keyboard, mouse) facilitated interaction. The 2D environments visually replicated their VR counterparts, developed in Unity3D. Input latency was benchmarked under 20 ms for optimal brain-computer interaction analysis [26].

3.3.4 Real-World Setup

Pottery was conducted using an electric pottery wheel with 1.5 kg of standard terracotta clay. Participants used traditional shaping tools and a water basin. An instructor delivered standardised tutorials and shape reference templates before sessions began. Spatial cognition tasks involved manipulating 3D wooden puzzle cubes, mental rotation cards, and physical maze boards, matched in complexity with virtual tasks.

Environmental conditions (lighting, seating, and noise levels) were maintained constant across laboratory spaces. All sessions were video recorded for behavioural annotation and subsequent brain informatics analysis.

3.4 Task Descriptions

3.4.1 Kinetic Pottery Task

Participants received instructions to create a vase using the given reference in 15 min across all conditions. In virtual reality, hand motions governed deformation forces. Tactile shaping in real-world situations encompassed changing torque, grip adjustments, and applied pressure variations. In flat-screen mode, participants employed a drag-and-drop mechanism to imitate clay manipulation. The metrics collected were task duration, error rate in form matched, and user input on effort and realism, assessed using a 5-point Likert scale.

3.4.2 Spatial-Cognitive Assessment

Participants executed the subsequent subtasks in each environment for an exhaustive brain informatics analysis:

Spatial Rotation Task: Participants engaged in the manipulation of 3D geometric shapes, such as cubes, cuboids, and other foundational forms, through methodical rotation and dissection to thoroughly comprehend their structural composition from multiple viewpoints. The assignment was conducted in both digital and physical media, with participants urged to actively analyse and manipulate the shapes to attain a more profound spatial comprehension of its geometric features and construction.

Reconstruction Task: Participants disassembled and reassembled skeletal components, focusing primarily on the rib cage to avoid distraction due to sophisticated anatomical structures.Performance metrics included assembly accuracy, structural correctness, and time-to-completion for both disassembly and reconstruction phases.

Maze Navigation: Guide an avatar or physical token through three-layered mazes of increasing complexity.

Each subtask lasted 6–8 min with randomised task order. Behavioural data (accuracy, time-to-completion) was logged and synchronised with EEG timestamps for brain informatics correlation analysis.

3.5 EEG Preprocessing and Analysis

Preprocessing was carried out using the MNE-Python framework [25], which is suited for brain informatics applications. The extensive pipeline consisted of:

Band-Pass Filtering: 0.1–50 Hz employing zero-phase FIR for eliminating slow drifts and high-frequency EMG interference.

Notch Filtering: A 50 Hz notch filter to remove power line interference.

Artefact Rectification: ICA decomposition (fastICA) was employed to separate artefacts. Components of eye blinks (frontal slow waveforms), ECG (R-wave patterns), and EMG (high-frequency bursts) were thoroughly excluded.

Channel Interpolation: Defective channels, identified by variance thresholds and spectral entropy, were interpolated via spherical spline approximation.

Re-referencing: Common Average Referencing (CAR) increased signal uniformity across channels.

Epoching: 1.2-s epochs (−200 ms pre-stimulus to +1000 ms post-stimulus) were recovered after each trial.

Baseline adjustment was conducted for a period from −200 to 0 ms for each epoch.Signal quality parameters (SNR, peak-to-peak variance) were monitored for each condition. Sessions with >20% noisy epochs were excluded from analysis to maintain brain informatics data integrity.

3.6 Behavioural and Cognitive Assessment Metrics

After each spatial learning condition, participants completed a 20-item multiple-choice quiz on spatial strategies and object properties. Questions progressed from basic observational inquiries about the structural characteristics of objects participants interacted with to increasingly complex functional assessments based on information presented within the VR learning environment, aligned with established cognitive assessment frameworks [24]. Quiz scores were normalised using z-score transformation. Participants also completed a subjective workload survey adapted from NASA-TLX to estimate perceived cognitive load [27].

For pottery tasks, qualitative scores were assigned by an art instructor on symmetry, completeness, and resemblance to reference shape. Participants remained anonymous, the instructor. Post-task reflections about comfort, presence, and realism were collected in a thorough brain informatics examination.

3.7 Statistical Analysis Framework

EEG spectrum data was gathered using Welch's method (window = 256, overlap = 50%) for brain informatics analysis [28]. Relative power was computed for the alpha (8–12 Hz), beta (13–30 Hz), theta (4–7 Hz), and delta (0.5–4 Hz) wavelength scales.

Within-subject comparisons of spectral power were performed using repeated-measures ANOVA with Bonferroni-adjusted post HOC contrasts. Behavioural data was analysed using paired t-tests (VR vs Flat-screen; Real vs VR), with effect sizes (Cohen's d) reported. Normality testing employed the Shapiro–Wilk and Levene's tests for homogeneity.

Correlation analyses (Pearson's r) explored relationships between EEG measures (theta power) and test scores for brain-computer interface applications. Exploratory factor analysis (EFA) was conducted on NASA-TLX items to cluster workload dimensions.

All analyses were conducted using Python (stats models, scipy, pandas) and JASP for statistical verification. Significance was defined as $p < 0.05$ for brain informatics applications.

4 Results and Interpretation

4.1 Overview of EEG Findings

The EEG data were analysed across four primary frequency bands: delta (0.5–4 Hz), theta (4–7 Hz), alpha (8–12 Hz), and beta (13–30 Hz), focusing on their relative power during task execution in each environment. Virtual reality conditions consistently demonstrated higher theta and beta activity compared to both flat-screen and real-world contexts, notably evident in frontal and parietal electrodes, signifying heightened cognitive burden and attentional engagement during immersive VR encounters.

Delta Band Activity: Delta activity, linked to sensorimotor integration and rhythmic movement, peaked during real-world pottery ($M = 0.18$, $SD = 0.04$) and spatial navigation ($M = 0.17$, $SD = 0.03$). The VR settings had the lowest delta activity ($M = 0.12–0.13$), signifying compromised rhythmic physical involvement due to insufficient proprioceptive and tactile feedback.

Theta Band Activity: Theta power, reflective of working memory and encoding, reached its peak during virtual reality spatial tasks ($M = 0.29$, $SD = 0.05$), considerably beyond flat-screen ($M = 0.21$, $SD = 0.04$) and real-world ($M = 0.20$, $SD = 0.03$) conditions ($F(2,16) = 6.84$, $p = 0.008$, $\eta 2 = 0.461$). This supports the hypothesis that immersive spatial tasks in VR demand enhanced cognitive control and memory resources.

Alpha Band Activity: Alpha suppression (inverse of power increase) is commonly interpreted as a marker of active cortical engagement. VR pottery exhibited increased alpha activity ($M = 0.30$, $SD = 0.03$), consistent with visual immersion and internal visualisation Flat-screen and real-world pottery revealed reduced alpha ($M = 0.25$–0.27), signifying a greater dependence on external sensory integration and reduced cognitive disengagement.

Beta Band Activity: Beta band power, linked to attention, motor planning, and decision-making, was most evident in VR tasks ($M = 0.24$–0.25), particularly during interactive pottery ($M = 0.25$, $SD = 0.02$), in contrast to real-world ($M = 0.20$–0.22) and flat-screen modes ($M = 0.21$–0.23). These findings suggest increased cognitive effort and involvement in motor planning during virtual interaction (Fig. 2).

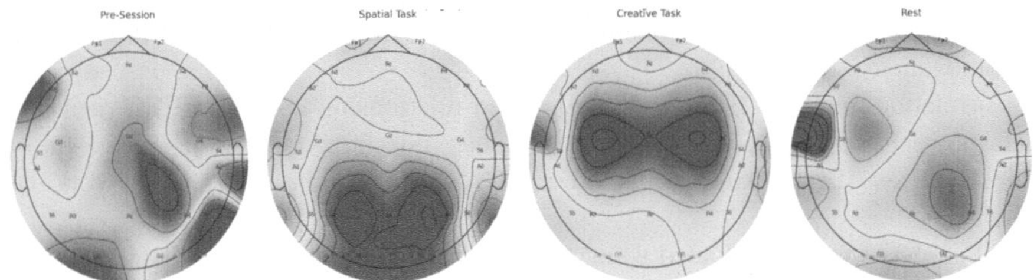

Fig. 2. Topographic EEG scalp maps at 50 ms post-stimulus spanning four experimental phases: Pre-Session (baseline), Spatial Task, Creative Task (pottery-related), and Rest. Each map illustrates the relative distribution of EEG power utilising the usual 10–20 methodology. In the Spatial Task, heightened theta activity is noted in the posterior-parietal areas (P3, Pz, P4, O1, O2), correlating with the involvement of spatial cognition. The Creative Task demonstrates increased delta power in central areas (C3, Cz, C4), indicating motor and imaginative processing. Rest has a consistent, low-amplitude pattern. These topographies exhibit unique neurophysiological characteristics associated with each cognitive state.

4.2 Behavioural Performance and Cognitive Assessment

Spatial Cognition Test Outcomes: After each spatial cognition session, participants undertook a multiple-choice assessment, which consisted of 20 questions. Mean scores were markedly inferior in VR ($M = 3.6$, $SD = 1.1$) relative to flat-screen ($M = 6.2$, $SD = 1.3$), $t(8) = -4.39$, $p = 0.002$, Cohen's $d = 1.47$. Despite higher neural engagement, performance suffered, possibly due to cognitive overload or unfamiliar interface mechanics.

Pottery Evaluation Scores: Art instructor evaluations (on a 10-point scale) based on her regular curriculum criteria rated real-world pottery highest ($M = 7.8$, $SD = 0.9$), followed by VR ($M = 6.1$, $SD = 1.2$), and flat-screen ($M = 5.3$, $SD = 0.8$). The variations between the real world and virtual reality were statistically significant ($p < 0.05$).

NASA-TLX Workload Scores: Participants indicated a greater perceived workload in virtual reality ($M = 72.4$, $SD = 8.5$) compared to flat-screen ($M = 59.1$, $SD = 6.7$) and real-world (M = 61.3, SD = 7.2) environments. The cognitive demand and frustration subscales were significantly heightened in virtual reality, corresponding with EEG-based increases in theta and beta power (Fig. 3).

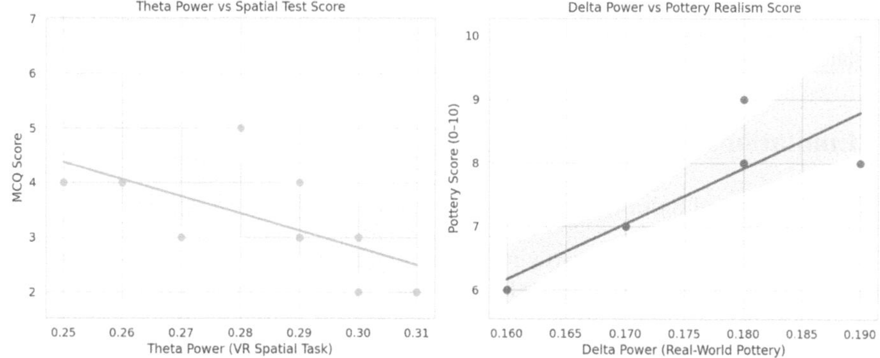

Fig. 3. **Left Plot**: Negative correlation between **Theta Power (VR Spatial)** and **Test Scores** suggesting higher cognitive load in VR leads to lower test performance. **Right Plot**: Positive correlation between **Delta Power (Pottery)** and **Pottery Realism Scores,** reflecting better somatosensory integration during real-world tasks.

4.3 EEG-Behavioural Correlation Analysis

A considerable negative relationship was identified between theta power and post-task test performance (r = −0.68, p = 0.04), suggesting that theta activity may represent cognitive engagement but also suggest overload in high-demand settings such as virtual reality. In contrast, delta activity had a positive correlation with pottery realism evaluations (r = 0.72, p = 0.02), underscoring the significance of tactile-motor synchrony in embodied tasks.

4.4 Brain Informatics Implications

Findings show that VR settings induce enhanced brain activation, especially in the theta and beta frequency bands, matching with elevated attentional demands, cognitive effort, and working memory involvement. However, this enhanced neural engagement does not consistently translate to superior learning outcomes. The disparity between EEG measures of involvement and test scores indicates an extent beyond which immersion may be unfavourable, probably due to overload or interface complexity.

Real-world tasks, enhanced by comprehensive sensory integration along with established motor schemas, showed higher performance, especially in fine-motor activities such as pottery. These findings emphasise the necessity for task-specific design in VR applications within brain-inspired computing frameworks: environments necessitating profound sensory-motor integration may derive greater advantages from real-world exposure, while abstract or spatially intricate tasks may benefit from meticulously regulated VR immersion.

5 Limitations and Methodological Considerations

5.1 Limitations of Sample Size

This study included only nine participants, limiting the potential for generalisation and statistical strength of the findings. Although power analysis validated the sample size for a pilot framework, the sample presented insufficient diversity considering characteristics such as age, VR experience, handedness, and learning styles. Limited sample sizes are susceptible to exaggerating effect sizes and elevating Type I and II errors. A comprehensive study should have at least 40–60 subjects, stratified by demographics and cognitive baselines, to provide a more detailed investigation of brain informatics.

5.2 Limitations of EEG Data

Despite the use of ICA-based artefact rejection and extensive preprocessing, EEG data acquired during movement-intensive tasks, particularly pottery, presented difficulties. Motion artefacts may have disguised or altered the underlying cognitive signals, despite quality control procedures. Subsequent research should incorporate motion capture synchronisation, real-time artefact monitoring, and powerful denoising techniques to enhance brain informatics applications.

5.3 Environmental Confounds

Real-world and virtual reality tasks were carried out in distinct physical environments, resulting in variations in light, temperature, noise levels, and posture. These unpredictable factors may affect participant behaviour and EEG activity. Subsequent investigations ought to standardise the physical configuration or execute all sessions within a single controlled atmosphere to enhance the collection of brain informatics data.

5.4 Counterbalancing and Sequence Effects

While the task order was partially randomly allocated, complete counterbalancing across all six task-environment pairings proved impractical within the pilot's scope. Order effects, such weariness, learning adaption, or novelty bias, may have impacted the results. Future designs must implement Latin square or complete randomisation methodologies and include statistical assessments for sequence effects.

5.5 Test Validity and Measurement Tools

The cognitive assessments administered after the session were created independently and lacked validation through conventional psychometric methods. The reliability, construct validity, and difficulty of calibration of these assessments are therefore uncertain. Future work should incorporate established instruments and assess their internal consistency (Cronbach's alpha) for brain informatics applications.

5.6 Missing Transfer and Retention Metrics

This pilot study evaluated learning immediately post-task but did not include delayed retention testing (24-h or 1-week follow-up). It additionally did not assess the transferability of acquired skills from virtual reality to real-world situations. To draw significant conclusions on educational impact, future research must assess longitudinal retention, practical applicability, and generalisation within brain-inspired computer frameworks.

6 Prospective Directions and Applications

6.1 Scalable Study Augmentation

The existing pilot framework will act as a model for a larger investigation encompassing 40–60 individuals, utilising stratified sampling based on gender, age groups (18–25, 26–35, 36–45), and educational background. A longitudinal approach will be utilised, encompassing updates at 24 h, 1 week, and 1 month to evaluate memory retention and knowledge transfer from virtual reality to real-world situations within brain informatics frameworks.

6.2 Integration of Multimodal Sensors

To improve ecological validity, subsequent studies should incorporate integrative biosensors (eye tracking, galvanic skin response, heart rate variability) alongside EEG for a thorough examination of brain informatics.

It additionally did not assess the transferability of acquired skills from virtual reality to real-world situations. To draw significant conclusions on educational impact, future research needs to evaluate longitudinal retention, practical applicability, and generalisation within brain-inspired computer models. This will allow multidimensional assessment of cognitive load, emotional arousal, and attention levels, particularly in high-immersion scenarios.

6.3 Adaptive VR-Based Learning Systems

Results support the need for intelligent learning platforms that adapt based on real-time brain metrics, representing advanced brain-computer interface applications. Leveraging EEG signals (rising theta or beta activity), AI-driven systems could dynamically modulate VR difficulty, pacing, or sensory load. This approach would optimize engagement while avoiding cognitive overload, thereby personalizing the VR learning experience in real time through a combination of neuroscience and artificial intelligence.

6.4 Integration into Educational Curriculum

The differential effects observed across environments indicate that VR can be selectively integrated into formal education through brain informatics principles. VR is ideal for teaching abstract spatial concepts (molecular geometry, anatomy, architecture) while real-world environments remain more suitable for motor training and hands-on crafts. Hybrid models (VR + real-world labs) can offer optimal learning outcomes.

6.5 Clinical and Therapeutic Utility

Beyond education, findings have implications for cognitive rehabilitation, occupational therapy, and anxiety treatment through brain informatics applications [29]. VR-based exposure therapy protocols can be refined using EEG biomarkers to calibrate emotional intensity and optimize therapeutic outcomes. Pottery and motor tasks simulated in VR may offer therapeutic benefits for individuals with motor impairments or PTSD, especially when real-life engagement is impractical.

6.6 Improved Human-VR Interface Design

The study highlights the importance of ergonomics, tactile feedback, and multisensory realism in brain-computer interaction design. Future VR hardware should prioritize spatial alignment, response latency, and feedback fidelity. Integration of soft haptic gloves, pressure-sensitive tools, and proprioceptive feedback modules will enhance realism and reduce cognitive dissonance during interaction, supporting brain-inspired computing principles.

6.7 Open Science and Collaborative Platforms

To ensure replicability and foster collaboration within the brain informatics community, future efforts will commit to open science practices. This includes pre-registering studies, publishing full protocols and preprocessing pipelines, and maintaining publicly accessible EEG datasets and annotated VR content. Collaborations across neuroscience, education, and human-computer interaction disciplines will amplify translational impact in neuroscience meets artificial intelligence applications.

7 Conclusion

This pilot study presents a foundational investigation into the differential impacts of real-world, flat-screen, and immersive VR environments on cognitive and motor learning, supported by comprehensive neurophysiological data from EEG recordings within a brain informatics framework. The results reveal that VR environments induce elevated theta and beta wave activity, suggesting heightened cognitive engagement and attentional demand. However, this neural activation does not uniformly translate into superior learning outcomes, representing a critical finding for brain-inspired artificial intelligence applications.

Lower post-task test scores in VR conditions point toward the risk of cognitive overload when immersive media is not properly calibrated for learner readiness or task suitability. Real-world tasks continue to outperform VR in scenarios requiring rich sensorimotor feedback, such as pottery, due to the authenticity of tactile and proprioceptive input. Conversely, VR demonstrates promise in enhancing spatial cognition and visual attention provided that task complexity, user interface design, and sensory load are carefully balanced through brain informatics principles.

EEG analysis not only provides insights into moment-to-moment neural engagement but also opens new avenues for developing adaptive, neuro-responsive learning platforms that embody the brain science meets artificial intelligence paradigm. By linking real-time brain signals with educational outcomes, future systems can be designed to accommodate individual differences in attention span, working memory capacity, and cognitive style through brain-computer interface technologies.

While this study is limited by its small sample size and methodological constraints, it offers preliminary evidence that immersive VR, when combined with real-time neurofeedback and thoughtful instructional design, holds substantial potential for revolutionizing education, cognitive rehabilitation, and human performance research within brain informatics applications. The integration of neurotechnology, AI, and immersive environments must be approached with scientific rigour, pedagogical insight, and ethical foresight [10] to ensure responsible and effective implementation.

Future work will require interdisciplinary collaboration, larger and more diverse participant samples, and longitudinal metrics of learning retention and transfer. As VR becomes increasingly accessible, understanding its neurological and psychological affordances through brain informatics approaches will be critical in designing next-generation cognitive training and educational ecosystems that truly embody the convergence of brain science and artificial intelligence.

Acknowledgments. The authors acknowledge the support of the GMERS SOLA Ethical Review Board and all participants who contributed to this research. Special thanks to the Satani Research Centre for providing research infrastructure and technical support for this brain informatics investigation.

References

1. Merchant, Z., Goetz, E.T., Cifuentes, L., Keeney-Kennicutt, W., Davis, T.J.: Effectiveness of virtual reality-based instruction on students' learning outcomes in K-12 and higher education: a meta-analysis. Comput. Educ. **70**, 29–40 (2014)
2. Slater, M., Sanchez-Vives, M.V.: Enhancing our lives with immersive virtual reality. Front. Robot. AI **3**, 74 (2016)
3. Török, Á., Kóbor, A., Honbolygó, F., Csépe, V., Nemeth, D.: What is the evidence that virtual reality is effective for spatial navigation-related tasks? An examination of neural and behavioral effects. Psychol. Res. **84**, 2157–2177 (2020)
4. Neumann, D.L., et al.: A systematic review of the application of interactive virtual reality to sport. Virtual Reality **22**, 183–198 (2018)
5. Rose, F.D., Brooks, B.M., Rizzo, A.A.: Virtual reality in brain damage rehabilitation: review. Cyberpsychol. Behav. **8**(3), 241–262 (2005)

6. Samadbeik, M., Bastani, P., Khoshgam, M., Garavand, A.: The applications of virtual reality technology in medical groups teaching. J. Adv. Med. Educ. Prof. **6**(3), 123–129 (2018)
7. Carl, E., et al.: Virtual reality exposure therapy for anxiety and related disorders: A meta-analysis of randomized controlled trials. J. Anxiety Disord. **61**, 27–36 (2019)
8. Parsons, T.D., Rizzo, A.A., Rogers, S., York, P.: Virtual reality in pediatric psychology. Pediatrics **140**(suppl. 2), S86–S91 (2017)
9. Allcoat, D., von Mühlenen, A.: Learning in virtual reality: Effects on performance, emotion and engagement. Res. Learn. Technol. **26** (2018)
10. Madary, M., Metzinger, T.K.: Real virtuality: a code of ethical conduct. Recommendations for good scientific practice and the consumers of VR-technology. Front. Robot. AI **3**, 3 (2016)
11. Freina, S., Ott, M.: A literature review on immersive virtual reality in education: State of the art and perspectives. In: Proceedings of the eLearning and Software for Education (eLSE), pp. 133–141 (2015)
12. Suh, A., Prophet, J.: The state of immersive technology research: a literature analysis. Comput. Hum. Behav. **86**, 77–90 (2018)
13. Sweller, J.: Cognitive load theory, learning difficulty, and instructional design. Learn. Instr. **4**(4), 295–312 (1994)
14. Makransky, G., Terkildsen, T.S., Mayer, R.E.: Adding immersive virtual reality to a science lab simulation causes more presence but less learning. Learn. Instr. **60**, 225–236 (2019)
15. Culham, J.C., Valyear, K.F.: Human parietal cortex in action. Curr. Opin. Neurobiol. **16**(2), 205–212 (2006)
16. Barsalou, L.W.: Grounded cognition. Annu. Rev. Psychol. **59**, 617–645 (2008)
17. Lederman, S.J., Klatzky, R.L.: Haptic perception: a tutorial. Atten. Percept. Psychophys. **71**(7), 1439–1459 (2009)
18. Klimesch, W.: EEG alpha and theta oscillations reflect cognitive and memory performance: a review and analysis. Brain Res. Rev. **29**(2–3), 169–195 (1999)
19. Brouwer, A.M., Hogervorst, M.A., van Erp, J.B.F., Heffelaar, T., Zimmerman, P.H., Oostenveld, R.: Estimating workload using EEG spectral power and ERPs in the n-back task. J. Neural Eng. **9**(4), 045008 (2012)
20. Zander, T.O., Kothe, C.: Towards passive brain–computer interfaces: applying brain–computer interface technology to human–machine systems in general. J. Neural Eng. **8**(2), 025005 (2011)
21. Burgess, N., Maguire, E.A., O'Keefe, J.: The human hippocampus and spatial and episodic memory. Neuron **35**(4), 625–641 (2002)
22. Tremmel, C., Herff, C., Sato, T., Rechowicz, K., Yamani, Y., Krusienski, D.J.: Estimating cognitive workload in an interactive virtual reality environment using EEG. Front. Hum. Neurosci. **13**, 401 (2019)
23. Mühl, C., Allison, B., Nijholt, A., Chanel, G.: A survey of affective brain computer interfaces: principles, state-of-the-art, and challenges. Brain-Comput. Interfaces **1**(2), 66–84 (2014)
24. Anderson, L.W., Krathwohl, D.R. (eds.): A Taxonomy for Learning, Teaching, and Assessing: A Revision of Bloom's Taxonomy of Educational Objectives. Longman, New York (2001)
25. Gramfort, A., et al.: MEG and EEG data analysis with MNE-Python. Front. Neurosci. **7**, 267 (2013)
26. Bailenson, J.: Experience on Demand: What Virtual Reality Is, How It Works, and What It Can Do. W. W. Norton & Company, New York (2018)

27. Hart, S.G., Staveland, L.E.: Development of NASA-TLX (task load index): results of empirical and theoretical research. Adv. Psychol. **52**, 139–183 (1988)
28. Welch, P.: The use of fast Fourier transform for the estimation of power spectra: a method based on time averaging over short, modified periodograms. IEEE Trans. Audio Electroacoust. **15**(2), 70–73 (1967)
29. Abreu, B.C., Seale, G.S., Temple, R.O., Sangole, A.P.: Rehabilitation, computers in cognitive (2006). https://doi.org/10.1002/0471732877.EMD225

The International Workshop on Neural Data Analysis for Brain-Computer Interfaces and Brain Disorders

The AppleCatcher Game: A Motor Imagery BCI Platform for Investigating Cortical Activation During Imagined Hand Movements

Erlend Skredsvig[1], Robin Kneider[2], and Marta Molinas[1](✉)

[1] Norwegian University of Science and Technology, 7491 Trondheim, Norway
marta.molinas@ntnu.no

[2] Department of Physics, Ecole Normale Supérieure, Lyon, France
robin.kineider@ens-lyon.fr

https://www.ntnu.edu/employees/marta.molinas

Abstract. The AppleCatcher game is an innovative brain-computer interface (BCI) designed to support hand rehabilitation in individuals with motor impairments. This EEG-based system enables users to control a virtual apple-catching game using motor imagery (MI) of hand movements, leveraging brain activity without requiring physical motion. By activating overlapping neural networks involved in motor execution and imagery, AppleCatcher aims to promote neuroplasticity and strengthen motor pathways. Unlike conventional MI-based BCIs that rely on EEG sensor-level data, AppleCatcher uses EEG source imaging (ESI) to localize brain activity at the cortical level. This approach enhances precision in monitoring motor-related regions, improving classification accuracy and reliability. The system thus serves both as a platform for studying motor function and recovery and as rehabilitation tool. Initial evaluations using a public EEG dataset for left/right hand motor imagery (MI) produced encouraging results. These were followed by live sessions involving 40 healthy participants during gameplay with the AppleCatcher interface. Among these, the top three subjects achieved classification accuracies of 88%, 86% and 83% using features extracted from sLORETA-based source power estimates and classified with Linear Discriminant Analysis (LDA). The overall average classification accuracy across all participants was 60%. Cluster analysis revealed three distinct groups based on BCI performance, with average accuracies of 79%, 59%, and 49%, respectively. Notably, for one subject, accuracy improved by 25% points between the first and fourth sessions, indicating potential training effects and progressive development of MI-related skills. These findings support the feasibility of the proposed MI-BCI system. Future work will include testing with stroke patients to assess the clinical applicability and rehabilitation potential of the platform.

Keywords: Motor Imagery (MI) · Brain Computer Interface (BCI) · EEG Source Reconstruction

A. Lombardi et al. (Eds.): BI 2025, LNAI 16348, pp. 113–125, 2026.
https://doi.org/10.1007/978-981-95-9578-5_9

1 Introduction

Motor impairments resulting from stroke, spinal cord injury, and other neurological conditions significantly impact an individual's quality of life, often limiting their ability to perform basic daily tasks. Rehabilitation techniques aimed at improving motor function in affected limbs are critical for promoting recovery and enhancing patients' independence. Traditionally, rehabilitation focuses on repetitive physical exercises to stimulate neural pathways involved in movement. However, recent advancements in neurotechnology have introduced brain-computer interfaces (BCIs) as promising tools for motor rehabilitation, particularly through the use of Motor Imagery (MI) - a process where individuals mentally simulate movements to engage similar neural networks used in actual movement. In an MI-based BCI, users imagine the kinesthetic sensation associated with moving specific limbs. The BCI system then analyzes the recorded EEG signals, using them as the control input for the BCI.

MI BCIs leverage the brain's inherent neuroplasticity, allowing individuals to "rehearse" movements even in the absence of physical activity, which can be especially beneficial for those with severe motor impairments. By using electroencephalography (EEG) to detect neural activity related to MI, BCIs offer a non-invasive and patient-centered approach to engage the brain's motor areas and potentially improve functional recovery. Research has demonstrated that MI and motor execution share common neural networks, allowing mental rehearsal to activate motor-related brain regions and promote adaptation and relearning [12,14,16].

Most BCIs rely solely on sensor space analysis [9], but this approach has limitations due to the low spatial resolution of EEG signals [13]. This results in spatial mixing in the measured EEG signal. EEG Source Imaging (ESI) methods can be used to estimate the sources activated on the brain cortex and provide an unmixed localization and time-courses of the underlying sources. Integrating ESI methods into MI-based BCIs has been shown to improve classification accuracy and surpass conventional analysis [1,3,4,15]. The AppleCatcher Game represents a novel application in this context, designed to make MI-based rehabilitation engaging and effective. By integrating MI tasks into an interactive, game-like environment, developed in the source space, this BCI system not only aims to motivate users but also to reinforce motor pathways crucial for hand function. The AppleCatcher Game translates EEG-detected MI signals into source space signals that will be used as commands from the users to catch virtual apples with imagined movements of the left or right hand, aiming to improve hand motor skills through neural stimulation. A recent study [10] found that individuals using an MI brain-computer interface (BCI) showed heightened neural activity in motor-related brain areas when imagining a grasping task with their affected hand, as compared to control subjects. They also discovered a link between motor function and visual-spatial processing, opening up promising new avenues for enhancing treatment approaches for stroke patients - potentially through engaging activities like games. The AppleCatcher system advances MI-based BCIs by using EEG source imaging to map brain activity at the cortical level, enabling more precise monitoring of motor regions. This improves classification accuracy and reliability, making the system valuable for both neuroscience research and motor rehabilitation. This paper explores the design and preliminary effectiveness of The AppleCatcher Game, highlighting its potential as a valuable tool for hand rehabilitation and motor function restoration.

2 Materials and Methods

2.1 The Game Experimental Paradigm

Apple Catcher is designed to be intuitive and user-friendly. The game-play objective is clear: the player uses motor imagery (MI) to imagine opening either the right or left hand to catch a falling apple. Figure 1 displays the game's user interface as seen by the player. At any given time, only one apple appears on the screen, and it always falls either to the left or the right side. A green progress bar at the bottom of the screen represents the apple's descent. Two orange vertical lines on the progress bar indicate the time window during which the player should perform the MI task. These markers also serve as reference points during data analysis, helping to align the timing of recorded brain activity with the event. Once the progress bar reaches the second marker, the collected EEG data is processed through the system's pipeline. It first undergoes preprocessing and feature extraction. The extracted features are then passed to the classifier, which predicts whether the player imagined opening the left or right hand. Based on the prediction, the corresponding virtual hand opens. If the prediction matches the correct side, the hand catches the apple, the player's score increases by one, and the game resets for the next apple. If the classifier makes an incorrect prediction (resulting in the wrong hand opening), the apple is missed and falls off the screen. This results in the failure count increasing by one, and the game resets for another attempt. This game-play cycle continues for a predefined number of rounds, with 20 rounds set as the default.

2.2 Data Collection During Live Game Session

This study involved 40 university students (28 males, 12 females). The study was carried out in accordance with the Declaration of Helsinki and all participants provided their informed consent prior to participation. The study was approved by the Norwegian Agency for Shared Services in Education and Research (Sikt, reference number 968653). The dataset was recorded at the Brain Cybernetics Lab facility of The Norwegian University of Science and Technology. EEG data were collected using a Mentalab Explore Pro wireless amplifier and a 32-channel EEG cap, following the 10-10 electrode placement system (as shown in Fig. 3.). Wet electrodes with an ear clip reference cable and conductive gel were used, and unnecessary electronic devices were removed from the experimental room to minimize interference. The EEG signal was sampled at 250 Hz. For each session a total of 200 trials were conducted, with 100 trials for the left hand and 100 trials for the right hand. The collected data were streamed in real time

Fig. 1. Apple Catcher game interface.

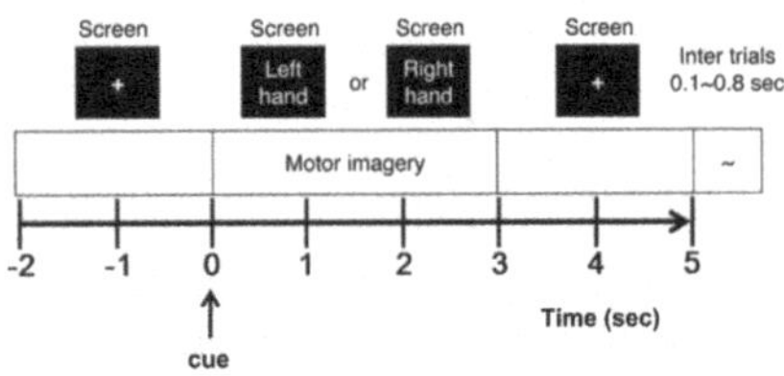

Fig. 2. Timeline of a single motor imagery trial from the offline MI-dataset. Figure taken from [2].

using the Lab Streaming Layer (LSL) protocol, which allowed instant access in Python through the pylsl library [7]. To ensure that the results of live trials could be compared to those obtained with the offline dataset, the data collection protocol was designed to closely replicate the procedures used by Cho et al. [2], with similar trial durations, rest periods and resembling visual instructions.

Each trial takes a total of 9 s, divided into three parts. For the first three seconds the subject is given time to identify which side the apple is falling, while resting and preparing to perform MI. Then, when the progress bar reaches the first marker after three seconds, the subject is asked to imagine the movement of catching the apple with the hand corresponding to the side the apple is falling on. This continues for three seconds until the progress bar reaches the second marker, signaling the end of the MI task. Data collected from these first six seconds are

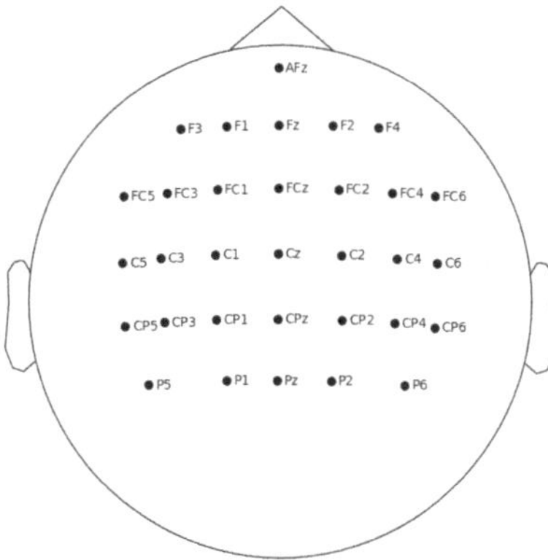

Fig. 3. Electrode placements for the 32-channel Mentalab Explore.

sent through the data processing pipeline and classified. The subject can then see whether the apple was caught, providing immediate feedback. The last three seconds are reserved for rest and preparation before the next trial. During the online data collection it is possible to choose whether the subject can see the apple falling from the start of each trial or not. This is done by drawing the background tree over the apple, concealing the position of the apple until right before the first marker. In the original version of the game, the player could see the apple all the way. The change was implemented to make live data collection more similar to that used in [2] and to explore whether a surprising stimuli elicits different results compared to a stimuli by which the player anticipates the side where the apple is falling.

2.3 Offline Evaluation with MI-BCI Dataset

For preliminary testing of the game, the left/right MI dataset created by Cho et al. [2] was used. The dataset comprises high-density EEG recordings collected from 52 participants using a 64-electrode cap positioned according to the international 10-10 system, with a sampling rate of 512 Hz. For each participant, 100 or 120 trials of left and right hand MI were recorded according to the protocol shown in Fig. 2. Each trial is seven seconds long. During the first two seconds, subjects were asked to look at a black screen with a fixation cross. An instruction of either "left hand" or "right hand" would then appear, and for the next three seconds subjects were asked to imagine hand movement of the corresponding hand. The screen would then revert to the black screen with a fixation cross for the last two seconds, allowing the subject to rest before the next trial. Between each trial there was a short break of random length.

3 Data Processing and Classification

The data processing pipeline, from raw samples to classification-ready features, is primarily based on the MNE Python library, which provides tools for EEG data processing, analysis, and visualization [5]. The same processing steps are applied to both the offline MI-dataset and live game data, differing only in the input size of the time series: 64×3584 for offline MI-dataset and 32×1500 for live game-play dataset. The following sections describe the processing steps using live data as a reference.

3.1 From Raw Data to Epochs

The raw data from the LSL stream are structured as an array, where each row corresponds to an EEG channel. Upon retrieval from the LSL buffer, timestamp correction is performed to ensure correct ordering of the samples. A finite impulse response (FIR) band-pass filter is then applied to the data (1–50 Hz), and a 50 Hz notch filter to reduce power-line noise. The data are then re-referenced to the average of all channels to remove common noise over all electrodes. To use the MNE library, the data must be converted into the *epochs* format, MNE's standard for time-locked data. The event time is set to 0 based on the first marker, and an epoch is created around it, with labels assigned according to the position of the apple. Accurate event onset timing is crucial for proper classification. A verification test, in which the subject clenched their jaw at the first marker in the game, confirmed the accuracy of the method by detecting the expected voltage spike.

3.2 Feature Extraction

The feature extraction method in this study is based on source reconstruction using sLORETA, which maps EEG signals back to their origin in the brain via an inverse solution [11]. Two key decisions precede extraction: selecting a time window and defining frequency bands. A short time window (typically 1–2 s post-event) captures Event-Related De-synchronization (ERD) [6], and its size and placement influence classification performance. For frequency bands, 7–11 Hz and 9–13 Hz were chosen due to their relevance for MI tasks and slightly better results than the conventional μ-rhythm. sLORETA was implemented in MNE Python by first computing a forward model using a standard BEM, followed by generating an inverse operator. For each band, the EEG epochs were band-pass-filtered, down-sampled, and then processed with the sLORETA inverse operator to yield source time course estimates (STCs). Following [1], average STC power was used as it outperformed raw STCs and electrode-space features. This resulted in an 8196×1 feature vector per band, which were concatenated for classification. Decimation and dimensionality reduction were applied to ensure computational efficiency, critical for real-time use.

3.3 Classification

Classification follows a three-step pipeline: feature standardization (zero mean, unit variance), dimensionality reduction via PCA (retaining 95% variance), and classification using LDA. In real-time game-play, the predicted label determines hand movement, while offline testing uses cross-validation. LDA was chosen based on [1], which showed it outperformed other classifiers when combined with source reconstruction. Its linear decision boundary aligns well with the contra-lateral brain responses expected in left-right MI tasks.

4 Results

4.1 MI-BCI Dataset Offline Results

The first testing of the classification pipeline was carried out using the offline MI data from the ten best performing subjects. Figure 4 presents a box plot of the cross-validated classification accuracies. For this analysis, the training and test sets were split in proportions of 80% and 20%, respectively. The results reveal that even among the "good" subjects, there is considerable variation in classification performance. This highlights the problem of large individual differences in the quality of MI signals. Nevertheless, the results clearly show that the pipeline is capable of reliably distinguishing between left and right MI, achieving an average classification accuracy of 85.0% $\pm$ 5.0%. These results provided a solid foundation for the next part of the study, where the pipeline was tested during live game play.

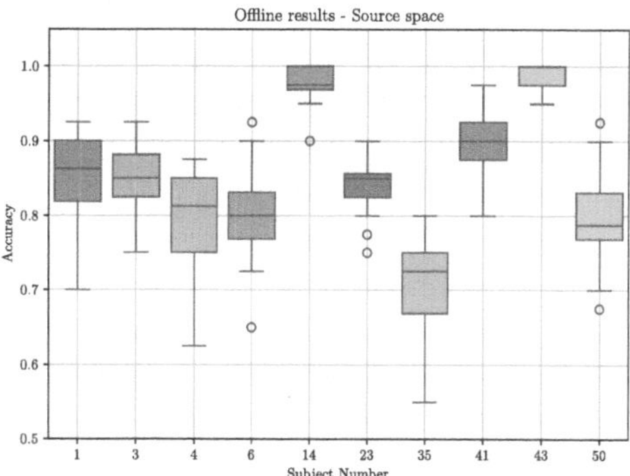

Fig. 4. Box plot of cross-validated classification accuracies for the ten best performing subjects in the offline MI-dataset.

4.2 Interactive Game Play Results

For each live session, a total of 100 samples were acquired for training the initial classifier, structured as five blocks of 20 samples each, with the subject consistently performing the correct hand-opening gesture during this phase. Following the initial training, the subject completed 10 testing rounds, each comprising 20 samples. After each test round, the corresponding data were appended to the training set, and a new classifier was trained at the beginning of the next round using the updated dataset. The entire procedure-from initial data recording through to the conclusion of the final testing round-lasted approximately 90 minutes per session. The classification accuracies for all 40 subjects are summarized in Fig. 5, with associated standard deviations. Detailed results from the live sessions are reported in Tables 1 and 2. In session 1, the average score was 12.8, corresponding to a classification accuracy of 64.0%±7.7%. In session 2, conducted one week later, the average score improved to 15.1, corresponding to an accuracy of 75.5% ±8.0%, reflecting an 11.5% point increase. A further improvement of 25% in accuracy was observed in session 4, conducted four months later. These results represent substantial gains in classification performance, demonstrating that even a single prior session can significantly enhance future performance. Despite these improvements, the standard deviation remained relatively consistent across sessions, suggesting that the primary sources of variability persisted. As discussed in Sect. 4.3, this variability can be mitigated by increasing the number of training samples.

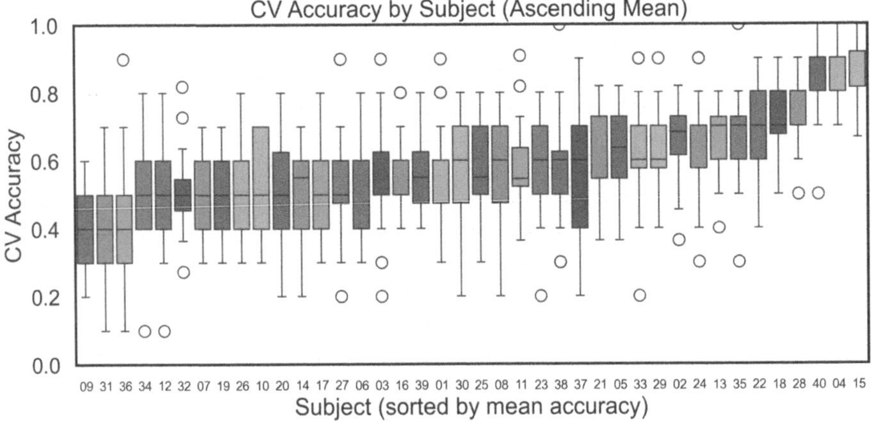

Fig. 5. Box plot of cross-validated classification accuracies for the ten best performing subjects in the offline MI-dataset.

To analyze the results in more detail, confusion matrices for each session are presented in Fig. 6. The matrices reveal a slight bias toward classifying the left hand over the right, with an approximate 55–45% split in both sessions. This bias

Table 1. First live session

Round	Score/20
1	15
2	10
3	12
4	12
5	12
6	14
7	12
8	12
9	14
10	15
Average Score	12.8
Accuracy	64%

Table 2. Second live session

Round	Score/20
1	16
2	18
3	16
4	13
5	12
6	17
7	15
8	17
9	14
10	13
Average Score	15.1
Accuracy	75.5%

is likely influenced by the neural characteristics of the test subject. However, it did not result in a dominant classification of the left hand, as the predicted hand varied between rounds. Importantly, the classifier consistently recognized both hands in every round, supporting the decision to balance the datasets. It is also worth noting that the data collection protocol was modified between the first two live sessions. As described in Sect. 2.2, the moment when the test subject first sees the apple can be adjusted. In session 1, the apple only became visible to the subject shortly before the first marker, whereas in session 2, the apple remained visible throughout its entire descent. Additionally, prior to session 2, the subject was asked to physically perform the movement, a step that was not included in session 1. These procedural differences likely influenced the observed results and will be further examined in the next phase of the study.

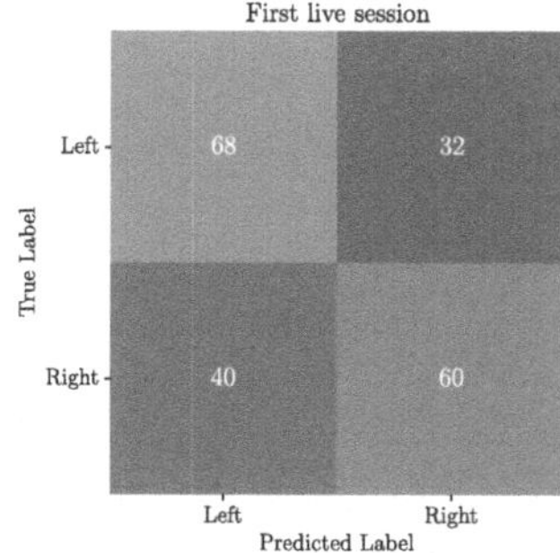

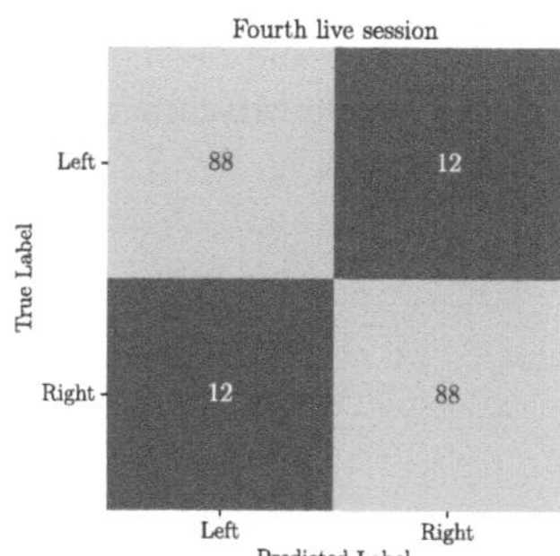

Fig. 6. Confusion matrices two live sessions (session 1 and 4). Each matrix compares the true and predicted labels for left and right MI.

4.3 Performance with Increasing Trials

In online BCI applications such as the Apple Catcher game, processing speed is a critical factor. Therefore, understanding how classification performance scales with the number of training samples is essential. Figures 7 and 8 present box plots of cross-validated classification accuracies for Subject 1 from the offline MI dataset and for Subject 40 during the second and fourth live sessions. The results demonstrate that increasing the number of training samples generally leads to higher classification accuracy. However, the rate of improvement diminishes as the number of samples approaches 200. Specifically, in Subject 40's second live session, accuracy reaches approximately 70% with only 100 training samples and shows minimal gains beyond this point. This suggests that the use of 100 training samples-as applied in the first two live sessions-is likely sufficient to initiate game-play with a reasonable level of accuracy. This trend is further supported by generalized model testing across the six best subjects, as illustrated in Fig. 9. The plots also reveal a reduction in variance with larger training sets, indicating improved robustness of the classifier to outliers and signal fluctuations. Ultimately, an effective classification model must balance the accuracy and stability benefits of additional training data with the need for low-latency processing in real-time BCI scenarios.

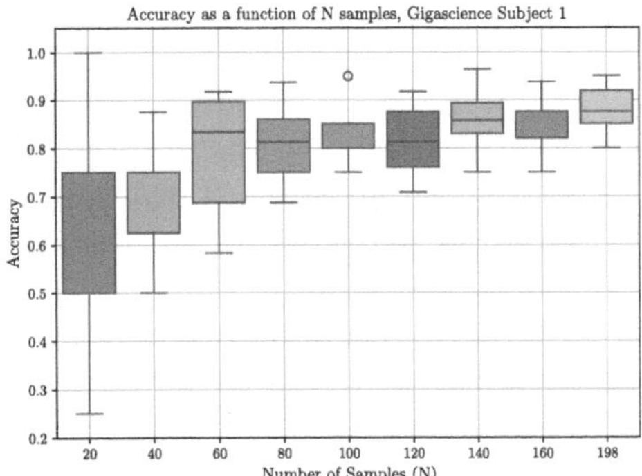

Fig. 7. Box plot of cross-validated classification accuracies with increasing sample sizes, for subject 1 of the offline MI-dataset.

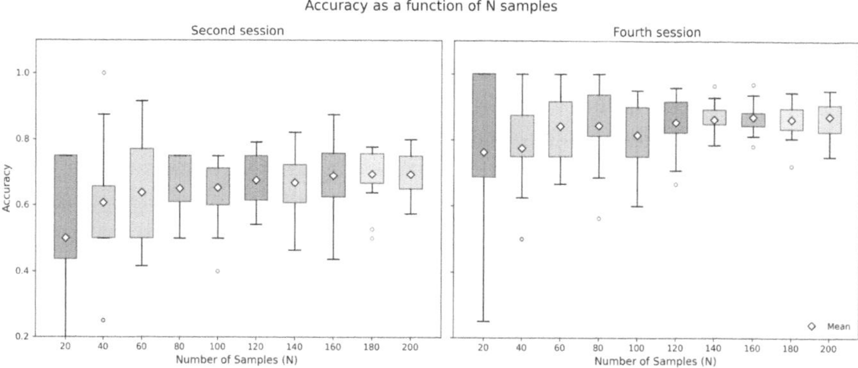

Fig. 8. Box plot of cross-validated classification accuracies with increasing sample sizes, for subject 40 on the second and fourth live sessions.

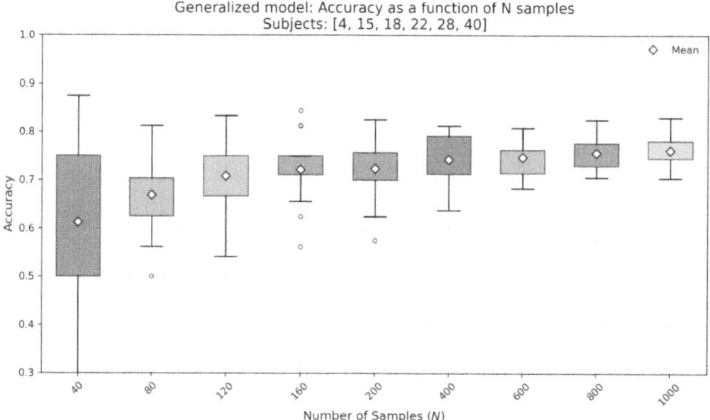

Fig. 9. Box plot of classification accuracies from a generalized model testing across the best six subjects from the live sessions with increasing sample sizes.

5 Conclusion

This study established a proof of concept for a motor imagery-based brain–computer interface (MI-BCI) game for neurorehabilitation and evaluated the feasibility of using EEG source imaging (ESI) for real-time MI classification. The system achieved promising offline and online results, with classification accuracies consistent with prior ESI-based studies. Among 40 participants, overall accuracy reached 60%, with top performers achieving 85%. A clustering analysis of all 40 subjects based on their classification accuracies revealed three distinct groups, corresponding to high, moderate, and low BCI aptitude, with average accuracies of 79%, 59%, and 49%, respectively. These findings highlight substantial inter-individual variability in motor imagery (MI) skills, suggesting that MI-based BCI performance varies widely among users. Further efforts are currently focused to investigate the underlying cognitive, neurophysiological, behavioral and experimental factors contributing to this variability (such as feature extraction window parameters), with the aim of improving personalization and efficacy of MI-based BCI systems. These findings confirm strong inter-individual variability in MI skills, emphasizing the need for personalization. The AppleCatcher game shows potential as a neurorehabilitation tool, warranting further validation with larger, more diverse populations and improved protocols focusing on artifact reduction, channel optimization, and 3D system refinement. Future work will focus on system refinement with a 3D version and virtual reality game interface, including validation using an EEG motor imagery dataset from acute stroke patients [8]. Improvements in data collection, artifact reduction, and channel optimization will be key to enhancing its performance and clinical applicability.

References

1. Soler, A.F., Naas, V., Giri, A., Molinas, M.: EEG source imaging enhances motor imagery classification. In: ESANN 2024 Proceedings, European Symposium on Artificial Neural Networks, Computational Intelligence and Machine Learning, Bruges, Belgium, pp. 577–582 (2024). https://doi.org/10.1016/j.neubiorev.2018.08.003
2. Cho, H., Ahn, M., Ahn, S., Kwon, M., Jun, S.C.: EEG datasets for motor imagery brain–computer interface. GigaScience **6**(7), gix034 (2017). https://doi.org/10.1093/gigascience/gix034
3. Edelman, B.J., Baxter, B., He, B.: EEG source imaging enhances the decoding of complex right-hand motor imagery tasks. IEEE Trans. Biomed. Eng. **63**, 4–14 (2016). https://doi.org/10.1109/TBME.2015.2467312
4. Giri, A., Kumar, L., Gandhi, T.K.: Cortical source domain based motor imagery and motor execution framework for enhanced brain computer interface applications. IEEE Sens. Lett. **5**(12), 1–4 (2021). https://doi.org/10.1109/LSENS.2021.3122453
5. Gramfort, A., et al.: MNE software for processing MEG and EEG data. Neuroimage **86**, 446–460 (2014). https://doi.org/10.1016/j.neuroimage.2013.10.027
6. Jeon, Y., Nam, C.S., Kim, Y.J., Whang, M.C.: Event-related (de)synchronization (ERD/ERS) during motor imagery tasks: Implications for brain–computer interfaces. Int. J. Ind. Ergon. **41**(5), 428–436 (2011). https://doi.org/10.1016/j.ergon.2011.03.005
7. Kothe, C.: chkothe/pylsl (2024). https://github.com/chkothe/pylsl. https://github.com/chkothe/pylsl, original-date: 2015-04-25T04:00:38Z
8. Liu, H., et al.: An EEG motor imagery dataset for brain computer interface in acute stroke patients. Sci. Data **11**(1) (2024). https://doi.org/10.1038/s41597-023-02787-8
9. Lotte, F., et al.: A review of classification algorithms for EEG-based brain–computer interfaces: a 10 year update. J. Neural Eng. **15**, 031005 (2018). https://doi.org/10.1088/1741-2552/AAB2F2
10. Ma, Z.Z., et al.: Motor imagery-based brain–computer interface rehabilitation programs enhance upper extremity performance and cortical activation in stroke patients. J. NeuroEngineering Rehabil. **21**(91) (2024). https://doi.org/10.1186/s12984-024-01387-w

11. Pascual-Marqui, R.D.: Standardized low-resolution brain electromagnetic tomography (sLORETA): technical details. Methods Find. Exp. Clin. Pharmacol. **24**(Suppl D), 5–12 (2002)
12. Pfurtscheller, G., Brunner, C., Schlogl, A., Lopes da Silva, F.: Mu rhythm (de)synchronization and EEG single-trial classification of different motor imagery tasks. NeuroImage **31**(1), 153–159 (2006). https://doi.org/10.1016/j.neuroimage.2005.12.003
13. Portillo-Lara, R., Tahirbegi, B., Chapman, C., Goding, J., Green, R.: Mind the gap: state-of-the-art technologies and applications for EEG-based brain–computer interfaces. APL Bioengineering **5**, 031507 (2021). https://doi.org/10.1063/5.0047237
14. Hardwick, R.M., et al.: Neural correlates of action: comparing meta-analyses of imagery, observation, and execution. Neurosci. Biobehav. Rev. **94**(2), 31–44 (2018). https://doi.org/10.1016/j.neubiorev.2018.08.003
15. Srisrisawang, N., Müller-Putz, G.R.: Applying dimensionality reduction techniques in source-space electroencephalography via template and magnetic resonance imaging-derived head models to continuously decode hand trajectories. Front. Hum. Neurosci. **16**, 137 (2022). https://doi.org/10.3389/fnhum.2022.830221
16. Hétu, S., et al.: The neural network of motor imagery: an ale meta-analysis. Neurosci. Biobehav. Rev. **37**(5), 930–949 (2013). https://doi.org/10.1016/j.neubiorev.2013.03.017

Classification of Motor Imagery Data Using TCN-Transformer

Miroslav Bártík, Duc Thien Pham(✉), and Roman Mouček

Department of Computer Science and Engineering, University of West Bohemia in Pilsen, Pilsen, Czech Republic

mbartik@students.zcu.cz, {ducthien,moucek}@kiv.zcu.cz

Abstract. Brain-Computer Interfaces (BCIs) represent a rapidly advancing field that enables communication between the brain and external devices. Motor Imagery (MI) and Motor Execution (ME) paradigms are particularly valuable for BCI applications, especially in neurorehabilitation contexts. This study introduces a novel hybrid TCN-Transformer architecture designed to automatically classify electroencephalography (EEG) signals from MI and ME tasks. The proposed model combines a Temporal Convolutional Network (TCN) for feature extraction with a Transformer encoder for modeling global temporal dependencies. We validated our approach through comprehensive experiments on three datasets: Shuqfa-103 (103 subjects), Brunner-9 (9 subjects), and Kodera-29 (29 subjects). The model demonstrated strong performance across multiple classification scenarios, achieving accuracies of 84.84% for 2-class classification and 64.57% for 4-class classification on the Shuqfa-103 dataset. Comparative analysis with existing studies shows the promising performance of the proposed model. Furthermore, the comparison of the classification results on separated MI and ME datasets was performed. The model was successfully integrated into a real-world neuroinformatics laboratory workflow, demonstrating its practical applicability for real-time EEG signal processing and classification.

Keywords: Motor Imagery · Motor Execution · Brain-Computer Interface · EEG · TCN-Transformer

1 Introduction

In today's world, there are multiple ways to interact with computers, from typing with fingers to using voice commands or even gestures. However, one of the most advanced methods emerging is the Brain-Computer Interface (BCI), which allows direct communication between the brain and a computer, bypassing traditional physical inputs altogether [11].

A BCI records brain activity and translates neural signals into commands that a computer or external device can interpret. One important paradigm within BCI technology is Motor Imagery (MI), which relies on detecting changes in brain

A. Lombardi et al. (Eds.): BI 2025, LNAI 16348, pp. 126–137, 2026.
https://doi.org/10.1007/978-981-95-9578-5_10

activity when a person imagines performing a movement, such as lifting a hand or walking. The imagination of movement itself activates similar brain regions to actual physical movement (motor execution - ME), making it a valuable technique for decoding intentions in a BCI system [9].

The MI paradigm holds particular promise in medical applications, especially in neurorehabilitation. For individuals who have suffered from brain injuries, stroke, or neurodegenerative diseases, MI-based BCIs offer potential pathways for recovery. By training patients to imagine movements, therapists can help them regain control of impaired limbs, bypassing damaged neural pathways [7]. This opens up new opportunities for non-invasive therapies that aid in restoring motor functions and improving the quality of life for people with physical disabilities.

The objective of this paper is to build upon the existing research, with a focus on introducing unexplored methods for processing and classifying brain signals, specifically electroencephalography (EEG) data. Additionally, the aim is to develop a method suitable for real-time BCI data processing within the workflow of a neuroinformatics laboratory.

2 State-of-the-Art

Kaviri and Vinjamuri [3] demonstrated that source localization methods can significantly enhance classification accuracy by projecting sensor-level EEG data into the source domain. Using dipole fitting, Minimum Norm Estimation (MNE), and beamforming, they improved the spatial resolution of MI signals obtained from a local dataset and achieved high classification accuracies, with dipole fitting yielding the best results (91.03%). A ResNet-CNN enhanced with attention and inception modules was employed to distinguish between left-hand, right-hand, and resting states.

Neha Sharma et al. [14] explored raw EEG classification using LSTM and Transformer architectures on the raw BCI competition III IVa and IV 2a datasets, aiming to reduce preprocessing and hardware demands. Their Transformer model reached 99.7% accuracy for binary classification and 84.0% for multiclass tasks, illustrating the potential of attention-based models in MI BCI.

Navneet Tibrewal et al. [16] compared traditional machine learning (ML) techniques to CNN-based DL approaches on an EEG dataset from 54 subjects who conducted the MI task during a BCI interaction [6]. While CSP+LDA achieved modest accuracy (52.56%), the CNN model outperformed it significantly (69.42% accuracy), particularly benefiting users with low signal quality.

Pham and Mouček [12] proposed a hybrid CNN-Transformer-LSTM model. The CNN component was used to extract time-invariant features from the input signals. The Transformer encoder then focused on modeling temporal dependencies, while the LSTM layer further processed sequential information to preserve context over time. Without data augmentation, the model achieved 78.51% accuracy for binary and 61.95% for multiclass classification on the Kodera-29 dataset [4].

Building upon prior advancements, we propose the TCN-Transformer architecture to enhance MI/ME classification using multi-channel EEG signals. This model combines TCN with Transformer mechanisms to efficiently extract temporal features and capture long-term dependencies within EEG data. By leveraging the strengths of both components, our approach effectively addresses challenges such as EEG signal variability, thereby contributing to the improvement of rehabilitation strategies for individuals with motor impairments.

3 Materials and Model

3.1 Datasets

The following three MI/ME datasets were used to build the TCN-Transformer architecture.

Shuqfa-103. Zaid Shuqfa et al. [15] addressed limitations in a large but underutilized motor imagery EEG dataset [13] by cleaning, restructuring, and standardizing it for research use. They reduced the subject count to 103 and reformatted the data into MATLAB-compatible files and CSVs, with a uniform sampling rate of 160 Hz and electrode placement based on the 10-10 system. The dataset includes two baseline runs and 12 task runs per participant (six for motor imagery and six for motor execution), each consisting of 15 trials. Every trial lasted 4 s, followed by a 4-s resting phase. The tasks involved left-fist movement, right-fist movement, both-fist movement, both-feet movement, and rest.

Brunner-9. C. Brunner et al. [2] compiled an EEG dataset known as the BCI Competition IV 2a dataset, which involves data from 9 participants. During the experiment, subjects were instructed to imagine four types of movements: right hand, left hand, both feet simultaneously, and tongue movements.

The recording of each subject was split into two sessions, each on a different day. Each session comprised six runs, with short breaks in between. Each run consisted of 48 trials, 12 trials for each of the four movements, resulting in a total of 288 trials per session. At the start of each session, a 5-min recording was made to assess the influence of electrooculography (EOG).

EEG signals were recorded using 22 electrodes placed according to the international 10–20 system. Additionally, 3 EOG (electrooculography) channels were recorded. Both recordings were sampled at 250 Hz. The data is stored in GDF (General Data Format for biomedical signals).

Kodera-29. Jakub Kodera et al. [4] created an EEG dataset that includes recordings from 29 healthy participants (18 females aged 18–23 and 11 males aged 21–26), who performed right-hand and left-hand motor imagery tasks.

Each session lasted approximately 10–15 min and consisted of alternating phases: a 10-s resting phase followed by a 20-s motor execution phase (to execute a movement, movement intention has to precede). These phases were repeated throughout the session. During the motor execution phase, participants were required to control a robotic arm, which followed a predefined circular trajectory.

The recordings were made using Ag/AgCl electrodes arranged according to the international 10–20 system. Conductive gel was applied under each electrode to reduce impedance. While data recording, a V-Amp amplifier was used, ensuring high-quality signals.

3.2 Model

This section introduces the TCN-Transformer architecture, a hybrid neural network model designed to address the challenges of EEG signal classification. In this hybrid approach, the TCN first processes the input sequence to extract the features. The Transformer encoder further refines these representations by modeling global dependencies. In this section, the key components of the model are described. The architecture diagram is displayed in Fig. 1.

TCN. Temporal Convolutional Networks (TCNs) represent a powerful architectural approach for a number of tasks containing temporal dependencies. The architecture employs dilated convolutions that enable exponentially large receptive fields, allowing the network to capture long-term dependencies in the data. This is achieved by increasing the dilation factor exponentially with network depth [1] [5].

A key strength of TCNs lies in their integration of modern convolutional design principles. The architecture uses residual connections to improve gradient flow through deep networks. Each residual block contains two layers of dilated causal convolutions followed by non-linearity through rectified linear units (ReLUs). Weight normalization is applied to the convolutional filters, and spatial dropout randomly zeroes entire channels during training to enhance regularization [1]. Together, these techniques enable TCNs to process long sequences effectively while maintaining stable gradients across the network [1].

Transformer Encoder. A Transformer neural network is a deep learning architecture primarily designed for handling sequential data. Introduced in [18], Transformers rely on self-attention mechanisms, allowing them to process entire sequences in parallel. This makes them highly efficient and scalable for tasks like machine translation, text generation, and even EEG signal analysis.

In this paper, a Transformer encoder is used. It consists of two sub-layers: a multi-head self-attention mechanism and a feed-forward neural network. A residual connection is applied around each sub-layer, followed by layer normalization. This means that the output of each sub-layer is computed as:

$$\mathrm{LayerNorm}(x + \mathrm{Sublayer}(x))$$

where $\mathrm{Sublayer}(x)$ represents the function implemented by the respective sub-layer itself [18].

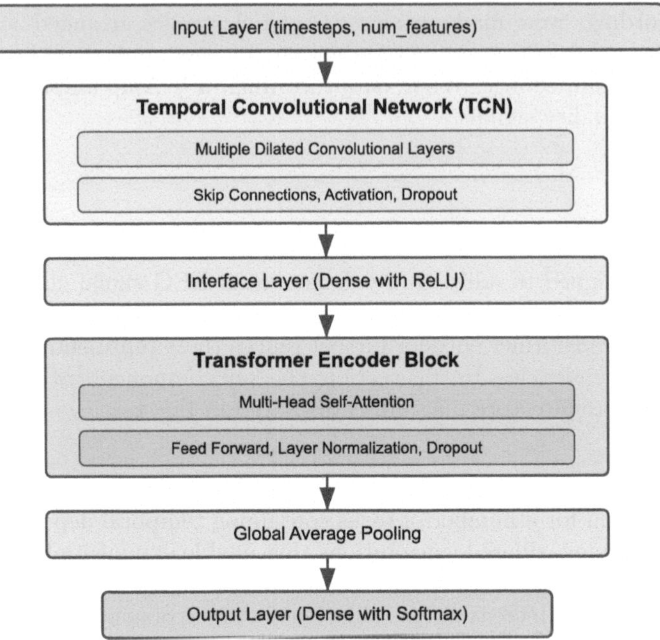

Fig. 1. Diagram of the TCN-Transformer architecture.

3.3 Training and Performance Evaluation

During training, we employed the Adam optimizer and utilized sparse categorical cross-entropy as the loss function. The initial learning rate was set at a configurable value with exponential decay scheduling that reduces the rate by a factor of 0.85 every 5 epochs. We incorporated the "ReduceLROnPlateau" callback that dynamically reduces the learning rate by half when validation loss fails to improve within the specified patience limit. Early stopping was implemented to prevent overfitting when the validation loss remained unchanged for the configured patience epochs, with automatic restoration of best weights. The dataset was split into training (70%), testing (20%), and validation (10%) subsets, with the validation set used to monitor performance after each epoch. Accuracy, precision, recall, and F1-score were utilized as evaluation metrics for multi-class EEG classification.

4 Results

4.1 Brunner-9

The first experiment was conducted using the Brunner-9 dataset. This experiment involved a 4-class classification task, where the model distinguished between four types of movement: right-hand movement, left-hand movement, simultaneous movement of both feet, and tongue movement. The classification results are presented in Table 1. The confusion matrix is presented in Fig. 2.

4.2 Shuqfa-103

The second experiment was conducted using the Shuqfa-103 dataset. This experiment included two separate classification scenarios: a 4-class classification and a 2-class classification. In the 4-class classification scenario, the model was trained to distinguish between right-fist movement, left-fist movement, both feet movement, and a resting state. In the 2-class classification scenario, the categories were simplified to movement versus rest, where all movement-related classes were merged into a single class and compared against the resting state. The results of both classification scenarios are depicted in Table 1. The confusion matrices for both classification scenarios are presented in Fig. 3.

The third experiment was conducted using the Shuqfa-103 dataset, which was divided into two subsets: motor execution (ME) and motor imagery (MI) data subsets. For both subsets, two classification scenarios were evaluated: a 4-class classification and a 2-class classification. The 4-class classification aimed to distinguish between right-fist movement, left-fist movement, both-feet movement, and a resting state. In contrast, the 2-class classification scenario focused on differentiating between movement and resting states only. The classification results are shown in Table 2. The confusion matrices are presented in Fig. 4 for the 4-class classification and Fig. 5 for the 2-class classification.

4.3 Kodera-29

The last experiment was conducted using the Kodera-29 dataset. This experiment involved a 3-class classification scenario in which the model distinguished between right-hand movement, left-hand movement, and resting state, and a 2-class classification scenario in which the model differentiated only between a movement and a resting state. The classification results are presented in Table 1. Figure 6 shows the confusion matrices for both classification scenarios.

4.4 Laboratory Use

The model was tested in a real-world scenario within the workflow of the neuroinformatics laboratory. Its integration into the laboratory's system was successful from a technical standpoint. The model operated without errors and was capable of continuously processing incoming data in real time. These results demonstrated that the model was technically robust and suitable for deployment within the existing workflow infrastructure.

4.5 Performance Comparison

Table 3 presents a performance comparison between the proposed TCN-Transformer model and several existing methods across two EEG datasets: Shuqfa-103 and Kodera-29. On the Shuqfa-103 dataset (2-class), the TCN-Transformer achieves an accuracy of 84.84%, outperforming the SSTAF model [10] by a margin of over 8% (the SSTAF model is so far the only model we

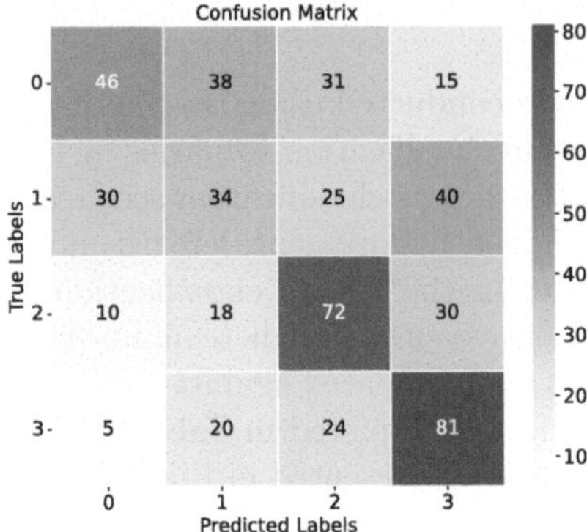

Fig. 2. Confusion matrix for the 4-class classification scenario using the TCN-Transformer model on the Brunner-9 dataset.

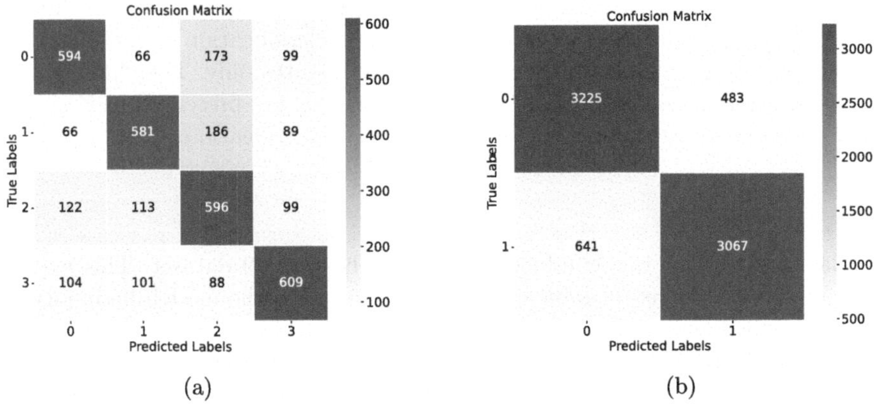

Fig. 3. Confusion matrix for (a) 4-class and (b) 2-class classification scenario using the TCN-Transformer model on the Shuqfa-103 dataset.

can compare due to the update to the Shuqfa-103 dataset). For the Kodera-29 dataset (2-class), the TCN-Transformer attains the best accuracy of 77.73%, outperforming traditional classifiers and deep learning models.

5 Discussion

In the first experiment, described in Sect. 4.1, the model achieved a modest classification performance on a Brunner-9 dataset. The confusion matrix displayed in Fig. 2 reveals substantial misclassifications among the first two classes (left-hand movement, right-hand movement), which suggests that the EEG patterns associated with respective movement types in this dataset may not be sufficiently consistent across subjects for the TCN-Transformer model.

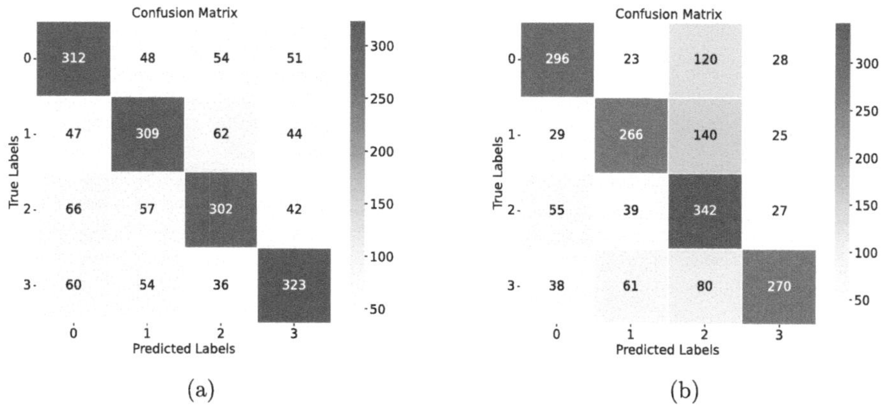

Fig. 4. Confusion matrix for the 4-class classification scenario using the TCN-Transformer model on (a) ME and (b) MI subsets on the Shuqfa-103 dataset.

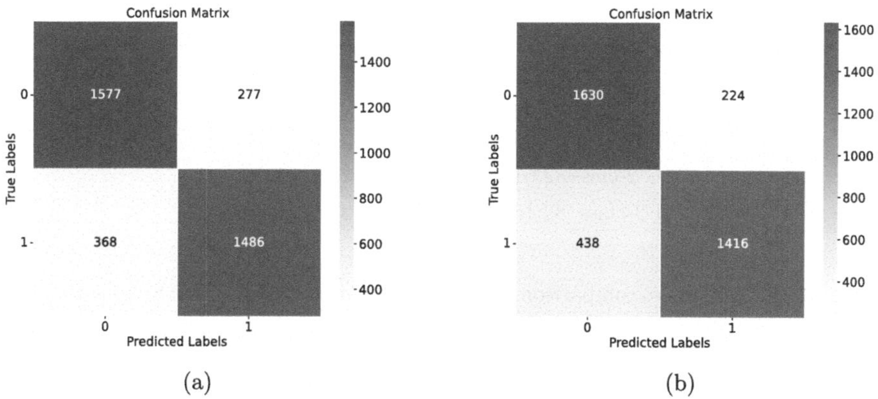

Fig. 5. Confusion matrix for the 2-class classification scenario using the TCN-Transformer model on (a) ME and (b) MI subsets on the Shuqfa-103 dataset.

Table 1. Classification results of the proposed TCN-Transformer model on three datasets.

Dataset	Scenario	Accuracy	Precision	Recall	F1-score
Shuqfa-103	4-class	64.57	64.91	64.59	64.67
Shuqfa-103	2-class	84.84	84.91	84.84	84.84
Brunner-9	4-class	44.89	44.41	44.86	43.97
Kodera-29	3-class	56.25	56.30	56.17	56.20
Kodera-29	2-class	77.73	77.78	77.73	77.72

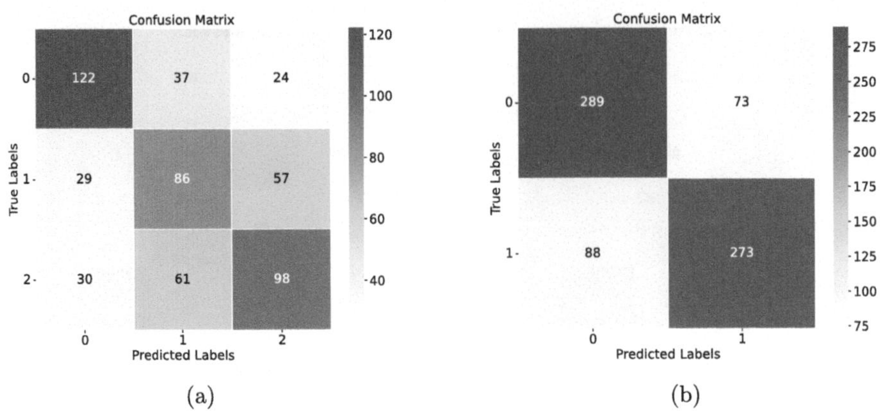

(a) (b)

Fig. 6. Confusion matrix for (a) 3-class and (b) 2-class classification scenario using the TCN-Transformer model on the Kodera-29 dataset.

Table 2. Classification results of the proposed TCN-Transformer model on MI and ME data separately, evaluated using the Shuqfa-103 dataset.

Scenario	Accuracy	Precision	Recall	F1-score
ME 4-class	66.74	66.78	66.74	66.74
MI 4-class	63.84	66.62	63.80	64.22
ME 2-class	82.61	82.68	82.61	82.59
MI 2-class	82.15	82.58	82.15	82.09

Table 3. Performance comparison with existing methods for the Shuqfa-103 and Kodera-29 datasets.

Dataset	Scenario	Studies	Accuracy	Precision	Recall	F1-score
Shuqfa-103	2-class	SSTAF [10]	76.83	-	-	73.52
		TCN-Transformer	**84.84**	**84.91**	**84.84**	**84.84**
Kodera-29	3-class	SVM [8]	40.35	40.43	39.82	39.48
		LDA [8]	35.26	35.34	35.32	35.20
		MLP [8]	32.94	33.03	33.00	32.49
		CNN [8]	**58.57**	**60.32**	**58.43**	**57.99**
		TCN-Transformer	56.25	56.30	56.17	56.20
Kodera-29	2-class	SVM [8]	57.28	57.28	57.26	57.24
		LDA [8]	50.51	50.53	50.52	50.49
		MLP [8]	51.12	51.16	51.13	50.55
		CNN [8]	76.00	76.73	76.05	75.86
		EEG-ITNet [17]	75.45	76.43	75.50	75.23
		TCN-Transformer	**77.73**	**77.78**	**77.73**	**77.72**

In contrast, the Shuqfa-103 dataset (Sect. 4.2) yielded significantly better results. The results indicate a much clearer separability between movement types and between movement and resting states. As expected, the 2-class task performed better, which is consistent with the reduced complexity and higher inter-class distinction. The confusion matrices displayed in Fig. 3 confirm that the model was more capable of correctly identifying resting and movement-related signals. A further breakdown into motor execution (ME) and motor imagery (MI) conditions, also discussed in Sect. 4.2, revealed better performance when using ME signals. This suggests that motor execution signals are typically stronger and more distinct than those generated during MI.

Lastly, with the Kodera-29 dataset, evaluated in Sect. 4.3, the model reached modest accuracy in 4-class classification, which indicates that further optimization may be needed. The 2-class scenario again yielded a much higher performance.

Table 3 shows that the proposed TCN-Transformer outperforms existing methods in most MI/ME classification tasks. On the Shuqfa-103 dataset (2-class), it improves accuracy from 76.83% to 84.84%, indicating strong and balanced performance. For the Kodera-29 dataset (2-class), it also achieves better accuracy (77.73%), surpassing traditional models and recent deep learning approaches like EEG-ITNet. However, in the 3-class setting, the model slightly underperforms compared to CNN [8], suggesting room for improvement in more complex tasks.

Across all datasets, it is evident that the model consistently performs better in binary classification scenarios than in multi-class tasks. This suggests that while the TCN-Transformer architecture is capable of learning meaningful EEG features, the increasing number of output classes introduces higher intra-class confusion, likely due to the inherent variability and subtlety of EEG signals across different motor tasks. It can be observed that the model performs better when trained and tested on larger datasets, as the most promising results were obtained with the Shuqfa-103 dataset, which is the largest among the three selected.

6 Conclusion

The proposed TCN-Transformer model achieved decent results across all three datasets. Notably, it performed particularly well on the Shuqfa-103 dataset, which is the largest one. The performance on Brunner-9 and Kodera-29, while slightly lower, still demonstrated the model's versatility and potential. TCN-Transformer outperformed state-of-the-art models in terms of classification accuracy, highlighting its effectiveness in capturing temporal and long-term dependencies in EEG signals. Furthermore, the model was successfully deployed in a neuroinformatics laboratory workflow, where it was able to classify real-time data.

Future work will focus on conducting an in-depth ablation study to better understand the contributions of each model component, as well as further validating the model's performance when deployed as part of a real-world BCI system.

Acknowledgments. This work was supported by the University specific research project SGS-2025-022 New Data Processing Methods in Current Areas of Computer Science (project SGS-2025-022).

References

1. Bai, S., Kolter, J.Z., Koltun, V.: An empirical evaluation of generic convolutional and recurrent networks for sequence modeling. arXiv preprint arXiv:1803.01271 (2018)
2. Brunner, C., Leeb, R., Müller-Putz, G., Schlögl, A., Pfurtscheller, G.: BCI competition 2008–graz data set a. Institute for knowledge discovery (laboratory of brain-computer interfaces), Graz Univ. Technol. **16**, 1–6 (2008)
3. Kaviri, S.M., Vinjamuri, R.: Integrating electroencephalography source localization and residual convolutional neural network for advanced stroke rehabilitation. Bioengineering **11**(10), 967 (2024). https://doi.org/10.3390/bioengineering11100967
4. Kodera, J., et al.: EEG motor imagery (2023). https://doi.org/10.5281/zenodo.7893847
5. Lea, C., Vidal, R., Reiter, A., Hager, G.D.: Temporal convolutional networks: a unified approach to action segmentation. In: European Conference on Computer Vision, pp. 47–54. Springer, Cham (2016). https://doi.org/10.1007/978-3-319-49409-8_7
6. Leeuwis, N., Paas, A., Alimardani, M.: Psychological and Cognitive Factors in Motor Imagery Brain Computer Interfaces (2021). https://doi.org/10.34894/Z7ZVOD
7. Miao, Y., et al.: BCI-based rehabilitation on the stroke in sequela stage. Neural Plast. **2020**(1), 8882764 (2020). https://doi.org/10.1155/2020/8882764
8. Mouček, R., Kodera, J., Mautner, P., Prucha, J.: Augmentation of motor imagery data for brain-controlled robot-assisted rehabilitation. In: Proceedings of the 17th International Joint Conference on Biomedical Engineering Systems and Technologies, pp. 812–819 (2024). https://doi.org/10.5220/0012575700003657
9. Mulder, T.: Motor imagery and action observation: cognitive tools for rehabilitation. J. Neural Transm. **114**, 1265–1278 (2007). https://doi.org/10.1007/s00702-007-0763-z
10. Muna, U.M., Shawon, M.M.H., Jobayer, M., Akter, S., Sabuj, S.R.: SSTAF: spatial-spectral-temporal attention fusion transformer for motor imagery classification. arXiv preprint arXiv:2504.13220 (2025)
11. Nicolas-Alonso, L.F., Gomez-Gil, J.: Brain computer interfaces, a review. Sensors **12**(2), 1211–1279 (2012). https://doi.org/10.3390/s120201211
12. Pham, D.T., Mouček, R.: Automatic motor imagery classification by CNN-transformer-LSTM using multi-channel EEG. In: European Conference on Artificial Intelligence (ECAI), pp. 4555–4562 (2024). https://doi.org/10.3233/FAIA241048
13. Schalk, G., McFarland, D., Hinterberger, T., Birbaumer, N., Wolpaw, J.: EEG motor movement/imagery dataset. Retrieved November **18**, 2011 (2009)

14. Sharma, N., Upadhyay, A., Sharma, M., Singhal, A.: Deep temporal networks for EEG-based motor imagery recognition. Sci. Rep. **13**(1), 18813 (2023)
15. Shuqfa, Z., Lakas, A., Belkacem, A.N.: Increasing accessibility to a large brain–computer interface dataset: Curation of physionet EEG motor movement/imagery dataset for decoding and classification. Data Brief **54**, 110181 (2024). https://doi.org/10.1016/j.dib.2024.110181
16. Tibrewal, N., Leeuwis, N., Alimardani, M.: Classification of motor imagery EEG using deep learning increases performance in inefficient BCI users. PLoS ONE **17**(7), e0268880 (2022). https://doi.org/10.1371/journal.pone.0268880
17. Titkanlou, M.K., Monjezi, E., Mouček, R.: A type of EEG-itnet for motor imagery EEG signal classification. In: Proceedings of the 17th International Joint Conference on Biomedical Engineering Systems and Technologies, pp. 257–262 (2024). https://doi.org/10.5220/0012569400003657
18. Vaswani, A., et al.: Attention is all you need. In: Advances in Neural Information Processing Systems, vol. 30 (2017)

An Ensemble of Lightweight Convolutional Neural Networks for EEG-Based Major Depressive Disorder Detection

Fatima Hussain, Muhammad Hussain(✉), and Saad AlAhmadi

Department of Computer Science, College of Computer and Information Sciences, King Saud University, Riyadh, Saudi Arabia
mhussain@ksu.edu.sa

Abstract. Major Depressive Disorder (MDD) is a prevalent mental illness and a leading cause of suicide, making early detection critical. The electroencephalogram (EEG) provides a non-invasive method for recording brain activity; however, current diagnostic methods rely on manual evaluation by neurologists, which can be subjective, labor-intensive, and time-consuming. While Machine Learning (ML) and Deep Learning (DL) have shown promise in medical diagnosis, many existing models for MDD detection lack generalizability due to a large number of learnable parameters, small datasets, and data leakage from Patient-Independent evaluation protocols. In this work, we propose an ensemble classifier of lightweight convolutional neural networks (CNNs) for MDD detection using EEG signals, designed with minimal learnable parameters to ensure efficiency and generalization. The method was evaluated on the MUMTAZ benchmark dataset using Leave-Some-Subject-Out Cross Validation (LSSOCV) to ensure robust performance, achieving an accuracy of 94.1%. This approach offers a practical tool to assist psychiatrists in the early and objective detection of MDD, supporting timely intervention.

Keywords: EEG Signal · Major Depression Disorder Detection · Ensemble Classification · Convolutional Neural Network

1 Introduction

Major Depressive Disorder (MDD) is a prevalent mental health condition that significantly impairs daily functioning. It is a leading cause of disease burden globally, and the World Health Organization predicts that it will become the foremost cause by 2030 [1]. The disorder imposes substantial personal, social, and economic costs. The accurate and timely diagnosis of MDD remains a significant clinical challenge. Traditional diagnostic approaches rely heavily on subjective assessments and self-reported symptoms, which can be influenced by stigma, recall bias, and variability in clinical presentation [2]. It highlights the importance of objective and reliable methods in supporting the diagnosis of MDD. EEG signals provide a reliable source of physiological data for diagnosis, unlike subjective measures such as surveys. Due to its simplicity and patient-friendly

A. Lombardi et al. (Eds.): BI 2025, LNAI 16348, pp. 138–149, 2026.
https://doi.org/10.1007/978-981-95-9578-5_11

nature, EEG is widely used in research [3], and recent studies have demonstrated its effectiveness in detecting MDD. However, manual analysis of EEG signals is laborious, time-consuming, and prone to error.

To overcome these issues, many automated methods based on traditional ML and DL approaches for MDD detection using EEG signals have been developed. The DL-based methods, such as those by Sharma et al. [4] and Bagherzadeh et al. [5], yield very good performance. However, these methods have been evaluated using a patient-independent evaluation (PIE) protocol, where the data from the same subject appear in the training, validation, and test sets, allowing the model to learn subject-specific noise in addition to MDD patterns. These methods have poor generalization due to the data leakage nature of the PIE protocol and are not suitable for clinical applications. To overcome this problem, several methods have been proposed [6–8, 10, 11, 15] and evaluated using Leave-Some-Subject-Out Cross-Validation (LSSOCV), where the training, validation, and test sets comprise data from different subjects. This approach aligns with clinical practice. Sun et al. [6] and Zandbagleh et al. [8] employed traditional ML techniques, which lack the capacity to capture the complexities of the EEG signal fully. Yang et al. [7] achieved good performance but are limited by the approach, which requires extensive feature engineering and channel selection, thereby reducing its real-world scalability. Xia et al. [10] designed a CNN-transformer model to achieve better generalization; however, its complexity is high relative to the size of the available MDD datasets. Similar efforts were made by Xu et al. [11]. Large models, such as EEGPT [15], can address some of these challenges; however, they have limitations, including the need for high-performance computing infrastructure and a large training dataset, which is typically not available in cases of MDD detection.

Addressing the above issues, we propose a deep learning-based ensemble classifier for MDD detection. We design a lightweight and computationally efficient CNN model as a base learner for the ensemble classifier. This model analyzes EEG signals spatially and temporally to learn discriminative features, achieving better performance than state-of-the-art methods (SOTA) using LSSOCV, making it suitable for clinical applications.

The remainder of this paper is organized as follows: Sect. 2 describes the dataset and the proposed method; Sect. 3 presents the evaluation protocol utilized and the experiment results; Sect. 4 compares the proposed method with SOTA methods; and Sect. 5 concludes the paper.

2 Material and Methods

This section begins with the mathematical problem formulation, followed by the dataset description and preparation, and concludes with the proposed model architecture.

2.1 Problem Statement and Formulation

We are given an EEG signal recorded non-invasively from the subject's skull using electrodes, over a fixed time window. It is required to assess the subject's mental state using this recording. Based on their mental state, the subject is either a healthy control (HC) or an individual diagnosed with major depressive disorder (MDD).

Let the EEG signal be recorded at a sampling rate r over a time interval t. The EEG segment can be represented as a matrix $x \in \mathbb{R}^{C \times T}$, where C denotes the number of EEG channels and $T = r \times t$ is the total number of samples in the EEG recording. The corresponding label $y \in Y$ denotes the subject's mental state, with the label set defined as $Y = \{HC, MDD\}$. The objective is to design a mapping function $f : \mathbb{R}^{C \times T} \rightarrow Y$ parametrized by θ, such that for any input signal x, the function predicts the correct label: $f(x; \theta) = y$.

This function f can be developed using conventional ML or DL approaches. DL outperforms traditional ML methods in several domains, including signal processing and, in particular, EEG processing [16].

2.2 Dataset Description and Preparation

The MUMTAZ Dataset [12] serves as the benchmark for training and evaluating the proposed method. This dataset was collected at the University Hospital Sains in Malaysia. It comprises EEG recordings from 64 subjects aged between 27 and 54 years. Of these, 34 patients were diagnosed with MDD and recorded before any medication, while 30 were age-matched healthy control subjects. The EEG signals were acquired using a standard 19-channel setup, in accordance with the international 10–20 system. Each recording is 10 min long, consisting of 5 min with eyes open (EO) and 5 min with eyes closed (EC), at a sampling rate of 265 Hz.

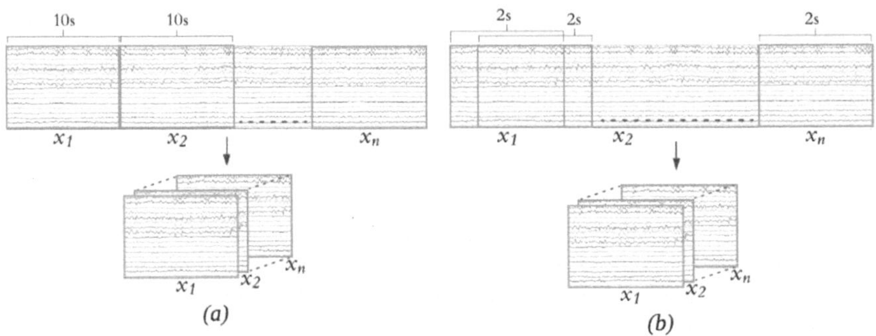

Fig. 1. (a) *Test data*: the EEG recordings of the test subjects are split into 10-s EEG trials using a non-overlapping window, (b) *Training data*: the EEG recordings of the training and validation subjects are split into 2-s trials using an overlapping window with a 75% overlap.

Using the 5-min EEG recordings captured under EC conditions, we create multiple EEG trials (EEG instances) to train and test the model. The model is designed to process short EEG trials of a small duration of s_1 seconds, enabling low parameter complexity and reducing the risk of overfitting while predicting the corresponding label. Through experimentation, we found that using s_1= 2 s with a 75% overlap between consecutive EEG trials, as illustrated in Fig. 1(b), effectively generates enough training instances for model learning. However, for inference, we use EEG trials of a large duration of s_2 seconds so that brain activation over a longer duration can be used to get a reliable prediction; empirically, we determined that s_2=10 s results in good performance. This means that test EEG trials of 10 s are created without overlapping to assess the network's performance, as shown in Fig. 1(a). At test time, the 10-s EEG trial is segmented into 2-s trials, as the model only receives 2-s trials. The labels of all 2-s sub-trials extracted from the 10-s trial are predicted and fused for the final decision.

2.3 Proposed Model

We design the model for the function f using an ensemble approach. There are two primary approaches to constructing an ensemble model, i.e., bagging and boosting. In the bagging strategy, *multiple diverse base learners* are trained on distinct subsets derived from the original dataset and used in parallel to predict the label of an instance. In contrast, we build an ensemble based on a single lightweight CNN model as a base.

EEG data, particularly from the clinical population affected by MDD, are characterized by high inter-subject variability, inherent non-stationarity, and a low sample size-to-high dimensionality ratio. Consequently, a bagging ensemble strategy is often preferred over a single complex model [17]. It is preferable due to its variance-reduction property, as well as its lightweight, segmented implementation, which offers a practical solution to the typical constraints of clinical EEG analysis.

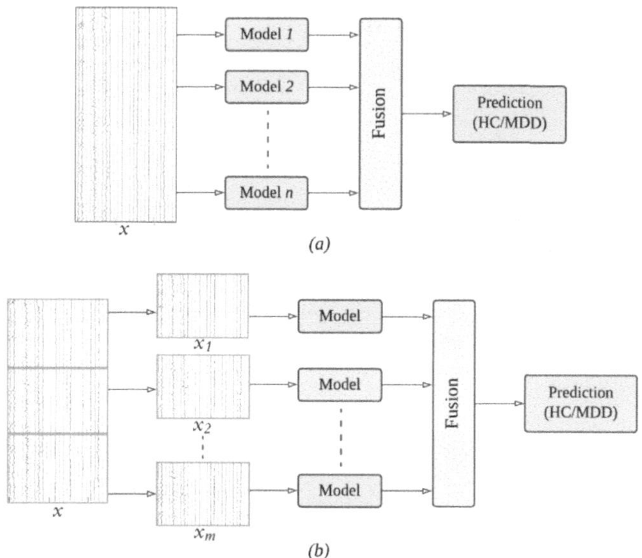

Fig. 2. (a) Traditional ensemble classifier, (b) The proposed ensemble model.

The traditional design of an ensemble classifier is illustrated in Fig. 2(a), where n distinct models (Model 1, Model 2, ..., Model n) serve as base learners. The EEG segment is passed independently into each base model, and their predictions are fused to make the final decision. This approach is computationally costly, as each model requires the full-length EEG trial (e.g., 10 s), thereby increasing model complexity and the number of parameters. Additionally, during inference, each model generates predictions based on the same input. This approach is also memory-intensive as it necessitates storing parameters for n separate models.

In contrast, we use another design shown in Fig. 2(b), where an EEG trial x of s_2 seconds is divided into sub-trials $x_1, x_2, .., x_m$, each of duration s_1 seconds so that $s_2 = m \times s_1$ seconds, where m is the number of total segments. Each segment x_i is passed to the same base model, and the predictions are fused. In this case, the diversity arises from the different segments $x_1, x_2, .., x_m$. The same base model independently analyzes different portions of the EEG signal to make the final decision. The key component of this design is the base learner, which we design as a lightweight CNN model. The formulation of the model illustrated in Fig. 2(b) is given by:

$y = f(x; \theta) = fusion(\phi(x_1; \theta), \phi(x_2; \theta), ..., \phi(x_m; \theta)),$

where ϕ denotes the base model. For *fusion*, different options are possible, we use a simple **majority decision function**. The base learner is described in detail in the following subsection.

This solution is computationally efficient as it requires training a model utilizing segmented EEG trials rather than full-length EEG trials, thereby reducing model complexity and the risk of overfitting. It is also spatially optimized, as only one model's parameters need to be stored in memory.

2.3.1 Backbone Lightweight CNN Model

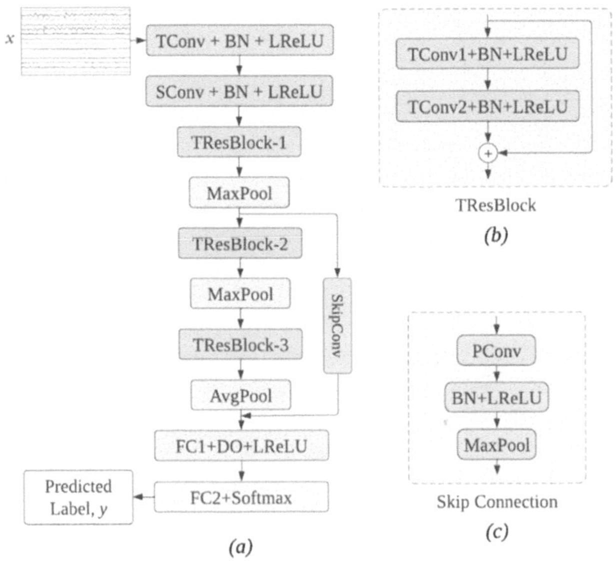

Fig. 3. (a) Lightweight CNN model architecture, and designs of (b) Temporal Residual Block (TResBlock) and (c) Skip Connection (SkipConv).

The proposed lightweight CNN base learner is illustrated in Fig. 3, and its specifications are presented in Table 1. It is composed of five distinct blocks: the Temporal Convolution block (*TConv*), the Spatial Convolution Block (*SConv*), the Temporal Residual Block (*TResBlock*), the Fully Connected Block (*FC*), and the Pooling Blocks (*MaxPoolandAvgPool*).

The *TConv* consists of three layers: a temporal convolution (Conv) layer, a batch normalization (BN) layer, and a Leaky ReLU (LReLU) activation layer. The Conv layer uses 20 convolution filters, each of size 1 × 11, to analyze the input along the temporal axis. The use of temporal convolution enables the model to effectively capture dynamic patterns and sequential dependencies over time, thereby enhancing its ability to recognize temporal features in the signal. The BN and LReLU help stabilize training by normalizing feature distributions and introducing non-linearity.

The *S Conv* also contains three layers: a spatial Conv layer, a BN layer, and LReLU activation. This Conv layer utilizes 20 filters of size 1 × 8, specifically designed to operate across the channel dimension. The spatial Conv focuses on the extraction of local features along the channels while preserving the temporal dimension. This process enhances the model's sensitivity to spatial patterns within the selected channels, resulting in a more informative feature representation.

The next block is *TResBlock*, which comprises two temporal modules consisting of sequential temporal Conv, BN, and LReLU layers. Notably, the Conv layers in both modules use the same filter size (1 × 5 in each *TResBlock*), ensuring consistent feature extraction. A skip connection directly adds the input to the block's output, supporting effective gradient flow and improving overall model stability. This entire block is repeated three times throughout the network, and with each repetition, the number of convolutional filters is progressively reduced, starting from 16, then 12, and ending with eight filters. This gradual reduction helps compress learned features, controls model complexity, and supports hierarchical feature abstraction for improved classification performance.

The *MaxPool* and *AvgPool* are employed to progressively reduce the spatial dimension of the feature maps, resulting in lower computational load and simplifying the model architecture. The first *MaxPool* decreases the dimensions from 1 × 512 × 16 to 1 × 255 × 16, followed by the second *MaxPool* layer, which further reduces them from 1 × 255 × 12 to 1 × 127 × 12. Finally, the *AvgPool* layer substantially compresses the dimensions from 1 × 127 × 8 to 1 × 2 × 8, eliminating redundancy.

The *SkipConv* enables direct transfer of information from earlier layers to later layers in the network. It includes a point-wise convolution layer (*PConv*) for reducing the input's dimension so it can be added to the output coming from the Temporal Residual blocks and Pooling Blocks. By allowing the gradients to bypass one or more layers, the skip connection facilitates stable backpropagation, helping mitigate the vanishing gradient problem. This architectural feature preserves important features across layers, enabling the training of deeper networks without significant loss of information or degradation in performance.

Finally, $FC1$ reduces the dimension of the feature maps from 1 × 2 × 8 to 1 × 1 × 10, and applies dropout to minimize the risk of overfitting, followed by an LReLU activation. This output is then passed to $FC2$, which contains two output neurons, each representing one of the possible outcomes. The SoftMax function is employed here to produce a probability distribution for each class (HC and MDD).

Table 1. Specification of the details of the lightweight CNN Model. KS: Kernel Size, KN: Kernel Number, BN: Batch Norm, DO: Dropout Layer, ACT: Activation Function, #LPs: Number of Learnable Parameters, TConv: Temporal Convolution, SConv: Spatial Convolution, TResBlock: Temporal Residual Block, SkipConv: Skip Convolution, PConv: Point-wise Convolution, and FC: Fully Connected Layer.

Block	Layer	KS	KN	Input Size	Output Size	BN/DO/ACT	#LPs
TConv	Input			8x512x1			
	TConv	1x11	20	8x512x1	8x512x20	BN/LReLU	280
SConv	SConv	8x1	20	8x512x20	1x512x20	BN/LReLU	3,260
*TResBlock*1	TConv1	1x5	16	1x512x20	1x512x16	BN/LReLU	1,648
	TConv2	1x5	16	1x512x16	1x512x16	BN/LReLU	1,328
	SkipConv	-		1x512x16	1x512x16	-	336
MaxPool				1x512x16	1x255x16	-	
*TResBlock*2	TConv1	1x5	12	1x255x16	1x255x12	BN/LReLU	996
	TConv2	1x5	12	1x255x12	1x255x12	BN/LReLU	756
	SkipConv			1x255x12	1x255x12		204
MaxPool				1x255x12	1x127x12		
*TResBlock*3	TConv1	1x5	8	1x127x12	1x127x8	BN/LReLU	504
	TConv2	1x5	8	1x127x8	1x127x8	BN/LReLU	344
	SkipConv			1x127x8	1x127x8	-	104
SkipConv	PConv	1x1	8	1x255x16	1x255x8	BN/LReLU	136
	MaxPool			1x255x8	1x127x8		16
AvgPool		-		1x127x8	1x2x8	-	
*FC*1		-		1x2x8	1x1x10	DO/LReLU	170
*FC*2		-		1x1x10	1x1x2	SoftMax	22
Total Learnable Parameters							10,104

2.4 Model Training

The model was learned using the Adam algorithm with a sparse categorical cross-entropy loss function, which is suitable for classification tasks. Training was configured for a maximum of 25 epochs, with early stopping (patience = 5). The initial learning rate was set to 0.0002 with a step decay factor of 0.1. The batch size was set to twice the sampling rate (2 × 256 Hz), and a dropout rate of 0.3 was used for regularization.

3 Experiments and Results

This section presents the evaluation protocol, experimental results, and performance metrics, demonstrating the method's effectiveness through a comprehensive analysis.

3.1 Evaluation Protocol

The evaluation protocol used in this study is the Leave-Some-Subject-Out cross-validation (LSSOCV). In this protocol, the EEG data are partitioned into training, validation, and test sets, ensuring that each set contains data from distinct subjects. This subject-wise separation is critical for preventing data leakage and guaranteeing the model learns generalized MDD-related patterns.

The evaluation was performed using a 10-fold cross-validation scheme employing LSSOCV. In each iteration, one fold was used for validation, one for testing, and the remaining eight folds for training. This process was repeated ten times, with a different test fold selected in each iteration, and final performance metrics were reported as the average of the evaluation results obtained across all repetitions.

For model training, EEG recordings are segmented into 2-s windows with a 75% overlap between consecutive segments. This overlapping window technique increases the number of training samples and enhances the model's ability to learn reliable features. During testing, EEG segments are divided into 10-s non-overlapping trials, which are further subdivided into m smaller trials for classification.

This protocol ensures rigorous evaluation by maintaining strict patient independence between data splits, leveraging cross-validation for robust performance assessment, and employing windowing techniques to maximize data utility for classification of HC and MDD subjects.

The evaluation metrics used in this study include accuracy, specificity, F1-score, area under the ROC curve (AUC), and ROC curve.

3.2 Results and Discussion

This subsection presents the performance outcomes of the proposed model across various electrode signal combinations and cross-validation folds. The results highlight the model's ability to distinguish between MDD and HC subjects, and the impact of different EEG channel selections on classification accuracy and reliability.

EEG signals were recorded from electrodes distributed across the subject's scalp. For model development, these signals were considered in various combinations. In total, 14 different signal groupings were evaluated, resulting in 14 separate models. These groupings included: all electrodes, the central electrodes, {FP1, T3}, {FP2, T4}, {FP1, FP2, T3, T4}, frontal electrodes, frontal-temporal electrodes, frontal-temporal left, frontal-temporal right, left hemisphere, occipital, parietal, right hemisphere, and temporal electrodes. This approach enabled a comprehensive assessment of how different spatial configurations of EEG data affect model performance.

Based on the evaluation of 14 different electrode combinations, the model trained on right hemisphere signals (FP2, F4, F8, C4, T4, P4, T6, O2) achieved superior performance across four of the five evaluation metrics, as illustrated in Fig. 4. This finding aligns with previous research indicating that hemispheric asymmetries, particularly in the right temporal and frontal regions, serve as strong predictors of MDD [13].

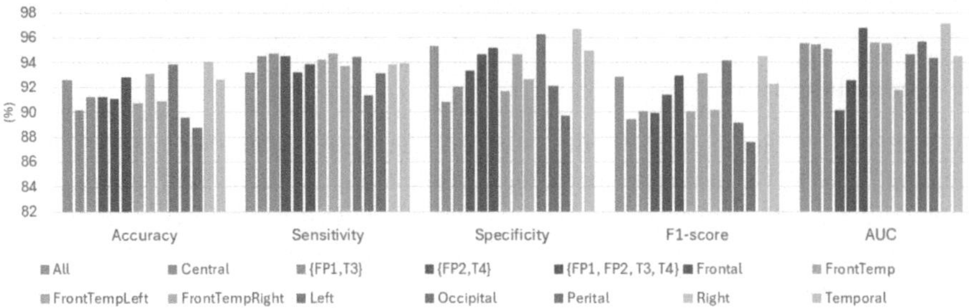

Fig. 4. Comparison of key metrics across the 14 models trained.

The parietal electrode model demonstrated the poorest performance across three key metrics: accuracy, F1-score, and specificity. This suboptimal performance may reflect the complex role of parietal regions in MDD. The occipital electrode model exhibited the lowest sensitivity, suggesting limited capability in correctly identifying MDD patients when relying solely on posterior brain activity. Additionally, electrodes FP2 and T4 yielded the lowest AUC score.

Due to the dominant performance of the right hemisphere, we further examine its performance on 10 folds, each trained and tested on different subjects, as shown in Table 2. Except for four folds, the model's performance is exceptionally good across all metrics.

Table 2. Breakdown of the performance of the right hemisphere across key metrics and cross-validation folds.

Folds	ACC%	Sen%	Sp%	F1%	AUC%
F_1	100	100	100	100	100
F_2	87.1	87.5	86.7	87	94.9
F_3	100	100	100	100	100
F_4	100	100	100	100	100
F_5	87.7	100	80.4	85.9	99.44
F_6	83.3	75	100	85.7	86.1
F_7	100	100	100	100	100
F_8	100	100	100	100	100
F_9	82.7	76	100	86.4	90.9
F_{10}	100	100	100	100	100
Avg	94.1	93.9	96.7	94.5	97.1

This observation is also depicted in the ROC curves shown in Fig. 5. We can observe that the curves are clustered near the top-left corner of the plot, indicating high sensitivity and low false positive rates across all folds except the four foldsF_2,F_5, F_6 and F_9. This suggests that the model consistently achieves strong discrimination between classes, with excellent generalizability and robustness across different subsets of the data.

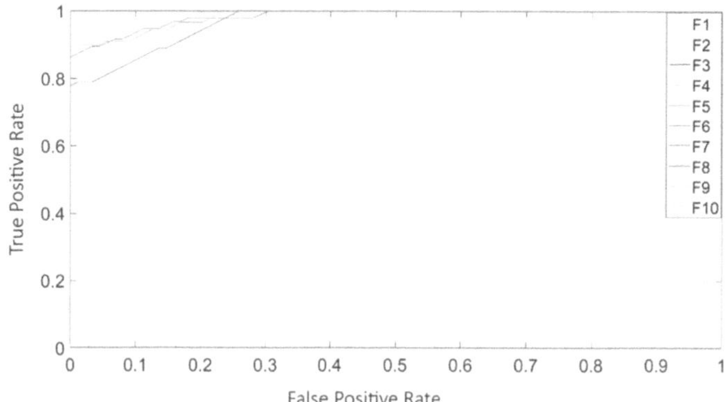

Fig. 5. ROC for the right hemisphere across folds F_1 through F_{10}.

The model's performance drops across folds F_2, F_5, F_6 and F_9 when subjects (MDD 15, 27, 5; HC 16, 24, 25) are included in the validation or test sets. In addition to general distributional differences, lower performance in these folds arises from pronounced inter-subject variability in EEG signal characteristics, a known challenge in neurophysiological classification [17]. EEG signals are highly susceptible to contamination from artifacts, noise, and dynamic behaviors. These factors introduce non-stationarity, challenging the model's ability to transfer learned representations and achieve robust classification. Furthermore, with a modest sample size, such outliers exert greater influence on fold-wise results, amplifying generalization limitations. While the model handles minor distributional differences, its inability to generalize to these extreme shifts suggests that the existence of these atypical patient cases limits the reliable deployment of this method in a real-world clinical setting. These findings suggest the need to explore robust domain adaptation or distribution alignment techniques to enhance robustness across heterogeneous patient populations.

4 Comparison with SOTA Methods

In Table 3, we compared the proposed method with those that employed the LSSOCV protocol on the MUMTAZ dataset. The method by Yang et al. [7] is a traditional ML approach, whereas the methods by Xia et al. [10] and Carrle et al. [9] are based on a DL approach. Among these methods, the one by Xia et al. [10] utilized a two-branch CNN to extract features and dense layers for classification. However, this approach was limited in its ability to integrate both temporal and spatial information effectively.

Our proposed model, which utilizes a lightweight CNN backbone within an ensemble framework, yielded significant performance gains over existing traditional ML and complex DL-based methods. The architecture's effectiveness is attributed to its ability to simultaneously capture both temporal and spatial features with a reduced parameter count, making it highly effective at extracting discriminative features for MDD classification. The resulting model excels in performance compared to SOTA methods on the MUMTAZ dataset.

Table 3. Comparison of the proposed method with current SOTA models. TC = Trial Length, #C = Number of channels.

Study	Method	TC/#C	ACC%	Sen%	Sp%
Yang et al. [7]	LZC + PSD	10/19	78.6	78.9	78.3
Xia et al. [10]	2D-CNN	5/19	91.06	91.33	89.68
Carrle et al. [9]	DeprNet	8/13	79.8	-	-
Proposed Method	**CNN-ensemble**	**2/8**	**94.1**	**93.9**	**96.7**

5 Conclusion and Future Work

Major depressive disorder (MDD) continues to pose significant challenges for individuals and society. This study demonstrates the effectiveness of an ensemble classifier comprising lightweight CNNs, utilizing raw EEG data for the detection of MDD. By leveraging both spatial and temporal convolutions, the model efficiently extracts key discriminative features associated with MDD. Our analysis revealed that EEG signals from the right hemisphere contributed most to accurate classification. The method's robustness was validated using the LSSOCV protocol on the MUMTAZ benchmark dataset, achieving an accuracy of 94.1%. This approach shows promise as a supportive tool for psychiatrists in the early detection of MDD.

However, several limitations remain. Channel selection for discriminative features was performed manually, and automating this process could enhance model performance. Additionally, the model operates as a black box, emphasizing the need for improved transparency and explainability to increase clinical trust. The method's performance degraded when there was a significant difference in the data distributions of the training and test sets.

Future work will focus on evaluating the current method on MODMA [14] and other benchmarks, exploring alternative backbone architectures, investigating the impact of various brain wave bands (sigma, theta, alpha, beta, gamma) on performance, and developing domain adaptation and explainable AI techniques to improve clinical reliability and applicability.

References

1. Malhi, G.S., Mann, J.J.: Depression. Lancet **392**(10161), 2299–2312 (2018). https://doi.org/10.1016/s0140-6736(18)31948-2

2. Fava, M., Kendler, K.S.: Major depressive disorder. Neuron **28**(2), 335–341 (2000). https://doi.org/10.1016/s0896-6273(00)00112-4
3. Alzubaidi, L., et al.: Review of deep learning: concepts, CNN architectures, challenges, applications, future directions. J. Big Data **8**(1) (2021). https://doi.org/10.1186/s40537-021-00444-8
4. Sharma, G., Joshi, A.M., Gupta, R., Cenkeramaddi, L.R.: DepCap: A smart healthcare framework for EEG based depression detection using time-frequency response and deep neural network. IEEE Access **11**, 52327–52338 (2023). https://doi.org/10.1109/access.2023.3275024
5. Bagherzadeh, S., Norouzi, M.R., Ghasri, A., et al.: Automated depression detection via cloud-based EEG analysis with transfer learning and synchrosqueezed wavelet transform. Sci. Rep. **15**, 18008 (2025). https://doi.org/10.1038/s41598-025-02452-7
6. Sun, S., Li, J., Chen, H., Gong, T., Li, X., Hu, B.: A study of resting-state EEG biomarkers for depression recognition. arXiv [Eess.SP] (2020). Retrieved from http://arxiv.org/abs/2002.11039
7. Yang, J., Zhang, Z., Xiong, P., Liu, X.: Depression detection based on analysis of EEG signals in multi brain regions. J. Integr. Neurosc. **22**(4) (2023). https://doi.org/10.31083/j.jin2204093
8. Zandbagleh, A., Sanei, S., Azami, H.: Implications of aperiodic and periodic EEG components in classification of major depressive disorder from source and electrode perspectives. Sensors **24**(18), 6103 (2024). https://doi.org/10.3390/s24186103
9. Carrle, F.P., Hollenbenders, Y., Reichenbach, A.: Generation of synthetic EEG data for training algorithms supporting the diagnosis of major depressive disorder. Front. Neurosci. **17**, 1219133 (2023). https://doi.org/10.3389/fnins.2023.1219133
10. Xia, M., Zhang, Y., Wu, Y., Wang, X.: An end-to-end deep learning model for EEG-based major depressive disorder classification. IEEE Access **11**, 41337–41347 (2023). https://doi.org/10.1109/access.2023.3270426
11. Xu, C., Fan, F., Shen, J., Wang, H., Zhang, Z., Meng, Q.: An EEG-based depressive detection network with adaptive feature learning and channel activation. In: Proceedings of the Annual Meeting of the Cognitive Science Society (2024). https://escholarship.org/uc/item/76b4c4qw
12. Mumtaz, W.: MDD patients and healthy controls EEG data (new). Figshare (2016). https://figshare.com/articles/dataset/EEG_Data_New/4244171
13. Liu, X., et al.: EEG-based major depressive disorder recognition by neural oscillation and asymmetry. Front. Neurosci. **18**, 1362111 (2024). https://doi.org/10.3389/fnins.2024.1362111
14. Cai, H., et al.: MODMA: A multi-modal open dataset for mental-disorder analysis. Sci. Data **9**(1) (2022). https://doi.org/10.1038/s41597-022-01211-x
15. Wang, G., Liu, W., He, Y., Xu, C., Ma, L., Li, H.: EEGPT: Pretrained transformer for universal and reliable representation of EEG signals. Adv. Neural Inf. Process. Syst. (2024). https://proceedings.neurips.cc/paper_files/paper/2024/hash/4540d267eeec4e5dbd9dae9448f0b739-Abstract-Conference.html
16. Gong, S., Xing, K., Cichocki, A., Li, J.: Deep learning in EEG: advance of the last ten-year critical period. IEEE Trans. Cogn. Dev. Syst. **14**(2), 348–365 (2022). https://doi.org/10.1109/tcds.2021.3079712
17. Unnisa, Z., Zia, S., Butt, U.M., Letchmunan, S., Ilyas, S.: Ensemble usage for classification of EEG signals a review with comparison. Lecture Notes in Computer Science, pp. 189–208 (2020).https://doi.org/10.1007/978-3-030-50353-6_14

A Novel Framework for Analyzing the Speed-Accuracy Trade-Off in Online P300-Based Brain-Computer Interfaces

Javier Jiménez(✉) and Francisco B. Rodríguez

Grupo de Neurocomputación Biológica, Departamento de Ingeniería Informática, Escuela Politécnica Superior, Universidad Autónoma de Madrid, Madrid, Spain
{javier.jimenez01,f.rodriguez}@uam.es

Abstract. This study addresses the daunting challenge of optimizing Brain-Computer Interfaces (BCIs) by focusing on the speed-accuracy trade-off, which is inherent in BCI systems due to the limited Signal to Noise Ratio (SNR) in electroencephalography (EEG) signals. To detect Event-Related Potentials (ERPs) like the P300, multiple trials are often averaged, improving SNR, but increasing the time required for data collection, thus slowing down the system. This trade-off has traditionally been analyzed using measures like the Information Transfer Rate (ITR), which combine speed and accuracy into a single measure, hindering the separate analysis of these factors. To address this limitation, this study introduces two new measures, *Gain* and *Conservation* (*Cons*), that separately characterize speed and accuracy, allowing BCI designers to optimize systems by adjusting these factors according to their specific needs. A new characterization procedure is proposed to assist BCI designers and users in selecting interfaces based on their preferences for speed and accuracy. The findings demonstrate how these tools can enable dynamic, online BCI optimization, offering a more flexible and interpretable approach to BCI design.

Keywords: brain data analysis · early stop · EEG pattern recognition · event-related potentials · BCI metrics

1 Introduction

Brain-Computer Interfaces translate brain signals into commands to control electronic devices. These brain signals are captured using neuroimaging techniques like electroencephalography (EEG), or magnetoencephalography (MEG), among others [6,14]. This work focuses on EEG, which records the instantaneous electrical activity of the scalp using a headset with multiple electrodes.

To control devices via EEG, the user's intention must be decoded, often through Event-Related Potentials (ERPs) like P300s, or Steady State Visual Evoked Potentials (SSVEPs), in addition to others [6,14]. Here, the P300-ERP, a distinct EEG deflection occurring about 300 ms after a stimulus, will be assessed.

A. Lombardi et al. (Eds.): BI 2025, LNAI 16348, pp. 150–161, 2026.
https://doi.org/10.1007/978-981-95-9578-5_12

The P300-ERP occurs involuntarily in response to rare, surprising stimuli among frequent ones—a setup known as the oddball paradigm [1]. This can involve various sensory modalities, including visual [8,10], or auditory [12], along with others [5]. This study is focused on the visual oddball paradigm, specifically the Rapid Serial Visual Presentation (RSVP) [10], where subjects attend to a target within a rapid stream of visual stimuli. However, due to the low Signal to Noise Ratio (SNR) of EEG signals, BCIs often require repeated trials to detect ERPs like the P300 through averaging. As shown in Fig. 1A, averaging more trials enhances P300 detection.

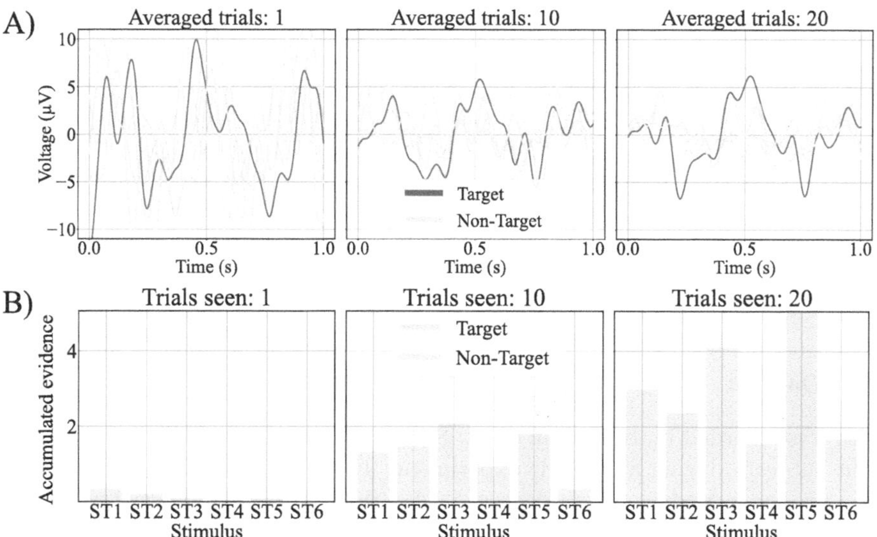

Fig. 1. A) SNR evolution of averaged EEG time series from the third subject's first session and run in Hoffmann et al. [8], showing clearer P300 detection as more trials (1, 10, 20) are averaged. B) Accumulated Bayesian Linear Discriminant Analysis (BLDA) probabilities for P300 classification across trials, using a model trained on all sessions from [8] except the first. Results shown for 1, 10, and 20 trials from the first session and run.

Adding trials boosts SNR but slows interaction, revealing a speed-accuracy trade-off. To consider this trade-off, metrics such as Information Transfer Rate (ITR) [16], Symbols Per Minute (SPM) [15], or BCI-Utility [4], combine speed and accuracy into a single score. However, while different tasks demand different needs, these metrics always combine speed and accuracy in the same way and within complex relationships, limiting adaptation. As an illustration, Dal Seno et al. [4] showed how the ITR exhibited high bitrates for a P300-Speller with which communication was unfeasible due to lack of accuracy. In contrast, this paper proposes two new measures to evaluate speed and accuracy independently, as well as a method to help choose different interfaces based on users' needs.

2 Materials and Methods

As noted previously, the main goal of this paper is to evaluate BCIs in light of the speed-accuracy trade-off with two new measurements addressing speed and accuracy separately, along with a characterization procedure to guide BCI selection. Then, the results of using these new measurements will be compared against the most commonly used BCI measure, the ITR. As far as the authors are concerned, previous work have focused on either BCI decoding accuracy (Cohen's Kappa coefficient, classification accuracy, etc. [11]) or speed-accuracy composite measures (ITR, BCI-Utility, etc. [4]), being the latter hard to condition towards faster or more accurate BCIs. In contrast, this work novelty lies on a new optimization strategy, highly inspired in the speed-accuracy trade-off, which facilitates BCIs' conditioning towards faster or more accurate interfaces.

In terms of the contents of this section, first, the employed dataset will be described (Sect. 2.1), followed by the preprocessing steps applied (Sect. 2.2) before feeding data into a machine learning algorithm to detect P300-ERP patterns (Sect. 2.3). Then, new evaluation criteria will be defined along with a widely known BCI measure in the literature (Sect. 2.4). Finally, a brief description of the experimental procedure to obtain the results will be presented in Sect. 2.5.

2.1 Dataset

Data was recorded by Hoffmann et al. [8], and consists of raw EEG signals from eight subjects during an RSVP experiment. The dataset comprises recordings from two separate days per subject, spaced within a two-week interval, with each day including two sessions, each consisting of six runs containing 20 to 25 trials. Data were sampled at 2048 Hz using a 32-electrode EEG headset (10–20 system) plus two mastoid references.

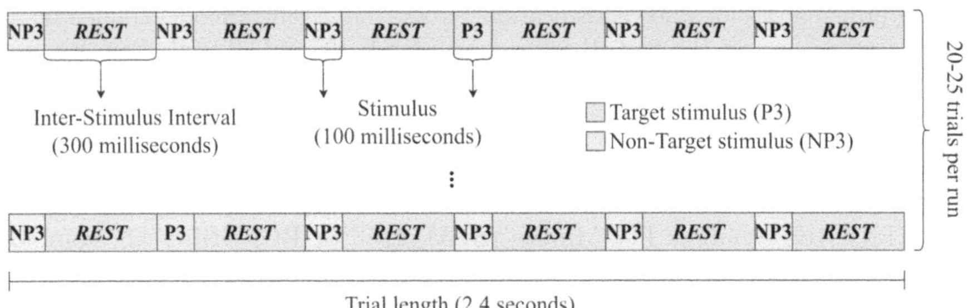

Fig. 2. RSVP experiment from Hoffmann et al. [8]. From the experiment, each run consisted of 20–25 trials in which six stimuli were shown in a random order. Just one of the six stimuli shown was the target one. Please note that only the target stimulus should generate the P300 wave in EEG recordings (P3), in contrast with the five non-target stimuli (NP3).

The experiment used an RSVP oddball paradigm [10] with one target and five non-target visual stimuli. Each image was shown for 100 ms, followed by a 300 ms blank period, in a randomized, non-repeating sequence over 20–25 trials (see Fig. 2).

2.2 Data Preprocessing

Most of the preprocessing steps were reproduced from [8] at run level, except for their winsorization and scaling phases, which were not employed to obtain the results of this paper. These were omitted to keep the preprocessing stage as simple as possible while maintaining most of the original interface's accuracy [8], however, this also resulted in a higher incidence of artefacts.

EEG data were preprocessed by first re-referencing the signals using the average of the reference electrodes. The signals were then band-pass filtered with a 6th-order Butterworth filter between 1–12 Hz which corresponded with the theta (4–8 Hz), alpha (8–12 Hz) and part of delta (<4 Hz) bands as they are known to contain most of the P300 activity [13]. After filtering, data were downsampled from 2048 Hz to 32 Hz to facilitate machine learning processing. Then, EEG signals were segmented into one second epochs starting at each stimulus onset to include the P300 response—as it is reported to occur 250–500 ms after each stimulus onset [13]. Each run was trimmed to 20 trials.

2.3 Bayesian Linear Discriminant Analysis to Detect P300-ERPs

Once preprocessed, the epoched time series were employed to fit a BLDA classifier to determine which epochs contain a P300-ERP. BLDA is a classification variant of Fisher's Linear Discriminant Analysis (LDA), which employs a Bayesian-framework to discriminate among LDA's projections, and it has been widely used to obtain successful P300-ERP detection results in the literature [8,10–12,15]. This classifier starts from a series of input vectors $\boldsymbol{x}$ and their labels y. Then it projects $\boldsymbol{x}$ to a more compact representation, $\boldsymbol{z}$, which maximizes the distance between the means of different classes while minimizing the variance of samples coming from the same class (see Fig. 4.9 in [7]). Once mapped, $\boldsymbol{z}$ is classified with Bayes' maximum a posteriori procedure as seen below:

$$P(y|\boldsymbol{z}) = \frac{P(\boldsymbol{z}|y) \times P(y)}{P(\boldsymbol{z})}. \tag{1}$$

Additionally, BLDA assumes the likelihood $P(\boldsymbol{z}|y)$ follows a multivariate Gaussian distribution whose covariance matrices, Σ, are all the same for all classification labels, simplifying the computation as:

$$\log P(\boldsymbol{z}|y) \propto -\frac{1}{2}(\boldsymbol{z} - \boldsymbol{\mu})' \Sigma^{-1} (\boldsymbol{z} - \boldsymbol{\mu}), \tag{2}$$

being $\boldsymbol{\mu}$ a vector with the means of all classes' projections and $(\cdot)'$ the transpose operation.

Now, all variables can be empirically obtained from the projections $\boldsymbol{z}$. But since the empirical covariance matrix, $\hat{\Sigma}$, is not a good estimator of Σ when the number of training samples is low [9], a shrinkage hyperparameter δ is also introduced in the following equation:

$$\Sigma_\delta = (1-\delta)\hat{\Sigma} + \delta \frac{Tr(\hat{\Sigma})}{d}\mathbf{I}(d), \tag{3}$$

being $Tr(\cdot)$ the trace of a matrix, $\mathbf{I}(d)$ the $d \times d$ identity matrix, and d the number of $\boldsymbol{z}$ features. This δ hyperparameter regularizes the covariance matrix Σ_δ and can be analytically computed through the Ledoit-Wolf's lemma [9], which will be employed to adjust the model.

2.4 Standard BCI Measures do not Provide a Clear Mechanism to Adjust the Speed-Accuracy Trade-Off

Although several measures, such as the ITR [16], variants of the ITR [2], the SPM [15], and the BCI-Utility [4], are used to evaluate BCIs in the literature, this paper will include just the original ITR [16] as it is commonly employed in BCI studies [3,5,8,12]. The ITR measures the efficiency of a BCI in transmitting information. This crucial metric, essential for applications demanding both speed and precision, is expressed in bits per minute, as defined by the following equation:

$$ITR(\frac{bits}{minute}) = B\frac{60}{\tau}, \tag{4}$$

being τ the time invested in seconds, $B = \log_2 N + P\log_2 P + (1-P)\log_2 \frac{1-P}{N-1}$ the number of bits transferred, $N = 6$ the number of possible decisions of the BCI in [8], and P the classifier's accuracy. However, the ITR relies on assumptions that limit its validity for typical BCI applications, such as treating BCIs as memoryless [17], a relevant limitation when employing early stopping algorithms that consider information from previous trials. It also fails to separate speed and accuracy, making it hard to balance the speed-accuracy trade-off. To address these issues, this paper introduces two new measures that independently evaluate improvements in speed and accuracy compared to a baseline BCI.

To measure the relative improvement in speed of a BCI against another, the *Gain* is defined as the relative amount of trials saved as shown in the following equation:

$$Gain(t, t^*) = \frac{t - t^*}{t}, \tag{5}$$

being t the number of trials required by the baseline BCI, and t^* the number of trials required by the proposed BCI.

Regarding the *Gain* usage, if a baseline BCI consumed $t = 20$ trials, and the proposed BCI consumed just $t^* = 5$, then $Gain(t = 20, t^* = 5) = 0.75$, highlighting it saved 75% of trials. In other words, the proposed BCI would be 75% faster than the baseline BCI.

Following the *Gain*, the *Conservation* is also defined to quantify the relative amount of preserved accuracy from a baseline BCI in the following equation:

$$Cons(i, i^*) = 1 - \frac{A(i) - A(i^*)}{A(i)}, \tag{6}$$

being $A(\cdot)$ the accuracy of a model $\in [0, 1]$ after stopping at a specific trial computed as the number of runs well classified divided by all the available runs, i the trial at which the baseline BCI stops, and i^* the trial at which the proposed BCI stops.

In terms of the *Cons* usage, consider a baseline BCI obtains $A(i) = 1$ after $i = 20$ trials, and the proposed BCI obtained just $A(i^*) = 0.75$ after $i^* = 5$ trials, then $Cons(i = 20, i^* = 5) = 0.75$, showing it preserved 75% of the original accuracy.

Unlike composite metrics like the ITR, these new measures support varied optimization strategies, favoring speed (*Gain*), accuracy (*Cons*), or trade-off equations like $\alpha Gain + (1 - \alpha) Cons$ where $\alpha \to 0$ bias BCIs towards higher accuracies and $\alpha \to 1$ towards faster BCIs. However, as they rely on a specific baseline BCI, they are not suitable for universal comparison but for user-centred adaptation. Finally, it should be noted that, for these equations to measure relative improvement, the baseline BCI must be slower and more accurate than the evaluated BCI—reflecting the relationship between speed and accuracy.

2.5 Validating *Gain* and *Conservation*: Characterization of the Speed-Accuracy Trade-off

To assess the suitability of the already defined BCI measures, the present work relies on a baseline BCI, here defined as the slowest and most accurate for Hoffmann et al. dataset [8]. This baseline BCI will require 20 trials to achieve the maximum P300-ERP detection accuracy.

In contrast, two early stop strategies are tested against the baseline using the proposed measures. While many exist [3], this paper implements a fixed-stop strategy (optimizing the stopping trial) and a threshold-based strategy (stopping at the first trial in which BLDAs' accumulated evidences reach an optimized threshold). Each strategy hyperparameter is optimized via Cross-Validation (CV) to maximize: ITR, *Gain*, *Cons*, or a balance of the last two measures.

Particularly, early stop models are optimized using a 3-fold CV, with each fold representing a full session. A BLDA model is trained on the training folds to detect P300-ERPs in the test fold, producing class probabilities, here called evidences, per EEG epoch. These evidences are accumulated across trials as shown in Fig. 1B, and the stimulus with the highest accumulated evidence is selected based on the number of trials determined by the early stopping strategy.

Finally, the entire process, including early stop optimization, model training, and performance evaluation, is repeated four times within a 4-fold CV procedure. This repetition ensures a robust validation of each proposed measure, allowing for a comprehensive comparison of their effectiveness relative to one another.

3 Results

This section first shows the proposed measures' behaviour in terms of the speed-accuracy trade-off (Sect. 3.1), followed by an overall study on all subjects from Hoffmann et al. [8] (Sect. 3.2). Before analyzing the results, it is important to note that the terms speed and *Gain* will be used interchangeably, as well as the concepts accuracy and *Cons*, since both measure BCIs' speed and accuracy, respectively.

3.1 Analyses of *Gain* and *Conservation* at the Individual Subject Level

The goal of this paper, using the *Gain* and *Cons* measures, is to characterize the speed-accuracy trade-off and provide a systematic procedure to help BCI developers and users actively control and tailor it based on specific needs. In brief, the speed-accuracy trade-off states that faster BCIs would also be less precise due to the low SNR of EEG signals. Therefore, the speed, quantified by the *Gain*, should be maximum when the accuracy, measured by the *Cons*, is minimum and vice-versa. It is possible to observe such behaviour in Fig. 3, where the proposed BCI measures show high *Gain* values corresponding with low *Cons* values, and the opposite, reflecting the speed-accuracy trade-off. Moreover, as it was mentioned at the end of Sect. 1, in Fig. 3A is possible to observe the ITR can assign high bitrates to hyperparameters which make communication almost unfeasible with very low *Cons* values, which are directly related with the overall BCI accuracy.

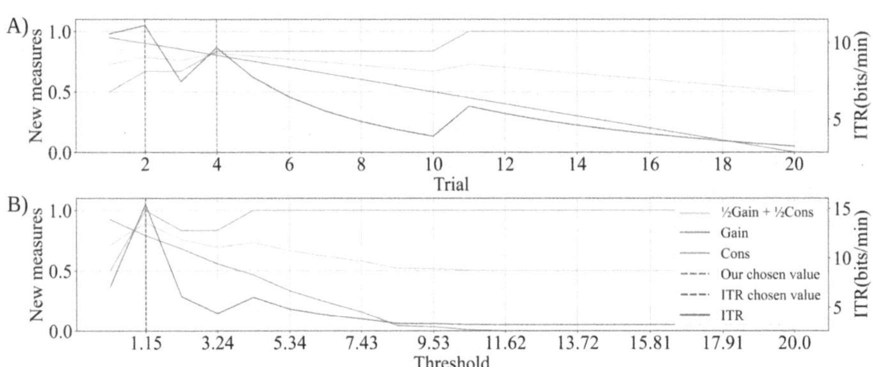

Fig. 3. Evolution of the proposed BCI measures for the described early stop strategies in terms of their hyperparameters for the first subject and first session of [8]. The ITR and $\frac{1}{2}Gain + \frac{1}{2}Cons$ optimized values are shown with blue and red dotted vertical lines, respectively. A) Fixed-stop strategy, here both ITR and $\frac{1}{2}Gain + \frac{1}{2}Cons$ optimize different trials to stop at. B) Threshold-based strategy, here both ITR and $\frac{1}{2}Gain + \frac{1}{2}Cons$ optimize a similar threshold to stop at.

With a better understanding of how *Gain* and *Cons* interact with the speed-accuracy trade-off, customized optimization strategies can be designed to balance speed and accuracy. For example, $\frac{1}{2}Gain + \frac{1}{2}Cons$ equally weights both speed and accuracy and delays decisions to achieve higher accuracy, unlike ITR which favors speed. However, results depend on the early stopping strategy used—as seen in Fig. 3B, *Gain* can change non-linearly, making selection more complex. Overall, strategies like $\alpha Gain + (1-\alpha) Cons$ appear promising for tailoring BCIs to prioritize either precision or speed depending on user needs.

Diving further into how these BCI optimization strategies make decisions, an analysis of each was carried out by extracting contour plots of them in terms of *Gain* and *Cons* pairs as shown in Fig. 4 for subjects one and four from Hoffmann et al. [8]. These contour plots show what combinations of *Gain* and *Cons* pairs would be optimized by each optimization strategy. Particularly, the more yellow the *Gain* and *Cons* pair is, the higher priority they will receive. On the left-side column, Fig. 4A shows ITR values as a function of *Gain* and *Cons* (in bits per minute), highlighting combinations that maximize the ITR in yellow. On the right-side column, Fig. 4B presents different linear combinations of *Gain* and *Cons* constrained between zero and one as they were appropriately normalized, those *Gain*-*Cons* pairs that maximize each linear combination are highlighted in yellow. Since Gain and Cons represent relative improvements over a baseline BCI, they are unitless.

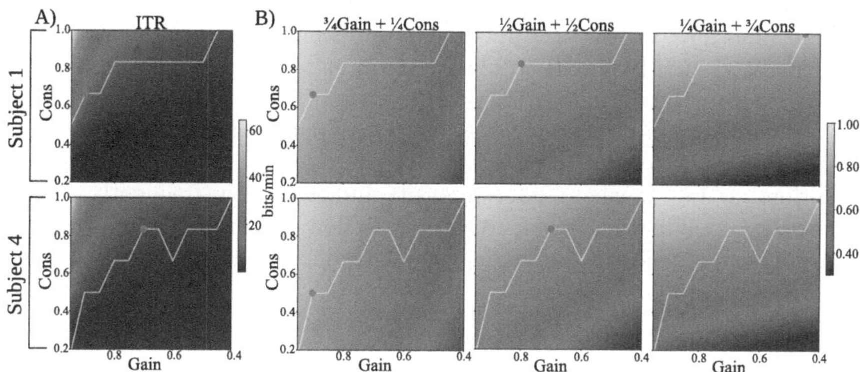

Fig. 4. Contour plots of different optimization strategies, specified on each column's title, in terms of the *Gain* and *Cons* evaluation criteria. The cyan curves represent the evolution of the fixed-stop strategy for a session, and the maximum value achieved on every grid by such curve is stressed out with a red dot. The top row corresponds with the first subject and first session, whereas the bottom row represents the fourth subject and fourth session of [8]. A) ITR contour plots measured in bits/min. B) Different optimization strategies based on linear combinations of the *Gain* and *Cons* measures.

Regarding Fig. 4A, it is possible to see that the ITR prioritizes the speed over the accuracy since the ITR values shrink drastically for lower values of *Gain* in contrast with lower values of *Cons*. However, studying such in terms of the ITR is remarkably difficult due to its non-linear nature, so different linear combinations of *Gain* and *Cons* are also posed in Fig. 4B. These linear combinations of *Gain* and *Cons* show contour plots of differently oriented hyperplanes, which prioritize either the *Gain* or the *Cons*, giving more control over the BCI.

In addition, the evolution of various pairs of *Gain* and *Cons* of a session is displayed as a cyan curve in all contour plots with a red dot indicating the maximum value of such curve in each grid. On one hand, it was observed that the linear combinations of *Gain* and *Cons* consistently selected optimization points that either maximized Gain, Cons, or achieved a balance between them (Fig. 4B). On the other hand, the ITR method prioritized speed in the case of the first subject, while opting for a more balanced combination with the fourth subject (Fig. 4A). This variability introduces greater uncertainty regarding the underlying selection criteria of the ITR approach in contrast with the *Gain* and *Cons* balance. In brief, it is possible to observe how these evolutions' maximum values are different in all contour plots, allowing for a fine-grained methodology when it comes to choosing the minimum number of trials to keep most of BCIs' accuracy.

3.2 Analyses of *Gain* and *Conservation* at the Population Level

The previous analyses were conducted at subject-level, so a broader evaluation was performed by combining results from all participants using the 4-fold CV procedure described in Sect. 2.5. As Hoffmann et al. dataset [8] includes data from 8 subjects, and 4 validation folds were evaluated for every triplet of subject, early stop method, and optimization strategy, this resulted in 32 pairs of optimized trials and accuracies for every early stopping and optimization strategies. Results for the fixed-stop early stopping method are shown as probability distributions in Fig. 5, where color intensity indicates how frequently certain accuracy-trial combinations occur—the more yellow the more likely—revealing each strategy's tendency to use more or fewer trials and achieve higher or lower accuracy.

Regarding the behaviour of the posed optimization strategies, it would be expected that those prioritizing accuracy would tend to consume more trials, but also accumulate around higher accuracies due to the speed-accuracy trade-off, and vice-versa. For example, consider the $\frac{3}{4}Gain + \frac{1}{4}Cons$ optimization strategy: such method will prioritize speed, so its number of required trials should gather around a few trials, but its accuracy should not be as high as the methods that optimize accuracy such as the $\frac{1}{4}Gain + \frac{3}{4}Cons$. These behaviours are successfully captured by the probability density functions estimated in Fig. 5. In essence, the density of strategies that prioritize speed (ITR and $\frac{3}{4}Gain + \frac{1}{4}Cons$) tend to expand across lower trials and accuracies, while strategies that prioritize accuracy ($\frac{1}{4}Gain + \frac{3}{4}Cons$) expand across higher trials and accuracies, and those which balances both ($\frac{1}{2}Gain + \frac{1}{2}Cons$) expand along both axes.

Finally, by analyzing these two-dimensional kernel density estimations in Fig. 5, BCI users and designers would be able to choose their ideal strategies

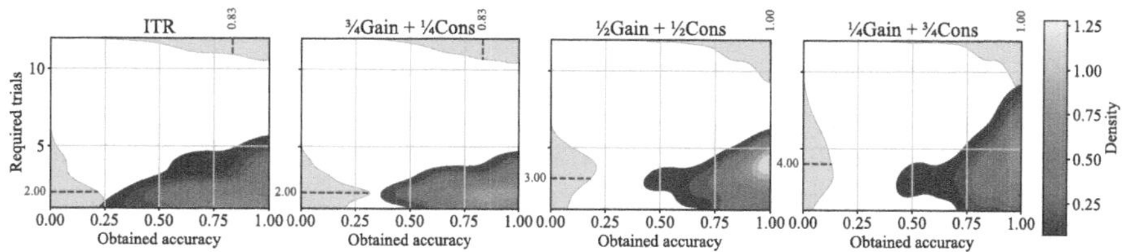

Fig. 5. Contour plots of two-dimensional kernel density estimation for multiple optimization strategies employing the fixed-stop technique. Every dimension kernel density estimation is shown on its respective axes with its median displayed as a dashed line. Each estimation was obtained with 32 samples from a 4-fold CV process on 8 subjects from [8].

based on their current priorities. For example, consider a scenario in which users would prioritize accuracy; for them, it would be interesting to consider the $\frac{1}{4}\,Gain$ + $\frac{3}{4}\,Cons$ optimization strategy, since its density gathers around higher accuracy values, whereas other strategies, such as the ITR, are shifted towards lower accuracies. Ultimately, these two-dimensional Kernel Density Estimations in Fig. 5, serve as a map to look for the desired qualities of a BCI system by leveraging the speed-accuracy trade-off in an interpretable way.

4 Discussion

This paper introduces a new way to characterize and exploit the speed-accuracy trade-off, with particular relevance for online BCI design. Because the *Gain* and *Cons* measures only depend on fixed baseline values and updated performance of the current BCI, they can be computed and optimized online. This enables researchers and developers to monitor performance and select BCIs that match user needs by prioritizing speed, accuracy, or a balance of both.

Nevertheless, the present work tested the proposed measures using only one dataset, one machine learning model and two simple early stopping strategies, so broader validation is still needed. Future work should evaluate additional datasets, P300-ERP detection models [11], and more advanced stopping methods [3]. Doing so would confirm the framework's generalizability and uncover further improvements in speed and accuracy for real-world BCIs.

Additionally, the optimal value of the weighting factor α in the proposed form $\alpha Gain + (1-\alpha) Cons$ is still uncertain. It could be preset to favor speed or accuracy, manually adjusted by a BCI practitioner, or dynamically adapted online. In a closed-loop system, the BCI could monitor factors like task urgency, user fatigue, or error rate to automatically tune α—choosing α close to zero to prioritize accuracy, or α close to one to emphasize speed. However, safeguards would be needed to prevent the system from overly favoring one objective and compromising overall communication reliability.

Finally, it has been observed that BCI measures such as the ITR, which integrate both speed and accuracy into a single metric, make it difficult to prioritize each factor individually, as they combine both in a non-linear manner. For example, optimizing BCIs' accuracy using the ITR would not be recommended, as it tends to prioritize speed over accuracy. This is shown in Fig. 5, where the ITR distribution shift towards fewer trials, and consequently, lower accuracies. In contrast, our new measurements provide a direct estimation of improvement against a baseline BCI which serves as guide to personalized BCI design. However, further testing has yet to be done to verify potential biases in variants of the ITR [2], the BCI-Utility [4], the SPM [15], and, in general, commonly used BCI measurements as it was shown with the ITR.

5 Conclusion

This paper introduced a new way to evaluate BCIs using two measures—*Gain* and *Cons*—to better manage the trade-off between speed and accuracy. These measures helped reveal that different optimization strategies naturally favor either speed or accuracy, and that the commonly used ITR metric is biased toward faster systems. Unlike ITR, *Gain* and *Cons* allow explicit control over this bias, enabling designers to prioritize speed, accuracy, or a balance between the two through an adjustable α parameter. Overall, the paper proposes a new framework for describing and tuning BCI behavior, paving the way for dynamic and adaptive closed-loop optimization.

Acknowledgments. This study was supported by the Predoctoral Research Grants of the Universidad Autónoma de Madrid (FPI-UAM) and by PID2023-149669NB-I00 (MCIN/AEI and ERDF – "A way of making Europe").

Disclosure of Interests. The authors have no competing interests to declare that are relevant to the content of this article.

References

1. Abiri, R., Borhani, S., Sellers, E.W., Jiang, Y., Zhao, X.: A comprehensive review of EEG-based brain-computer interface paradigms. J. Neural Eng. **16**(1), 011001 (2019). https://doi.org/10.1088/1741-2552/aaf12e
2. Arslan, S.S., Sinha, P.: Information transfer rate in BCIs: towards tightly integrated symbiosis. Biomed. Signal Process. Control **87**, 105466 (2024). https://doi.org/10.1016/j.bspc.2023.105466
3. Bianchi, L., Liti, C., Liuzzi, G., Piccialli, V., Salvatore, C.: Improving P300 Speller performance by means of optimization and machine learning. Ann. Oper. Res. **312**(2), 1221–1259 (2022). https://doi.org/10.1007/s10479-020-03921-0
4. Dal Seno, B., Matteucci, M., Mainardi, L.T.: The utility metric: a novel method to assess the overall performance of discrete brain-computer interfaces. IEEE Trans. Neural Syst. Rehabil. Eng. **18**(1), 20–28 (2010). https://doi.org/10.1109/TNSRE.2009.2032642
5. Duan, X., Guo, S., Chen, L., Wang, M.: A P300 brain-computer interface for lower limb robot control based on tactile stimulation. J. Med. Biol. Eng. **43**(1), 22–31 (2023). https://doi.org/10.1007/s40846-022-00766-9

6. Edelman, B.J., et al.: Non-invasive brain-computer interfaces: state of the art and trends. IEEE Rev. Biomed. Eng. **18**, 26–49 (2025). https://doi.org/10.1109/RBME.2024.3449790
7. Hastie, T., Tibshirani, R., Friedman, J.: Linear methods for classification. In: The Elements of Statistical Learning: Data Mining, Inference, and Prediction, pp. 101–137. Springer, New York (2009). https://doi.org/10.1007/978-0-387-84858-7_4
8. Hoffmann, U., Vesin, J.M., Ebrahimi, T., Diserens, K.: An efficient P300-based brain-computer interface for disabled subjects. J. Neurosci. Methods **167**(1), 115–125 (2008). https://doi.org/10.1016/j.jneumeth.2007.03.005
9. Ledoit, O., Wolf, M.: A well-conditioned estimator for large-dimensional covariance matrices. J. Multivar. Anal. **88**(2), 365–411 (2004). https://doi.org/10.1016/S0047-259X(03)00096-4
10. Lees, S., et al.: A review of rapid serial visual presentation-based brain-computer interfaces. J. Neural Eng. **15**(2), 021001 (2018). https://doi.org/10.1088/1741-2552/aa9817
11. Lotte, F., et al.: A review of classification algorithms for EEG-based brain-computer interfaces: a 10 year update. J. Neural Eng. **15**(3), 031005 (2018). https://doi.org/10.1088/1741-2552/aab2f2
12. Ogino, M., Hamada, N., Mitsukura, Y.: Simultaneous multiple-stimulus auditory brain-computer interface with semi-supervised learning and prior probability distribution tuning. J. Neural Eng. **19**(6), 066008 (2022). https://doi.org/10.1088/1741-2552/ac9edd
13. Polich, J.: Updating P300: an integrative theory of P3a and P3b. Clin. Neurophysiol. **118**(10), 2128–2148 (2007). https://doi.org/10.1016/j.clinph.2007.04.019
14. Ramsey, N.F., Millán, J. (eds.): Brain-Computer Interfaces, Handbook of Clinical Neurology, vol. 168, 1st edn. Elsevier, San Diego (2020)
15. Schreuder, M., Höhne, J., Treder, M., Blankertz, B., Tangermann, M.: Performance optimization of ERP-based BCIs using dynamic stopping. In: 2011 Annual International Conference of the IEEE Engineering in Medicine and Biology Society, pp. 4580–4583 (2011). https://doi.org/10.1109/IEMBS.2011.6091134
16. Wolpaw, J.R., Birbaumer, N., McFarland, D.J., Pfurtscheller, G., Vaughan, T.M.: Brain-computer interfaces for communication and control. Clin. Neurophysiol. **113**(6), 767–791 (2002). https://doi.org/10.1016/S1388-2457(02)00057-3
17. Yuan, P., Gao, X., Allison, B., Wang, Y., Bin, G., Gao, S.: A study of the existing problems of estimating the information transfer rate in online brain-computer interfaces. J. Neural Eng. **10**(2), 026014 (2013). https://doi.org/10.1088/1741-2560/10/2/026014

The Special Session on Spatio-Temporal Brain Data Modelling: New Approaches to Understanding Brain Dynamics

A Novel Approach, a Modified Phase-Based Analysis to Assess the Behavioral and Neural Effects of tDCS Across Three Brain Regions

Chayapol Sae-chueng[1], Nakorn Chukasemrat[1], Poopa Kaewbuapan[2], Sirawaj Ithiphuripat[2], and Duanghathai Wiwatratana[2(✉)]

[1] Darunsikkhalai Science School SciUS Program, King Mongkut's University of Technology Thonburi (Bangkuntien), 49 Soi Thian Thale 25, Bang Khun Thian–Chai Thale Road, Tha Kham, Bang Khun Thian, Bangkok 10150, Thailand

[2] Neuroscience Center for Research and Innovation, Learning Institute, King Mongkut's University of Technology Thonburi (KMUTT), Bangkok 10140, Thailand

duanghathai.wiw@kmutt.ac.th

Abstract. Transcranial direct current stimulation (tDCS) is a non-invasive neuromodulation technique that has shown promise for enhancing cognitive functions such as attention and working memory, yet its effects remain inconsistent across studies. This study introduces a *modified phase-based analysis* to capture the temporal dynamics of tDCS-induced changes in both behavior and brain activity. Nineteen healthy adults performed a visual working memory task under active and sham stimulation targeting the left and right posterior parietal cortex (lPPC, rPPC) and right dorsolateral prefrontal cortex (rDLPFC). Trials were chronologically divided into Early, Middle, and Late phases to examine evolving cognitive states over time.

Behavioral outcomes-hit rate and reaction time-did not differ significantly between stimulation and sham, suggesting stable performance across conditions. However, event-related potential (ERP) analyses revealed phase-dependent neural modulations: rDLPFC stimulation showed a trend toward reduced Contralateral Delay Activity (CDA) in the Early phase and enhanced P3 amplitude in the Late phase, indicating improved memory efficiency and consolidation, while lPPC stimulation tended to increase N2PC amplitude during the Early phase, reflecting enhanced attentional allocation.

These findings demonstrate that even without overt behavioral effects, tDCS can induce temporally specific neural changes. The modified phase-based analysis provides a sensitive framework for linking behavioral stability with dynamic ERP modulations, offering new insights into how tDCS influences attention and working memory across time.

C. Sae-chueng, N. Chukasemrat and D. Wiwatratana—Equal contribution.
P. Kaewbuapan and S. Ithiphuripat—Senior author.

A. Lombardi et al. (Eds.): BI 2025, LNAI 16348, pp. 165–175, 2026.
https://doi.org/10.1007/978-981-95-9578-5_13

Keywords: Electroencephalography (EEG) · Transcranial Direct Current Stimulation (tDCS) · Working Memory Capacity

1 Introduction

Transcranial direct current stimulation (tDCS) is a non-invasive brain stimulation technique that has received growing attention for its potential to modulate cortical excitability and influence cognitive functions such as attention and memory [6,13,21]. By delivering a weak direct current to targeted brain regions, tDCS can either enhance or suppress neuronal activity depending on the stimulation polarity [18,22]. This method has been widely applied in cognitive neuroscience to explore mechanisms of working memory, attentional control, and learning [5,16]. However, despite extensive research, the cognitive and neural outcomes of tDCS remain mixed and, at times, contradictory—some studies report significant performance enhancements, while others find minimal or no effects [13,14,21].

This variability in findings has prompted the need for more refined experimental designs and analysis methods that can more effectively detect subtle changes in cognitive processing. Traditional analyses in tDCS–EEG studies often rely on repetition-based trial segmentation, which classifies trials by their ordinal positions within repeated blocks (e.g., trials 1–2, 3–4, 5–7) [4]. While this approach captures short-term shifts in cognitive states, it may overlook longer-term learning effects, task adaptation, and cumulative fatigue across the session [27].

To address these limitations, the present study employed a modified phase-based analysis framework. Rather than grouping trials by repetition, we segmented them chronologically into three equal-duration phases: Early (trials 1–20), Middle (21–40), and Late (41–60). This temporal structure allows for a continuous and time-sensitive assessment of how cognitive strategies evolve as participants engage with the task [27]. By aligning behavioral and ERP data within this framework, we aim to capture dynamic changes in neural processes such as attention deployment, working memory maintenance, and memory consolidation—effects that may be masked in conventional analyses [5].

We examined the effects of tDCS applied to three target brain regions—the left posterior parietal cortex (lPPC), right posterior parietal cortex (rPPC), and right dorsolateral prefrontal cortex (rDLPFC)—alongside a sham control condition. Behavioral outcomes were assessed through hit rate and reaction time (RT), while neural activity was measured via EEG, focusing on event-related potentials (ERPs) known to reflect distinct cognitive operations: contralateral delay activity (CDA) for working memory maintenance [19,25], N2PC for attentional selection [12], and P3 for memory updating and decision-related processing [22].

While the behavioral results did not reveal statistically significant differences between stimulation and sham conditions, ERP analyses using the phase-based approach uncovered time-varying neural modulations. Specifically, rDLPFC stimulation showed a trend toward reduced CDA amplitude during the early phase (which may reflect enhanced memory efficiency), and a trend toward elevated P3 amplitude during the late phase (which could indicate improved memory consolidation) [22,25]. Meanwhile, lPPC stimulation appeared to increase N2PC amplitude in the early phase, pointing to enhanced attentional deployment at task onset [12].

2 Materials and Methods

Nineteen neurologically healthy young adults were recruited from the King Mongkut's University of Technology Thonburi (KMUTT) community to participate in the study.

2.1 tDCS Stimulation

We used the Mindalive Oasis Pro tDCS device with conductive rubber electrodes and sponge pads placed over them. We prepared a saline solution by mixing approximately 30 g NaCl in 200 mL distilled water (about 15% w/v) to act as the conductive medium. After soaking the sponge pads in the solution, we inserted the electrodes into them. We positioned the anodal electrode over the target stimulation site and placed the cathodal electrode on the contralateral cheek. This placement minimizes confounding cortical stimulation and helps ensure current flow remains lateralized to the target region. To ensure stability, we secured the electrodes using rubber bands attached to the EEG cap.

We divided the stimulation into four conditions: (1) left PPC, (2) right PPC, (3) right DLPFC, and (4) sham stimulation. We counterbalanced the order of stimulation across sessions. Each day, we stimulated only one brain region and ensured at least a three-day rest period before the next session. For the first three conditions, we applied stimulation at 2 mA for 20 min. In the sham condition, we applied 2 mA for 30 s and then turned off the device.

2.2 Working Memory Task

Participants finished a visual working memory task intended to assess their capacity to encode and retrieve information about color and shape in a controlled environment. Each trial consisted of 3 sequential screens which remained for 900–2000 ms depending on screen, with a fixation point present in every screen to ensure participants maintained their gaze at a central location throughout the task (Fig. 1). Participants completed 4 rounds. One round contained 14 blocks. One block contained 60 trials. Although each round contained 14 blocks ($4 \times 14 = 56$ total blocks, 60 trials each), only the subset of trials that fell within the 20-minute stimulation window was analyzed. Each block (60 trials) was internally divided into Early (1–20), Middle (21–40), and Late (41–60) phases for phase-based analysis.

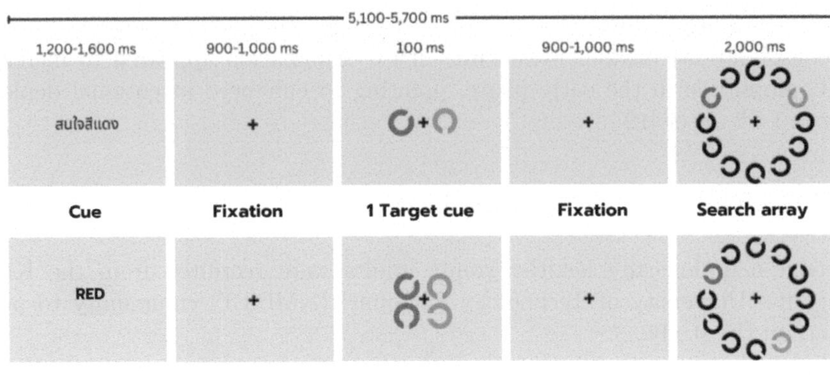

Fig. 1. Schematic of the visual working memory task procedure. Each trial began with a color cue display (e.g., RED) for 1,200–1,600 ms, followed by a fixation screen for 900–1,000 ms. A target cue was then presented for 100 ms, either as one or two colored-shape combinations (setsize 1 or 2), depending on the condition. After another fixation interval (900–1,000 ms), a search array was displayed for 2,000 ms, containing multiple colored-shape items arranged in a circular layout. A central fixation cross was maintained throughout.

2.3 EEG Section

EEG was recorded from 64 scalp electrodes (BioSemi). The EEG data were processed using EEGLAB [7]. ERP components were selected based on their functional roles: CDA [25], N2PC [12], and P3 [22].

2.4 Data Analysis

Behavioral Data Processing. Behavioral data were processed in MATLAB by extracting trial-by-trial performance for each subject. In contrast to the original repetition-based analysis by Carlisle et al. (2011), which grouped trials according to their ordinal positions within individual repetition runs (early: trials 1–2, intermediate: trials 3–4, late: trials 5–7), we adopted a modified phase-based analysis. Our approach aggregates trials across all repetition lengths into three chronological phases—Early (trials 1–20), Middle (21–40), and Late (41–60)—(see Fig. 2). Each phase consists of 20 trials, providing a more comprehensive assessment of longer-term, cumulative shifts in attentional control and memory utilization across extended task engagement. For each condition, we calculated hit rate (accuracy) and reaction time (RT) for correct responses. To reduce individual variability, subject-wise normalization was applied by subtracting each subject's mean across conditions and re-adding the overall group mean. This normalization centers individual performance relative to personal baselines, minimizing between-subject variability and ensuring that group-level effects primarily reflect stimulation-related differences.

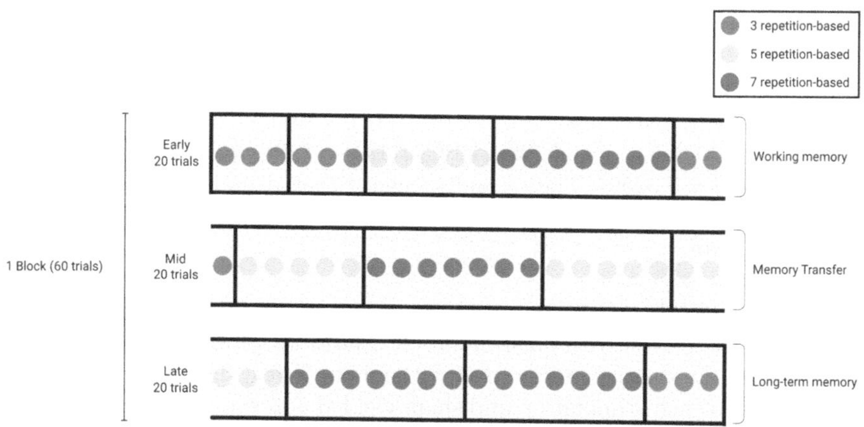

Fig. 2. Schematic representation of repetition-based versus phase-based analysis methods. Each block consists of 60 trials, comprising stimuli with 3 (green), 5 (yellow), or 7 (red) repetitions presented in pseudo-random order. In the traditional repetition-based analysis, trials are analyzed based on repetition frequency regardless of temporal order, potentially masking learning-related dynamics. In contrast, the phase-based analysis segments trials into three consecutive 20-trial epochs: Early (working memory phase), Mid (memory transfer phase), and Late (long-term memory phase).

Statistical Analysis. We applied repeated-measures ANOVA with linear mixed-effects models in MATLAB to evaluate the influence of stimulation site and trial order, treating subjects as random factors. Both main effects and interaction effects were tested. Additionally, paired t-tests compared each stimulation condition to the sham baseline within each trial phase (Early, Middle, Late). Bonferroni correction was applied when necessary.

EEG and ERP Component Analysis. EEG data were preprocessed to remove artifacts using independent component analysis (ICA). The signals were segmented into epochs time-locked to stimulus onset, maintaining the same temporal structure applied in behavioral data—Early, Middle, and Late phases. We extracted three ERP components from fixed time windows: CDA (300–1000 ms), N2PC (180–300 ms), P3 (250–500 ms). Mean amplitudes were calculated and compared between stimulation and sham using paired t-tests across all trial phases.

3 Results

3.1 Behavior Results

Hit Rate (HR). Across all trial phases, hit rates observed under each stimulation condition (lPPC, rPPC, and rDLPFC) and the sham condition (black line) (Fig. 3) showed largely overlapping 95% confidence intervals, indicating comparable performance levels. Statistical analysis confirmed the absence of significant differences between each stimulation and sham across all temporal segments: early (lPPC: $t(18) = 0.308$, $p = 0.7620$; rPPC: $t(18) = -0.293$, $p = 0.7728$; rDLPFC: $t(18) = 0.340$, $p = 0.7375$), middle (lPPC: $t(18) = -0.257$, $p = 0.7998$; rPPC: $t(18) = 0.577$, $p = 0.5710$; rDLPFC: $t(18) = -0.643$, $p = 0.5280$), and late (lPPC: $t(18) = 0.655$, $p = 0.5209$; rPPC: $t(18) = 1.361$, $p = 0.1905$; rDLPFC: $t(18) = 1.010$, $p = 0.3259$). These results suggest that stimulation of the parietal and prefrontal regions did not yield significant changes in hit rate performance compared to sham.

Reaction Time (RT). Reaction time outcomes also revealed similar trends across stimulation sites, with all stimulation conditions producing slightly faster responses than the sham condition, but without statistical significance. The comparison between each stimulation and sham yielded non-significant results across all trial segments: early (lPPC: $t(18) = 0.724$, $p = 0.4784$; rPPC: $t(18) = 0.753$, $p = 0.4613$; rDLPFC: $t(18) = 0.380$, $p = 0.7085$), middle (lPPC: $t(18) = 1.128$, $p = 0.2742$; rPPC: $t(18) = 1.718$, $p = 0.1092$; rDLPFC: $t(18) = 0.718$, $p = 0.4823$), and late (lPPC: $t(18) = 1.009$, $p = 0.3262$; rPPC: $t(18) = 1.042$, $p = 0.3111$; rDLPFC: $t(18) = 0.486$, $p = 0.6327$). Although numerical differences were observed—most notably under lPPC and rPPC stimulation—the lack of statistical significance suggests no robust effect of tDCS on reaction time.

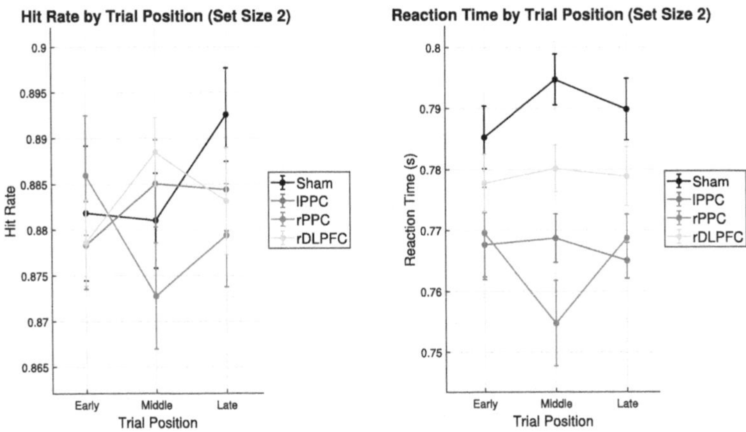

Fig. 3. Hit rate and reaction time across trial positions. Left panel shows mean hit rate, and right panel shows mean reaction time (in seconds) across early, middle, and late trial phases for each stimulation site (sham, lPPC, rPPC, rDLPFC). Error bars indicate ±1 SEM. Although some numerical differences were observed, none of the comparisons reached statistical significance.

3.2 Brain Signal Results

CDA Component. In the lPPC stimulation condition, the CDA amplitudes (Fig. 4) appeared largely similar to sham, with considerable overlap in their 95% confidence intervals. Statistical analyses confirmed the absence of significant differences between conditions across trial phases: early ($t(18) = 1.736$, $p = 0.0996$), middle ($t(18) = 1.164$, $p = 0.2598$), and late ($t(18) = 1.586$, $p = 0.1301$).

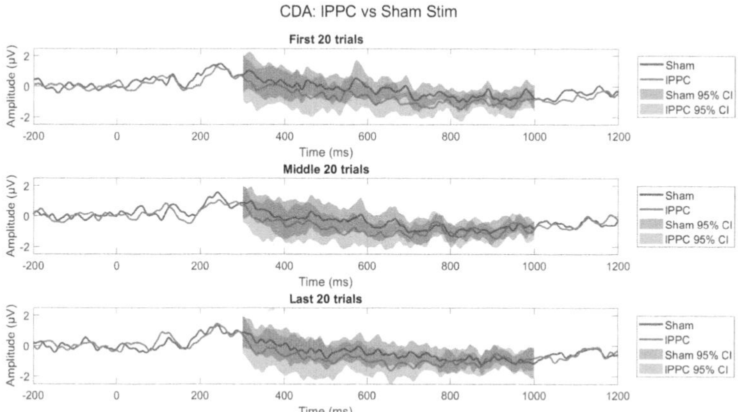

Fig. 4. Comparison of contralateral delay activity (CDA) amplitude between the lPPC stimulation and sham conditions across three trial blocks: first 20 trials, middle 20 trials, and last 20 trials.

N2PC Component. Under lPPC stimulation, the N2PC amplitude (Fig. 5) appeared more negative than sham within the typical N2PC time window (approximately 180–300 ms). This trend was consistent, especially in the early phase, but did not reach significance: early ($t(18) = -2.015$, $p = 0.0591$), middle ($t(18) = -1.122$, $p = 0.2764$), late ($t(18) = -0.938$, $p = 0.3607$).

P300 Component. For P3 (Fig. 6), rDLPFC stimulation showed waveforms closely aligned with sham. Statistical comparisons showed no significant differences: early ($t(18) = 0.383$, $p = 0.7060$), middle ($t(18) = 0.691$, $p = 0.4982$), and late ($t(18) = -1.433$, $p = 0.1689$).

4 Discussion

This study examined how transcranial direct current stimulation (tDCS) modulates attention and working memory using a modified phase-based analysis that aligns behavioral stability with evolving ERP dynamics across Early, Middle, and Late task phases. Compared to traditional repetition-based grouping [4], the phase-based approach captured gradual adaptation, fatigue, and strategy shifts over longer time windows [27], while preserving clear links between component-specific ERPs and cognitive operations [5,19,22].

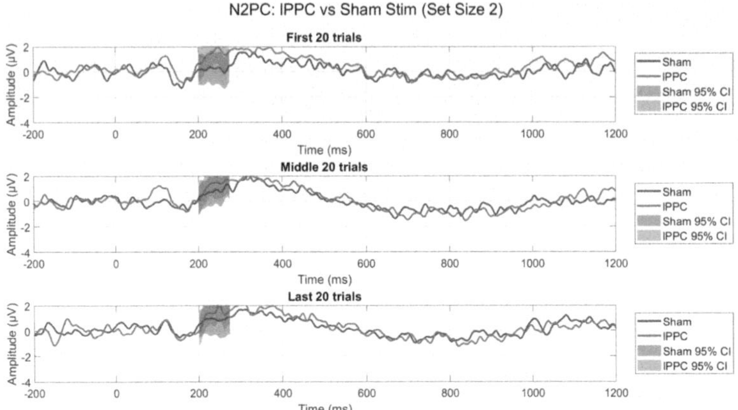

Fig. 5. N2PC amplitude comparison between the lPPC stimulation and sham conditions across three trial blocks: first 20 trials, middle 20 trials, and last 20 trials. Note: N2PC is typically negative-going.

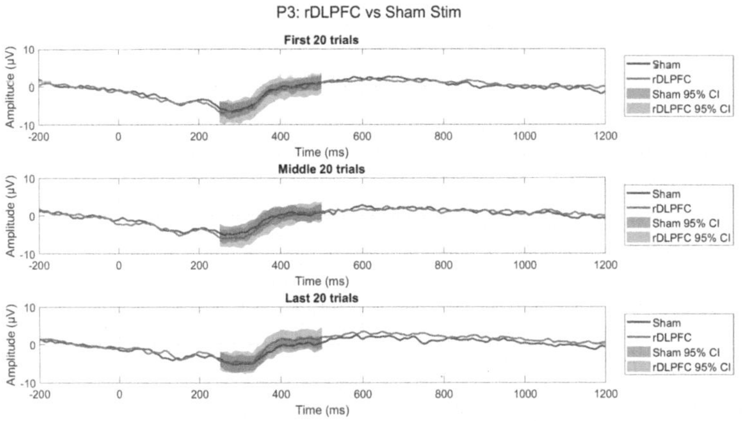

Fig. 6. P3 amplitude comparison between rDLPFC stimulation and sham conditions across three trial blocks: first 20, middle 20, and last 20 trials.

Behavior Versus ERP Sensitivity. Consistent with mixed behavioral findings in healthy samples [13,14,21], hit rate and reaction time did not differ significantly between active and sham stimulation across phases. Nonetheless, ERPs revealed temporally specific modulations: under right dorsolateral prefrontal cortex (rDLPFC) stimulation, CDA tended to be reduced early while P3 tended to be enhanced late; under left posterior parietal cortex (lPPC) stimulation, N2pc tended to increase early. Such dissociations—stable behavior with evolving neural signatures—mirror prior reports that tDCS can alter cortical processing even when overt performance remains unchanged [20,26].

Interpreting CDA Trends (Early Phase, rDLPFC). CDA is widely taken to index the quality or quantity of information maintained in visual working memory [25] and is sensitive to neural efficiency rather than load alone [9,19]. Thus, the observed early trend toward lower CDA under rDLPFC stimulation may reflect more efficient encoding or maintenance for equivalent accuracy—an interpretation consistent with prior work showing that prefrontal stimulation enhances working-memory efficiency [3,21,28]. Similar reductions in CDA amplitude with maintained accuracy have been interpreted as improved resource allocation under optimized frontal control [9].

Late-Phase P3 (rDLPFC). We also observed a trend for larger P3 amplitudes late in the task following rDLPFC stimulation. P3 is sensitive to memory updating, decisional evidence, and consolidation processes [22]. Frontal tDCS has been shown to increase P3 amplitude without necessarily changing behavior, indicating more efficient stimulus evaluation and context updating [26]. Meta-analytic evidence also supports that tDCS reliably modulates P3 amplitude and latency across cognitive tasks [20]. Our late-phase P3 trend therefore aligns with a time-dependent facilitation of updating and consolidation mechanisms by prefrontal stimulation.

Early N2pc (lPPC). The enhanced N2pc trend early in the block under lPPC stimulation aligns with the parietal cortex's role in attentional selection and priority mapping. Causal studies show that parietal stimulation can sharpen covert selection (indexed by N2pc) and speed visual search even with minimal behavioral differences overall [15,23,24]. However, other studies report null or mixed attentional effects, underscoring montage and task dependence [8]. Our phase-based segmentation likely captured an onset-specific attentional boost (Early phase) that might be obscured in time-collapsed analyses.

Why a Phase-Based Lens Matters. Together, these results suggest that (i) prefrontal stimulation can optimize working-memory operations early (reduced CDA) and bolster updating and consolidation later (larger P3), and (ii) parietal stimulation enhances early attentional deployment (larger N2pc). Phase-specific ERP changes thus reveal coherent neural mechanisms—encoding/maintenance → selection → updating—that remain hidden when averaging across the session. This supports recent recommendations to treat ERPs as sensitive biomarkers for stimulation efficacy and as mechanistic bridges between null behavioral outcomes and latent neural changes [1].

Limitations and Future Directions. The present study used conventional tDCS (2 mA, 20 min); stimulation effects can depend on current intensity, electrode montage, and individual neuroanatomy [26]. Future work should combine the phase-based design with high-definition tDCS, current-flow modeling, and increased task difficulty (to avoid ceiling effects). Additionally, preregistered ERP endpoints (CDA, N2pc, P3) and concurrent eye-tracking could further disentangle attentional versus memory-consolidation dynamics [5,23].

Acknowledgments. Grants from the National Research Council of Thailand and the Program Management Unit for Human Resources & Institution, the Office of National Higher Education, Science Research and Innovation Policy Council supported this work.

References

1. Assecondi, S., et al.: Event-Related Potentials as markers of efficacy for non-invasive brain stimulation. Front. Hum. Neurosci. **16**, 867566 (2022). https://doi.org/10.3389/fnhum.2022.867566
2. Bikson, M., et al.: Safety of transcranial direct current stimulation: evidence based update 2016. Brain Stimul. **9**(5), 641–661 (2016)
3. Brunoni, A.R., Vanderhasselt, M.A.: Working memory improvement with non-invasive brain stimulation of the dorsolateral prefrontal cortex: A systematic review and meta-analysis. Brain Cogn. **86**, 1–9 (2014)
4. Carlisle, N.B., Arita, J.T., Pardo, D., Woodman, G.F.: Attentional templates in visual working memory. J. Neurosci. **31**(25), 9315–9322 (2011)
5. Choe, K.W., Coffey, E.B.J., Brady, D.K., Reilly, J.: Measuring engagement during learning using EEG and eye-tracking. Cogn. Neurodyn. **10**(4), 263–275 (2016)
6. Corbetta, M., Shulman, G.L.: Control of goal-directed and stimulus-driven attention in the brain. Nat. Rev. Neurosci. **3**(3), 201–215 (2002)
7. Delorme, A., Makeig, S.: EEGLAB: an open source toolbox for analysis of single-trial EEG dynamics including independent component analysis. J. Neurosci. Methods **134**(1), 9–21 (2004)
8. Dubravac, M., Meier, B.: Stimulating the parietal cortex by tDCS: no effects on attention and memory. AIMS Neurosci. **8**, 33–46 (2021). https://doi.org/10.3934/Neuroscience.2021002
9. Feldmann-Wüstefeld, T., Vogel, E.K., Awh, E.: Contralateral delay activity indexes working memory storage and resource allocation. Psychophysiology **55**, e13033 (2018). https://doi.org/10.1111/psyp.13033
10. Fertonani, A., Miniussi, C.: Transcranial electrical stimulation: what we know and do not know about mechanisms. Neuroscientist **23**(2), 109–123 (2017)
11. Fregni, F., et al.: Cognitive effects of repeated sessions of transcranial direct current stimulation in patients with depression. BMC Neurosci. **12**(1), 2 (2005)
12. Gazzaley, A., Nobre, A.C.: Top-down modulation: bridging selective attention and working memory. Trends Cogn. Sci. **16**(2), 129–135 (2012)
13. Hill, A.T., Fitzgerald, P.B., Hoy, K.E.: Effects of anodal tDCS on working memory: a systematic review and meta-analysis. Brain Stimul. **9**(2), 197–208 (2016)
14. Horvath, J.C., Forte, J.D., Carter, O.: Quantitative review finds no evidence of cognitive effects in healthy populations from single-session tDCS. Brain Stimul. **8**(3), 535–550 (2015)
15. Hsu, T.-Y., et al.: Right posterior parietal tDCS modulates attentional deployment in visual search. Neuroimage **98**, 306–315 (2014). https://doi.org/10.1016/j.neuroimage.2014.04.067
16. Kastner, S., Ungerleider, L.G.: Mechanisms of visual attention in the human cortex. Annu. Rev. Neurosci. **23**, 315–341 (2000)
17. Kiss, M., Driver, J., Eimer, M.: Reward priority of visual target singletons modulates ERP signatures of attentional selection. Psychol. Sci. **20**(2), 245–251 (2009)

18. Kuo, M.-F., Nitsche, M.A.: Effects of transcranial electrical stimulation on cognition. Clin. EEG Neurosci. **43**(3), 192–199 (2012)
19. Luck, S.J.: An Introduction to the Event-Related Potential Technique (2nd ed.). MIT Press (2014)
20. Mendes, A.J., et al.: Modulation of the cognitive event-related potential P3 by transcranial direct current stimulation: a meta-analysis. Neurosc. Biobehav. Rev. **132**, 1049–1066 (2022). https://doi.org/10.1016/j.neubiorev.2021.12.043
21. Polanía, R., Nitsche, M.A., Ruff, C.C.: Studying and modifying brain function with non-invasive brain stimulation. Nat. Neurosci. **21**(2), 174–187 (2018)
22. Polich, J.: Updating P300: an integrative theory of P3a and P3b. Clin. Neurophysiol. **118**(10), 2128–2148 (2007)
23. Reinhart, R.M.G., Woodman, G.F.: Enhancing long-term memory with stimulation tunes visual attention in one trial. Proc. Natl. Acad. Sci. U.S.A. **112**, 13647–13652 (2014). https://doi.org/10.1073/pnas.1421320111
24. Tseng, P., et al.: Transcranial direct current stimulation over right posterior parietal cortex improves change detection in visual search. J. Neurosci. **32**, 10554–10561 (2012). https://doi.org/10.1523/JNEUROSCI.1462-12.2012
25. Vogel, E.K., Machizawa, M.G.: Neural activity predicts individual differences in visual working memory capacity. Nature **428**(6984), 748–751 (2004)
26. Vögtle, A., Svaldi, J., Schmitz, F.: Repetitive anodal tDCS to the frontal cortex increases P300 amplitude without behavioral change. Brain Sci. **12**, 1545 (2022). https://doi.org/10.3390/brainsci12111545
27. Wascher, E., Getzmann, S., Falkenstein, M.: Frontal theta activity reflects distinct aspects of mental fatigue. Biol. Psychol. **96**, 57–65 (2014)
28. Zaehle, T., Sandmann, P., Thorne, J.D., Jäncke, L., Herrmann, C.S.: tDCS of the prefrontal cortex modulates working memory performance: behavioral and electrophysiological evidence. BMC Neurosci. **12**(1), 2 (2011)

Author Index

A. Lombardi et al. (Eds.): BI 2025, LNAI 16348, p. 177, 2026.
https://doi.org/10.1007/978-981-95-9578-5

The manufacturer's authorised representative in the EU is Springer Nature Customer Service Centre GmbH, Europaplatz 3, 69115 Heidelberg, Germany. If you have any concerns regarding our products, please contact ProductSafety@springernature.com

Printed and bound by CPI Group (UK) Ltd, Croydon, CR0 4YY

07/07/2026

02160906-0001